WRITING ANALYTICALLY

writing analytically

David Rosenwasser
Jill Stephen

Muhlenberg College

Harcourt Brace College Publishers

Fort Worth   Philadelphia   San Diego   New York   Orlando   Austin   San Antonio
Toronto   Montreal   London   Sydney   Tokyo

PUBLISHER	*Christopher P. Klein*
ACQUISITIONS EDITOR	*John P. Meyers*
SENIOR DEVELOPMENTAL EDITOR	*Karl Yambert*
PROJECT EDITOR	*Kathryn Stewart*
PRODUCTION MANAGER	*Diane Gray*
ART DIRECTOR	*Sue Hart*
COVER IMAGE	*Neal Parks* © 1995 Horizon #3, 63" x 38", oil stick on canvas. email: nparks@ccnet.com,http://www.ccnet.com/~nparks
PHOTO CREDITS	Figure 1.1, p. 13/Erich Lessing/Art Resource, New York; Figure 7.2, p. 127/Jeff Widener/Wide World Photos
LITERARY CREDITS	"Playing by the Antioch Rules," p. 74/Copyright © 1993 by The New York Times Company. Reprinted by permission.

Supplements: Harcourt Brace & Company may provide complimentary instructional aids and supplements or supplement packages to those adopters qualified under our adoption policy. Please contact your sales representative for more information. If as an adopter or potential user you receive supplements you do not need, please return them to your sales representative or send them to: Attn: Returns Department, Troy Warehouse, 465 South Lincoln Drive, Troy, MO 63379.

Address for Editorial Correspondence: Harcourt Brace College Publishers, 301 Commerce Street, Suite 3700, Fort Worth, TX 76102

Address for Orders: Harcourt Brace College Publishers, 6277 Sea Harbor Drive, Orlando, FL 32887 1-800-782-4479, or 1-800-433-0001 (in Florida)

ISBN: 0-15-501889-2

Library of Congress Catalog Card Number: 96-75317

Printed in the United States of America

7 8 9 0 1 2 3 4 5   0 1 6   9 8 7 6 5 4 3

What This Book Is and What It Offers

Writing Analytically is a book about how to have ideas and develop them effectively. It offers a book-length treatment of analysis, a form of thinking and writing required in most college courses (and beyond) but frequently overshadowed in writing texts by an emphasis on argument, expressive writing, or the traditional rhetorical modes.

The text takes from the process approach to writing a concern with the stages that a writer goes through in composing an essay—emphasizing conceptual revisions as an ongoing rather than a late-stage activity. It takes from the critical-thinking movement a concern with such logical matters as reasoning back to premises and the careful consideration of evidence. It combines these two approaches to offer a guided tour of the thought processes inherent in analytical thinking. It treats thinking skills not in isolated exercises but in the context of the writing process, offering step-by-step accounts of how analyses are produced.

Writing Analytically is deeply committed to the concept of writing to learn—that is, to the notion that writing is a tool that can facilitate and enrich understanding. Thus, the book emphasizes ways of using writing to figure out what things mean. It encourages writers to assume an exploratory stance toward ideas and evidence: to delay their judgments in favor of understanding, to treat their ideas as hypotheses to be tested rather than as self-evident truths, and to share their thought processes with readers.

The book has been designed with several audiences in mind. It can serve as the primary text in a beginning or advanced composition course, or as a supplemental text in writing-intensive courses across the curriculum. We have deliberately created a text that does not require the instructor to organize a course around it, and that can be used as much or as little as the instructor sees fit. The book is really for anyone who wishes to learn how to use writing as a tool of thought.

Writing Analytically is collaboratively written by two people who codirect a Writing Across the Curriculum (WAC) program at a liberal arts college. It reflects our experience in teaching writing to students and in leading seminars on writing instruction for faculty. Our work with both groups has taught us that (1) analysis as a mode of thinking is essential to learning, (2) there are elements of effective analytical writing common to all disciplines, and (3) the area of consensus among faculty about writing is larger and more significant than the differences.

So, while the book respects disciplinary difference, it does not lead with difference. Instead, it attempts to forge a common language for talking about writing that does not over rely on the technical jargon of any one discipline. The book does, however, acknowledge that different disciplines have their own emphases and formats. We attempt to locate difference—and common ground—not just from our own perspective but from that of professors in other disciplines. Throughout the text you will find sections labeled "Voices from Across the Curriculum" that quote these professors on such matters as reasoning back to premises, determining what counts as evidence, constructing introductions and conclusions, and using the first-person *I*.

A Note to Instructors on How to Use This Book

Although the chapters of *Writing Analytically* build on one another if read sequentially, they are also designed to stand independently, so that they can be used in any order. You will note that the book contains neither exercises nor readings (other than the student drafts that illustrate our drafting and revising strategies). A separate Instructor's Manual provides suggested activities and writing assignments for each chapter, along with alternative ways of sequencing the chapters, guidelines for commenting on and evaluating papers, and advice on teaching practices conducive to success in a writing course.

Some users of *Writing Analytically* in a composition course might want to teach it in conjunction with a book of readings for students to use as models and subject matter, although we believe this is not necessary. The ways of thinking that the book invites can be applied to many kinds of materials—newspapers, magazines, films, primary texts (both fiction and nonfiction), television, popular culture, historical documents, advertising, photographs, political campaigns, conversations, athletic events, and so on.

Composition courses unified by some kind of theme (representations of the American family over time, for example, or of teenagers and rites of passage) or subject matter (such as congressional budget debates or philosophical treatises on the existence of God) would work well with this book. So would research-based composition courses, and courses primarily concerned with critical-thinking and -reading skills.

For instructors in Writing Across the Curriculum (WAC) and Writing In the Disciplines (WID) courses, course content will provide the materials that students will analyze in their writing. Although writing itself is not the central subject of such courses, it is an essential part of the learning process. The kind of writing that the book focuses on is especially well-suited for content courses with a writing component, since our emphasis is less on writing per se than on how to use writing to enhance understanding.

Our work with both Composition and WAC/WID faculty has taught us that most of them don't want the manufactured sequence of topics they find in textbooks, but more information about how to construct topics of their own that will elicit genuine thinking from students. So, *Writing Analytically* devotes its entire second chapter to topic construction, in which we explain to students how to make questions and responses to questions more analytical. (You will find the same kind of advice, addressed explicitly to instructors in checklist form, in the teaching suggestions for Chapter 2 in the Instructor's Manual.)

A goal of this book is to free instructors and students to talk throughout the writing process (not just at the end) about the content of papers without first having to go over such general matters as what a thesis is or when and how to quote sources or use examples. By troubleshooting the kinds of writing problems that students are likely to encounter, the book aims to make conferences between student and instructor as productive as possible.

Writing Analytically prescribes strategies on such matters as evolving a thesis, using evidence, and revising and editing, but its intention is not to impose a system that either students or professors must follow in every particular. Rather, we hope to provide a basis for conversation—between faculty and students, between students and students, and especially between writers and their own writing.

Chapter Outline

Chapter 1, "What Is Analytical Writing?" defines analysis and discusses how it resembles and differs from other forms of writing, such as summary and argument. It also shows how to determine what kind of writing the language of a paper topic calls for.

Chapter 2, "Constructing Effective Topics," treats topic construction as part of the writing process rather than as a prelude to it. It shows writers how to avoid oversimplifying their responses to standard types of topics, such as compare/contrast, define, and agree/disagree.

Chapter 3, "Questions of Format," explains the rationale for disciplinary formats and offers advice on how to use these as tools for thinking rather than just as ways for organizing final drafts.

Chapter 4, "Finding and Developing a Thesis," shows how to arrive at a thesis and make it evolve in response to evidence.

Chapter 5, "Recognizing and Fixing Weak Thesis Statements," isolates the basic types of weak theses, explains why they inhibit effective analysis, and shows how to fix them—especially those that rely on personal likes and dislikes and overly categorical thinking.

Chapter 6, "Introductions and Conclusions," demonstrates basic strategies for constructing introductions and conclusions, and targets some common problems. It relies heavily on "Voices from Across the Curriculum," since disciplinary differences are often most evident in beginnings and endings.

Chapter 7, "Analyzing Evidence," promotes a model of analysis in which writers restrict the pool of evidence and examine it in great detail. The chapter stresses the importance of reasoning from observations to implications to conclusions, and of constantly testing and refining theories of what the evidence means rather than leaping to overly broad generalizations.

Chapter 8, "Using Sources," puts the emphasis in research-writing on using rather than just documenting sources. It shows how to converse with sources rather than plugging in unanalyzed quotations and summaries as "answers."

Chapter 9, "Revising for Style," concentrates on the choices of words and sentence structures available to writers as they revise drafts for greater clarity and effect. It discusses such matters as the pros and cons of using the active voice versus the passive voice, the role of jargon, and the effect of word order on emphasis.

Chapter 10, "Revising for Correctness," offers a brief guide to grammar and usage. It illustrates those errors most likely to interfere with coherence and gives tips for recognizing and fixing them. The chapter also contains a glossary of grammatical terms. Taken together, the last two chapters cover most of the problems routinely encountered in producing a final draft.

Two appendixes appear at the end of the book. Appendix A illustrates various documentation styles, including the MLA, APA, number-reference, and Chicago styles, and contains information about documenting electronic sources. Appendix B comprises glossaries of the most common logical terms and fallacies.

Acknowledgments

Our thanks go first to the faculty of Muhlenberg College, without whom this textbook would never have been conceived. The insights they shared with us in the summer seminars on writing across the curriculum and the questions they raised have changed the way we think about writing.

Additional thanks are owed to the colleagues who read parts of the manuscript, notably Grant Scott; to all of the students (especially Marie Goldzung, David Killeen, Alyssa Picard, Robert Pileggi, and Christopher Smith) and faculty who have contributed papers from across the disciplines for our fund of examples; and to the students in our classes who told us what worked for them in the book and what didn't. We are especially grateful to the six Muhlenberg colleagues who contributed to the "Voices from Across the Curriculum" sections: Giacomo Gambino, James Marshall, Robert Milligan, Richard Niesenbaum, Fred Norling, and Alan Tjeltveit (who also led us through APA style). Further thanks are due to Dean Richard Hatch for the funds to attend the CCC and WPA conferences, and to him and the Faculty Scholarship Committee for providing us with summer research grants. We also wish to acknowledge the generous support given to us and the writing program by the former Dean of the College, Nelvin Vos.

We express our gratitude to the numerous reviewers who provided insightful comments and suggestions on successive drafts of the manuscript: Beverly Ann Chin (University of Montana), Christine R. Farris (Indiana University), John Hanes (Duquesne University), Nancy Hayward (Indiana University of Pennsylvania), Georgina Hill (Andrews University), Deborah Holdstein (Governors State University), Bruce Leland (Western Illinois University), Todd Lundberg (Cleveland State University), James A. Merrill (Oxnard College), John N. Miller (Normandale Community College), Joan Mullin (University of Toledo), Bruce W. Speck (University of Memphis), Sharon Stockton (Dickinson College), Jacqueline Wheeler (Arizona State University), and James D. Williams (Governors State University).

At Harcourt Brace, our thanks go to John Grashoff for persuading us to submit a book proposal; to Stephen Jordan for accepting it and, along with Marty Smith, for guiding us through the early stages of composition; and to John Meyers for his advice and encouragement as the book entered its final stages. Thanks also go to Steve Welch and especially Kathryn Stewart for shepherding our book through production; to Sue Hart for designing it; and to Diane Gray for keeping everyone on schedule.

Our spouses, Mark and Deborah, and children, Lesley, Sarah, and Elizabeth, deserve special thanks for their continued interest and support. Above all, we thank our developmental editor, Karl Yambert, for his critical acuity, generosity, and wit.

David Rosenwasser and Jill Stephen are Associate Professors of English at Muhlenberg College in Allentown, Pennsylvania, where they have codirected a Writing Across the Curriculum (WAC) program since 1987. They began teaching writing to college students in the early 1970s—David at the University of Virginia and then at the College of William and Mary, and Jill at New York University and then at Hunter College (CUNY). *Writing Analytically* has grown out of their undergraduate teaching, their direction of the college writing center, and, more directly, the seminars on writing and writing instruction that they have offered to faculty across the curriculum at Muhlenberg.

CONTENTS IN BRIEF

Preface   V

Chapter 1   WHAT IS ANALYTICAL WRITING?   1

Chapter 2   CONSTRUCTING EFFECTIVE TOPICS   17

Chapter 3   QUESTIONS OF FORMAT   41

Chapter 4   FINDING AND DEVELOPING A THESIS   55

Chapter 5   RECOGNIZING AND FIXING WEAK THESIS STATEMENTS   81

Chapter 6   INTRODUCTIONS AND CONCLUSIONS   95

Chapter 7   ANALYZING EVIDENCE   115

Chapter 8   USING SOURCES   137

Chapter 9   REVISING FOR STYLE   159

Chapter 10   REVISING FOR CORRECTNESS   189

Appendix A   DOCUMENTATION STYLES   210

Appendix B   GLOSSARY OF LOGICAL TERMS AND FALLACIES   229

Index   243

CONTENTS

PREFACE   v

CHAPTER 1

WHAT IS ANALYTICAL WRITING?   1

ANALYSIS IS A SEARCH FOR MEANING   1
  ANALYSIS IS MORE THAN BREAKING A SUBJECT INTO ITS PARTS   2
  ANALYZING DIFFERS FROM JUDGING   3
  Voices from Across the Curriculum: Ideas versus Opinions   4
  ANALYSIS MAKES THE IMPLICIT EXPLICIT   4
  ANALYSIS IS A PROCESS OF ASKING YOURSELF QUESTIONS   5
USE PREWRITING TO FIND WORKABLE QUESTIONS   7
COMMON CHARGES AGAINST ANALYSIS   7
  COMMON CHARGE 1: "ANALYSIS KILLS ENJOYMENT"   7
  COMMON CHARGE 2: "ANALYSIS FINDS MEANINGS THAT ARE
    NOT THERE"   8
  COMMON CHARGE 3: "SOME SUBJECTS WEREN'T MEANT TO
    BE ANALYZED"   9
DISTINGUISHING ANALYSIS FROM EXPRESSIVE WRITING
 AND ARGUMENT   9
  ANALYSIS VERSUS ARGUMENT IN WRITING ASSIGNMENTS   10
  ANALYSIS AND SUMMARY   12
  ANALYSIS AND PERSONAL ASSOCIATION   14
GUIDELINES FOR WRITING ANALYTICALLY   14

CHAPTER 2

CONSTRUCTING EFFECTIVE TOPICS   17

ASSIGNED VERSUS OPEN TOPICS   17
MAKING A TOPIC ANALYTICAL: LOCATING AN AREA OF
 UNCERTAINTY   18
  WHAT IT MEANS TO HAVE AN IDEA   19
SEVEN RULES OF THUMB FOR HANDLING COMPLEXITY   19
  RULE 1: REDUCE SCOPE   20
  RULE 2: STUDY THE WORDING OF TOPICS FOR UNSTATED QUESTIONS   20
  RULE 3: SUSPECT YOUR FIRST RESPONSES   21
  RULE 4: BEGIN WITH QUESTIONS, NOT ANSWERS   21
  RULE 5: FOCUS ON UNEXPECTED SIMILARITIES AND DIFFERENCES   22
  RULE 6: WRITE ALL OF THE TIME ABOUT WHAT YOU ARE STUDYING   22
  RULE 7: EXPECT TO *BECOME* INTERESTED   22
USING PREWRITING TO FIND AND INTERPRET TOPICS   22
  FREEWRITING   23

FOCUSED FREEWRITING   23

JOURNALS   24

MAKING YOUR RESPONSE TO TOPICS MORE ANALYTICAL   24

THE SUMMARY TOPIC   25

Advantages of Summary   25

Problems with Summary   25

Strategies for Using Summaries Analytically   26

Strategy 1: Rank the Items in Your List   26

Strategy 2: Shift the Focus from What? to How? and Why?   26

Strategy 3: Pursue Only Selected Features of Your Subject   27

THE PERSONAL RESPONSE TOPIC   27

Advantages of Personal Response   27

Problems with Personal Response   28

Strategies for Using Personal Responses Analytically   28

Strategy 1: Trace Your Responses Back to Their Causes   28

Strategy 2: Assume That You May Have Missed the Point   29

Strategy 3: Achieve Critical Detachment   29

Strategy 4: Locate the Topic within a Limiting Context   31

BINARIES: EITHER/OR QUESTIONS   31

Advantages of Binaries   31

Problems with Binaries   31

Strategies for Using Binaries Analytically   32

Strategy 1: Locate a Range of Opposing Categories   32

Strategy 2: Analyze and Define the Opposing Terms   33

Strategy 3: Question the Accuracy of the Binary   33

Strategy 4: Change "Either/or" to "The Extent to Which"   33

COMPARISON/CONTRAST AND DEFINITION TOPICS   34

Advantages of Comparison/Contrast and Definition Topics   34

Problems with Comparison/Contrast and Definition   34

Strategies for Using Comparison/Contrast Analytically   35

Strategy 1: Discuss Revealing Similarities and Differences   35

Strategy 2: Argue for the Significance of a Key Comparison   36

Strategy 3: Use One Side of the Comparison to Illuminate the Other   36

Strategy 4: Imagine How One Side of Your Comparison Might
   Respond to the Other   36

Strategies for Using Definition Analytically   37

Strategy 1: Test the Definition against Evidence   37

Strategy 2: Explore Competing Parts of the Definition   37

Strategy 3: Use a Definition from One Source to Critique Another   37

Strategy 4: Shift from What? Questions to How? and Why? Questions   38

GUIDELINES FOR CONSTRUCTING EFFECTIVE TOPICS   38

CHAPTER 3

QUESTIONS OF FORMAT

THE TWO FUNCTIONS OF FORMATS: PROCESS AND PRODUCT	42
WHAT'S WRONG WITH FIVE-PARAGRAPH FORM?	44
FORMATS IN COLLEGE WRITING	46
Voices from Across the Curriculum: **Formats in the Natural and Social Sciences**	47
USING FORMATS IN EXPLORATORY DRAFTS	49
COMMON THOUGHT PATTERNS: INDUCTION AND DEDUCTION	50
GUIDELINES FOR USING FORMATS IN ANALYTICAL WRITING	52

CHAPTER 4

FINDING AND DEVELOPING A THESIS   55

DEVELOPING A THESIS IS MORE THAN REPEATING AN IDEA	55
MAKING A THESIS EVOLVE: THE THESIS AS CAMERA LENS	57
MAKING A THESIS EVOLVE: A BRIEF EXAMPLE	57
Voices from Across the Curriculum: **The Evolving Thesis as Hypothesis and Conclusion**	58
OVERVIEW OF THE CHAPTER'S EXAMPLES	60
FINDING A THESIS IN AN EXPLORATORY DRAFT	60
Extended Analysis: **VELÁZQUEZ'S INTENTIONS IN *LAS MENINAS***	60
STRATEGIES FOR FINDING A THESIS IN AN EXPLORATORY DRAFT	63
Strategy 1: Check for Competing or Multiple Theses	63
Strategy 2: Check for Evidence That Does Not Seem to Be Adequately Accounted for by Your Thesis	64
Strategy 3: Use Conflicting Evidence to Evolve Your Thesis	64
Strategy 4: Develop the Implications of Your Evidence and of Your Own Observations as Fully as You Can by Repeatedly Asking "So What?"	65
Strategy 5: Make Connections—Put the Evidence Together	66
STEP-BY-STEP SAMPLE REVISION	67
KNOWING WHEN TO STOP	68
DEVELOPING A THESIS THROUGH SUCCESSIVE COMPLICATIONS	68
Extended Analysis: **EDUCATING RITA**	69
PLACING AND DEVELOPING THE THESIS IN A FINAL DRAFT	71
DEVELOPING A THESIS BY REASONING BACK TO PREMISES	73
REASONING BACK TO PREMISES: A BRIEF EXAMPLE	73
Extended Analysis: **PLAYING BY THE ANTIOCH RULES**	74
STRATEGIES FOR DEVELOPING THE THESIS BY REASONING BACK TO PREMISES	77
Voices from Across the Curriculum: **Reasoning Back to Premises**	79
GUIDELINES FOR FINDING AND DEVELOPING A THESIS	79

CHAPTER 5

RECOGNIZING AND FIXING WEAK THESIS STATEMENTS   81

FIVE KINDS OF WEAK THESES AND HOW TO FIX THEM   81

WEAK THESIS TYPE 1: THE THESIS MAKES NO CLAIM   82

WEAK THESIS TYPE 2: THE THESIS IS OBVIOUSLY TRUE OR IS A STATE-
MENT OF FACT   82

WEAK THESIS TYPE 3: THE THESIS RESTATES CONVENTIONAL
WISDOM   83

WEAK THESIS TYPE 4: THE THESIS MAKES AN OVERLY BROAD CLAIM   85

WEAK THESIS TYPE 5: THE THESIS ADVANCES UNSUBSTANTIATED
OPINION   86

THE DANGERS OF CATEGORICAL THINKING   89

TWO WAYS TO IMPROVE THE LOGIC OF YOUR THESIS
STATEMENTS   89

WAY 1: QUALIFY YOUR CLAIMS   90

WAY 2: CHECK FOR UNSTATED ASSUMPTIONS   91

THE RELATIONSHIP BETWEEN ARGUMENT AND
INTERPRETATION   91

GUIDELINES FOR RECOGNIZING AND FIXING WEAK THESIS
STATEMENTS   93

CHAPTER 6

INTRODUCTIONS AND CONCLUSIONS   95

THE FUNCTION OF INTRODUCTIONS   96

Voices from Across the Curriculum: **Putting the Thesis in Context**   97

Voices from Across the Curriculum: **Using Procedural Openings**   99

HOW MUCH TO INTRODUCE UP FRONT   101

TYPICAL PROBLEMS THAT ARE SYMPTOMS OF DOING TOO MUCH   101

Digression   101

Incoherence   102

Prejudgment   102

Voices from Across the Curriculum: **Limiting Introductory Claims**   103

OPENING GAMBITS: A FEW SOLUTIONS   103

Gambit 1: Challenge a Commonly Held View   104

Gambit 2: Begin with a Definition   104

Gambit 3: Offer a Working Hypothesis   104

Gambit 4: Lead with Your Second-Best Example   104

Gambit 5: Exemplify the Topic with a Narrative   105

THE FUNCTION OF CONCLUSIONS   106

Voices from Across the Curriculum: Ways of Concluding   107

Voices from Across the Curriculum: Discussion Sections of Reports   109

SOLVING TYPICAL PROBLEMS IN CONCLUSIONS   112

Redundancy   112

Raising a Totally New Point   112

Overstatement   112

Anticlimax   113

GUIDELINES FOR INTRODUCTIONS AND CONCLUSIONS   113

CHAPTER 7
ANALYZING EVIDENCE   115

LINKING EVIDENCE AND CLAIMS   115

THE FUNCTION OF EVIDENCE   115

THE FALLACY THAT FACTS CAN SPEAK FOR THEMSELVES   116

UNSUBSTANTIATED CLAIMS   117

POINTLESS EVIDENCE   119

Voices from Across the Curriculum: What Counts as Evidence? 121

ANALYZING EVIDENCE IN DEPTH   124

10 ON 1 VERSUS 1 ON 10   124

DEMONSTRATE THE REPRESENTATIVENESS OF YOUR EXAMPLE   128

PAN, TRACK, AND ZOOM: THE FILM ANALOGY   130

Extended Analysis: FLOOD STORIES: APPLYING THE FILM ANALOGY
IN REVISION   130

LOOK FOR DIFFERENCE WITHIN SIMILARITY   134

FACING THE FEAR   135

GUIDELINES FOR ANALYZING EVIDENCE   136

CHAPTER 8
USING SOURCES   137

SECONDARY SOURCES ARE A FORM OF EVIDENCE   137

THE CONVERSATION ANALOGY   138

WHY USE SOURCES AT ALL?   139

Voices from Across the Curriculum: Finding Sources   140

Voices from Across the Curriculum: Citing Sources   142

SIX TECHNIQUES FOR INTEGRATING QUOTATIONS INTO
YOUR PAPER   143

TECHNIQUE 1: ACKNOWLEDGE SOURCES IN YOUR TEXT, NOT JUST
  IN CITATIONS   143
TECHNIQUE 2: SPLICE QUOTATIONS ONTO YOUR OWN WORDS   143
TECHNIQUE 3: SPLICE QUOTATIONS IN A WAY THAT IS GRAMMATICALLY
  CORRECT   143
TECHNIQUE 4: USE ELLIPSES TO SHORTEN QUOTATIONS   144
TECHNIQUE 5: CITE SOURCES AFTER QUOTATIONS   145
TECHNIQUE 6: USE A CITATION FORM APPROPRIATE TO THE DISCIPLINE   145
SIX STRATEGIES FOR CRITICAL ANALYSIS OF SOURCES   145
STRATEGY 1: MAKE YOUR SOURCES SPEAK   146
STRATEGY 2: USE YOUR SOURCES TO ASK QUESTIONS, NOT JUST TO
  PROVIDE ANSWERS   147
STRATEGY 3: CONVERSE WITH YOUR SOURCES   148
STRATEGY 4: FIND YOUR OWN VOICE IN THE CONVERSATION   151
STRATEGY 5: SUPPLY ONGOING ANALYSIS OF SOURCES (DON'T WAIT
  UNTIL THE END)   152
Voices from Across the Curriculum: Integrating Sources   152
Extended Analysis: THE FLIGHT FROM TEACHING   153
STRATEGY 6: WHEN THE LANGUAGE IS IMPORTANT, QUOTE
  (DON'T PARAPHRASE)   156
GUIDELINES FOR USING SOURCES   158

CHAPTER 9

REVISING FOR STYLE   159

CONCEPTUAL VERSUS TECHNICAL REVISION   159
WAIT TO FOCUS ON TECHNICAL REVISION   160
USE TECHNICAL REVISION AS A FORM OF CONCEPTUAL REVISION   160
WHAT IS STYLE?   161
LEVELS OF STYLE: WHO'S WRITING TO WHOM AND WHY
  DOES IT MATTER?   162
Formal and Informal Styles   163
REVISING WORD CHOICE (DICTION)   163
GETTING THE RIGHT WORD   164
Shades of Meaning   164
What's Bad about *Good* and *Bad* (and Other Broad Terms)   165
Concrete and Abstract Diction   165
Hint Box: *Latinate Diction*   166
USING AND AVOIDING JARGON   167

USING PRONOUNS: THE PERSON QUESTION   168

    The First-Person *I:* Pro and Con   169

    Voices from Across the Curriculum: **The First-Person *I***   169

    The Second-Person *You* and the Imperative Mood   170

REVISING SENTENCE STRUCTURE (SYNTAX)   171

    ACTIVE AND PASSIVE VOICES: DOING AND BEING DONE TO   171

        Passive Voice: Pro and Con   172

        Passive Voice and Scientific Writing (Avoiding *I*)   172

    STATIC VERSUS ACTIVE VERBS: *TO BE* OR NOT *TO BE*   173

    COORDINATION, SUBORDINATION, AND THE ORDER OF CLAUSES   175

        Coordination   175

        Reversing the Order of Coordinate Clauses   175

        Subordination   176

        Reversing Main and Subordinate Clauses   176

    CUTTING THE FAT   177

    Hint Box: *Expletive Constructions*   177

    THE SHAPES OF SENTENCES   178

        How to Recognize the Four Basic Sentence Types   179

        Parallel Structure   181

        The Periodic Sentence: Snapping Shut   182

        The Cumulative Sentence: Starting Fast   184

CONSISTENCY OF TONE   185

    Voices from Across the Curriculum: **Diction and Syntax**   186

GUIDELINES FOR STYLISTIC REVISION   187

CHAPTER 10

REVISING FOR CORRECTNESS   189

BASIC WRITING ERRORS (BWEs)   189

NINE BASIC WRITING ERRORS AND HOW TO FIX THEM   190

    BWE 1: SENTENCE FRAGMENTS   190

    Hint Box: *Dashes and Colons*   192

    BWE 2: COMMA SPLICES AND FUSED (OR RUN-ON) SENTENCES   193

    BWE 3: ERRORS IN SUBJECT-VERB AGREEMENT   195

    Hint Box: *Nonstandard English*   196

    BWE 4: SHIFTS IN SENTENCE STRUCTURE (FAULTY PREDICATION)   197

    BWE 5: ERRORS IN PRONOUN REFERENCE   198

        Pronoun-Antecedent Agreement   198

        Ambiguous Reference   198

Hint Box: *Sexism and Pronoun Usage*   199
   Broad Reference   199
    BWE 6: MISPLACED MODIFIERS AND DANGLING PARTICIPLES 200
    BWE 7: ERRORS IN USING POSSESSIVE APOSTROPHES   201
    BWE 8: COMMA ERRORS   202
    BWE 9: SPELLING/DICTION ERRORS THAT INTERFERE WITH MEANING 204
GLOSSARY OF GRAMMATICAL TERMS   205
GUIDELINES FOR REVISING FOR CORRECTNESS   208

APPENDIX A
DOCUMENTATION STYLES   210

SECTION I: IN-TEXT CITATIONS   211
  MLA IN-TEXT CITATIONS   211
  APA IN-TEXT CITATIONS   212
SECTION II: END-OF-TEXT LISTS OF REFERENCES (MLA AND APA)   214
  MLA WORKS CITED   214
  APA REFERENCES   219
SECTION III: DOCUMENTING ELECTRONIC SOURCES   222
  MLA DOCUMENTATION OF ELECTRONIC SOURCES   223
  APA DOCUMENTATION OF ELECTRONIC SOURCES   224
SECTION IV: OTHER DOCUMENTATION STYLES   225
  THE NUMBER-REFERENCE SYSTEM   225
  THE CHICAGO STYLE   226
SECTION V: BIBLIOGRAPHY OF STYLE MANUALS   227

APPENDIX B
GLOSSARY OF LOGICAL TERMS AND FALLACIES   229

PRODUCING GOOD THINKING: SOME NECESSARY
  HABITS OF MIND   230
GLOSSARY OF LOGICAL TERMS   231
GLOSSARY OF LOGICAL FALLACIES   237
  DERAILERS   237
  CHAIN PROBLEMS   239
INDEX   243

WRITING ANALYTICALLY

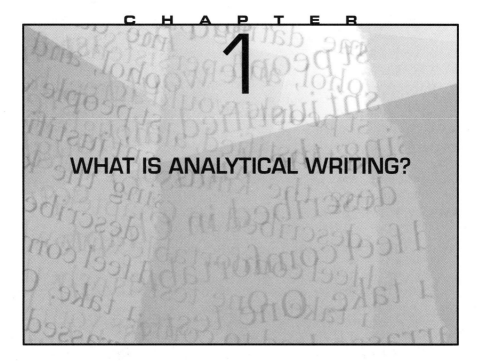

1

WHAT IS ANALYTICAL WRITING?

O F ALL THE SKILLS you acquire as a writer and thinker, analysis is likely to have the greatest impact on the way you learn. This is so because the more that you write analytically, the more actively and patiently you will think. The patience comes from recognizing that ideas and understanding can be methodically courted, that they are a product not just of sudden flashes of insight but of specific mental skills. Thinking is a process, an activity. Ideas don't just happen; they're made.

Like any activity, thinking can be performed with more strength and efficiency once you become more aware of yourself doing it. Most of us actually learn to ignore much of our own thinking and the details that would give us something to think about. This process of mental numbing is rather like what happens when you become so habituated to your surroundings and your routine ways of moving through them that you cease to see them. (Consider, for example, how much more you found yourself noticing about your campus or neighborhood before you started finding your way around as if on automatic pilot.) Learning to write analytically is primarily a matter of becoming more aware of the act of thinking.

ANALYSIS IS A SEARCH FOR MEANING

To analyze something is to ask what that something *means*. It is to ask *how* something does what it does or *why* it is as it is. The fact is that most people already analyze all the time, but they often don't realize that this is what they're doing. While analysis, the mainstay of serious thought, is the kind of thinking you'll most often be asked to do in your courses, it is also one of the most common of our mental activities.

If, for example, you find yourself being followed by a large dog, your first response, other than breaking into a cold sweat, will be to analyze the situation. What does being followed by a large dog mean for me, here, now? Does it mean the dog is vicious and about to attack? Does it mean the dog is curious and wants to play? Similarly, if you are losing at a game of tennis or you've just left a job interview or you are looking at a painting of a woman with three noses, you will begin to analyze. How can I play differently to increase my chances of winning? Am I likely to get the job, and why (or why not)? Why did the artist give the woman three noses?

ANALYSIS IS MORE THAN BREAKING A SUBJECT INTO ITS PARTS

Whether you are analyzing an awkward social situation, an economic problem, a painting, a substance in a chemistry lab, or your chances of succeeding in a job interview, the process of analysis is the same: divide the subject into its defining parts, its main elements or ingredients, and consider how these parts are related, both to each other and to the subject as a whole. In the case of the large dog, you might notice that he's dragging a leash, has a ball in his mouth, and is wearing a bright red scarf. Having broken your larger subject into these defining parts, you would try to see the connections among them and determine what they mean, what they allow you to decide about the nature of the dog: possibly somebody's lost pet, playful, probably not hostile, unlikely to bite me.

Analysis of the painting of the woman with three noses, a subject more like the kind you might be asked to write about in a college course, would proceed in the same way. Your result—ideas about the nature of the painting—would be determined, as with the dog, not only by noticing its various parts but also by your familiarity with the subject. If you knew little about painting, scrutiny of its parts would not tell you, for instance, that it is an example of the movement called cubism. You would, however, still be able to draw some analytical conclusions—ideas about the meaning and nature of the subject. You might conclude, for example, that the artist is interested in perspective or in the way we see, as opposed to realistic depictions of the world.

One common denominator of all effective analytical writing is that it pays close attention to detail. We analyze because our global responses, say, to a play or a speech or a social problem, are too general. If you comment on an entire football game, you'll find yourself saying things like "great game," which is a generic response, something you could say about almost anything. This "one-size-fits-all" kind of comment doesn't tell us very much except that you probably liked the game. In order to say more, you would necessarily become more analytical— shifting your attention to the significance of some important piece of the game, such as "they won because the offensive line was giving the quarterback all day to find his receivers" or "they lost because they couldn't defend against the safety blitz." This move from generalization to analysis, from the larger subject to its key components, is characteristic of the way we think. In order to understand a subject, we need to discover what it is "made of," the particulars that contribute most strongly to the character of the whole.

If all analysis did, however, was take subjects apart, leaving them broken and scattered, the activity would not be worth very much. The student who presents a paper to his or her professor with the words "Go ahead, rip it apart" reveals a disabling misconception about analysis—that, like dissecting a frog in a biology lab, analysis takes the life out of its subjects.

Clearly, analysis means more than breaking a subject into its parts. When you analyze a subject you ask not just "what is it made of?" but also "how do these parts help me to understand the meaning of the subject as a whole?" A good analysis seeks to locate the life of its subject, the ideas that energize it.

ANALYZING DIFFERS FROM JUDGING

As a general rule, you should seek to understand the subject you are analyzing *before* moving to a judgment about it. If you are analyzing a judgment you've already made, you will need to suspend that judgment for a while, detaching yourself from your position enough to check that you are seeing it clearly. Suspending judgment is, however, a singularly difficult thing for most people to do. This is because, as the psychologist Carl Rogers and others have argued, our natural tendency is to evaluate. Walking out of a movie, for example, most people will immediately voice their approval or disapproval, usually in either/or terms: I liked it *or* didn't like it; it was right/wrong, good/bad, interesting/boring. The other people in the conversation will then offer their own evaluation plus their judgment of the others' judgments: I think it was a good movie and that you are wrong to think it was bad. And so on.

There are several problems with this kind of reflex move to evaluation. First, such comments, because they are so general, really don't say much of significance about the subject. The fact that you liked or didn't like a movie probably says more about you—your tastes, interests, biases, and experiences—than it does about the film. Although you might go on to substantiate your judgment, saying that you thought the leading man was miscast or the dialogue too long-winded, these further comments tend to be motivated more by your desire to defend your position than to understand what the film was trying to accomplish.

Although evaluation can lead to analysis, you will usually see more in your subject if you begin the other way around. Try to figure out what your subject means before deciding how you feel about it. People are more comfortable when they can match new information to what they already know and to their habitual ways of reacting. But, the mental pathways we've grown accustomed to traveling, guided by family or friends or popular opinion, can become so automatic that we stop thinking. If you can break the evaluation reflex and press yourself to analyze before judging a subject, you will often be surprised by how much your initial responses change.

IDEAS VERSUS OPINIONS

An idea is not the same thing as an opinion. The two are closely re-lated, since both, in theory, are based on reasoning. Opinions, however, often take the form of judgments, the reflections of our personal attitudes and beliefs. While having ideas necessarily involves your attitudes and be-liefs, it is a more disinterested process than opinion making. The formula-tion of ideas, which is one of the primary aims of analysis, involves questioning; by contrast, opinions are often habitual responses, mental re-flexes like the jerk your knee makes when someone taps it lightly with a hammer.

When a writing assignment asks for your ideas about a subject, it is usually not asking for your opinion, what you think *of* the subject, but for your reasoning on what and how the subject means. The following obser-vations from a political science professor explain why and how he warns student writers to be wary of opinions:

Writers need to be aware of the distinction between an argument which seeks support from evidence, and mere opinions and assertions. Students taking politi-cal science courses often come with the assumption that in politics one opinion is as good as another. (Tocqueville thought this was a peculiarly democratic dis-ease.) From this perspective any position a political science professor may take on controversial issues is simply his or her opinion to be accepted or rejected by stu-dents according to their own beliefs/prejudices. The key task, therefore, is not so much the substitution of knowledge for opinions, but substituting well-constructed arguments for unexamined opinions.

What is an argument and how might it be distinguished from opinions? Several things need to be stressed: (1) The thesis should be linked to evidence drawn from relevant sources: polling data, interviews, historical material, etc. (2) The thesis should make as explicit as possible its own ideological assumptions. (3) A thesis, in contrast to mere statement of opinion, is committed to making an argument, which means that it presupposes a willingness to engage with others. To the extent that writers operate on the assumption that everything is in the end an opinion, they have no reason to construct arguments; they are locked into an opinion.

—G. Gambino, Professor of Political Science

ANALYSIS MAKES THE IMPLICIT EXPLICIT

A definition of analytical writing to which this book will return repeatedly is that it makes explicit (overtly stated) what is implicit (merely suggested) in both your subject and your own thinking. This process of converting suggestions into direct statements is essential to analysis, but it is also the feature of analyzing least understood by beginning writers. They fear that, like the emperor's new clothes, implications aren't really "there" but are instead the phantasms of an overactive imagination. "Reading between the lines" is the common and telling phrase that expresses this anxiety. We will have much more to say about the charge that analysis makes something out of nothing—the spaces between the lines—rather than out of what is there in black and white. But for now, let's look at a hypothetical example of this process of drawing out implications. This will suggest not only how it's done but also how often we do it in our everyday lives.

Imagine that you are driving down the highway and find yourself analyzing a billboard advertisement for a brand of beer. Such an analysis might begin with your noticing what the billboard photo contains, its various "parts"—six young, athletic, and scantily clad men and women drinking beer while pushing kayaks into a fast-running river. At this point, you have produced not an analysis but a summary—a description of what the photo contains. If, however, you go on to consider what the particulars of the photo *imply*, your summary would become analytical.

You might say, for example, that the photo implies that beer is the beverage of fashionable, healthy, active people, not just of older men with large stomachs dozing in armchairs in front of the television. Thus, the advertisement's meaning goes beyond its explicit contents; your analysis would lead you to convert to direct statement meanings that are suggested but not overtly stated, such as the advertisement's goal of attacking a common, negative stereotype about its product (that only fat, lazy men drink beer). The naming of parts that you do in analysis is not an end unto itself; it allows you to better understand the nature of your subject. The implications of the "parts" you name are an important part of that understanding.

ANALYSIS IS A PROCESS OF ASKING YOURSELF QUESTIONS

Although the process of analysis always involves the same basic moves—determining the significant parts of a topic and how they are related—there is no set formula, no single set of steps for arriving at an analysis. The steps a writer goes through in constructing an analysis rarely occur in the order that they appear in the finished essay. This is because analysis, like all forms of writing, requires a lot of experimenting. The essays you read are the carefully arranged and rearranged products of a messy and much less linear process.

When you start analyzing, you don't know for sure where you're going or how you will get there. Instead you ask questions like the following (not necessarily in this order):

- Which details are significant and which aren't? Why?
- What is the significance of a particular detail? What does it mean?
- What else might it mean?
- How do the details fit together? What do they have in common?
- What does this pattern of details mean?
- What else might this same pattern of details mean? How else could it be explained?

- What details don't seem to fit? How might they be connected with other details to form a different pattern?

- What does this new pattern mean? How might it cause me to read the meaning of individual details differently?

The process of posing and answering such questions—the analytical process—is one of trial and error. Learning to write well is largely a matter of learning how to frame questions. One of the main things you acquire in the study of an academic discipline is knowledge of the kinds of questions that the discipline typically asks. For example, an economics professor and a sociology professor might observe the same phenomenon, such as a sharp decline in health benefits for the elderly, and analyze its causes and significance in different ways. The economist might consider how such benefits are financed and how changes in government policy and the country's population patterns might explain the declining supply of funds for the elderly. The sociologist might ask about attitudes toward the elderly and about the social structures that the elderly rely on for support.

Whatever questions you ask, the answers you propose will often produce more questions. Like signposts on a trail, details (data) that initially seem to point in one direction may, on closer examination, lead you someplace else. Dealing with these realities of analytical writing requires patience, but it will also make you a more confident thinker, since you'll come to know that your uncertainty is a normal and necessary part of writing. Good ideas rarely spring to life of their own accord, like the lightbulb going on over the head of a cartoon thinker. Because the purpose of analytical writing is to figure something out, you shouldn't expect to know at the outset exactly where you are going, how all of your subject's parts fit together, and to what end.

In general, only the most practiced analytical thinkers can arrive at their best ideas before they begin to write. The common observation "I know what I want to say; I'm just having trouble getting it down on paper" is a half-truth at best. Getting words on paper almost always alters your ideas and leads you to discover thoughts you didn't know you had. If you expect to have all the answers before you begin to write, you are more likely to settle for relatively superficial ideas. And, when you try to conduct all of your thinking in your head, you may arrive at an idea but not be able to explain how you got there.

Writing allows us to follow our mental trails and to experiment with alternate routes without losing track of where we've been. This is important because the process of having ideas rarely moves steadily forward, traveling in an uninterrupted line from point to point like a connect-the-dots picture. Instead, thinking and writing are *recursive* activities, which means that we move forward by looking backward, by repeatedly going over the same ground, looking for wrong turns, uncovering signposts we may have missed, and reinterpreting signposts passed earlier because of what we later discovered. To figure out where we're going, we often need to revisit where we've been. Without writing, in all but the most carefully trained memories, the way back keeps vanishing, sometimes leaving us stranded.

USE PREWRITING TO FIND WORKABLE QUESTIONS

The tentative and exploratory nature of good analytical thinking makes it especially important to incorporate some kind of prewriting into your writing process. If you move directly from thinking about your subject to writing a draft, you will almost inevitably produce an overly general analysis. The pressures of time tempt most of us to move to a conclusion about a subject before we've spent enough time examining a subject. The solution to this problem is to *slow down*. Spend some time simply recording what you notice about your subject, and don't worry about where these observations might lead. By opening up your thinking in this way, you will discover more data to think with, more possible starting points from which to develop an idea. And, you will be less likely to get trapped into seeing only those features of your subject that support the first conclusion you come to.

One of several advantages to writing your observations down is that you can look back and remember your initial responses to the subject. In your prewriting phase, you should also write down all of the questions that occur to you; a good paper is essentially the answer to a good question, an explanation of some feature or features of your subject that needed explaining. If you don't take the time to look for questions, you might end up writing a tidy but relatively pointless paper.

When you shift from prewriting to writing a first draft, you may not—and most likely will not—have all the answers, but you will waste significantly less time chasing ill-focused and inadequately considered ideas than might otherwise have been the case. Good analytical papers retain an open and exploratory stance toward their subjects and share the process of discovery with their readers, but very few writers can begin a draft without first doing some writing aimed at finding a workable starting point and eliminating less fruitful pathways.

COMMON CHARGES AGAINST ANALYSIS

Once you accept the challenge of thinking and writing analytically—the careful, recursive, and nonjudgmental observation of your subject and of your own thoughts that analysis requires—you can expect to encounter another obstacle. Although analysis is an activity we call on constantly in our everyday lives, many people are deeply suspicious of it. "Why can't you just enjoy the movie rather than picking it apart?" they'll say. Or, "Oh, you're just making that up!" You may even be accused of being an unfeeling person if you adopt an analytical stance, since it is typical of this anti-intellectual position to insist that feeling and thinking are separate and essentially incompatible activities.

CHARGE 1: "ANALYSIS KILLS ENJOYMENT"

The danger of allowing yourself to fall into these common attitudes about analysis is that they can cause you to give up on the process of thinking and writing analytically almost as soon as you start. Or you'll write analytically for your courses but allow yourself to be embarrassed out of the activity everywhere else. The antidote to this, as with other problems, is to analyze it. Why, for example, should enjoyment and understanding be incompatible? At the experiential level, all one needs to do to raise doubts about this charge is to listen to the conversation of football fans after a game. If analysis is interfering with their enjoyment, they apparently haven't noticed. But citing such examples doesn't fairly answer the charge.

At the root of the analysis-kills-the-fun complaint is the idea that analysis is critical—in the sense of disapproving and negative. From this point of view, the basic activity of analysis (asking questions), along with its deliberate delaying of evaluation, seems skeptical, uncommitted, and uncaring. But raising questions and working out the possible meanings of significant details are not necessarily negative, nor do they require a complete absence of feeling. In fact, analytical thinkers tend to be more dedicated than most people to understanding, and thus to being sensitive to rather than attacking a subject. Understanding is not the enemy of enjoyment, at least not for people who enjoy thinking. In any case, the global "I like it/I don't like it" move is less common to people who have learned to think analytically because they are more likely to make careful distinctions—deciding to like some features of a subject (for well-explained reasons) while disliking others.

CHARGE 2: "ANALYSIS FINDS MEANINGS THAT ARE NOT THERE"

What about the charge that analysis "reads into" a subject things that aren't there ("reading between the lines")? Proponents of this view of analysis are, in effect, committing themselves to the position that everything in life means what it says and says what it means, that meanings are always obvious and thus don't require interpretation. Although the pursuit of implication can become a problem if a writer comes to believe that meaning is solely a matter of individual interpretation, the idea that all communication is a matter of direct statement is equally extreme and easily open to question.

The following experiment will demonstrate how much even everyday conversation depends on our ability to perceive what is not explicitly "there." Try writing down as much detail as you can remember about a recent, relatively brief conversation, using as many of the actual words as you can remember. Then write a summary (as opposed to a word-for-word restatement) of what you think got said in the interaction between the speakers. What, if anything, did you think was being communicated that a literal (word-for-word) account of the conversation would not capture?

We should acknowledge that analysis sometimes does draw out the implications of things that are not there, usually when the omission of some part of a subject runs counter to our expectations and thus is conspicuous in its absence. An analysis of the Nancy Drew mysteries, for example, might attach significance to the absence of a mother in the books, particularly in light of the fact that biological mothers, as opposed to wicked stepmothers, are pretty rare in other stories involving female heroines and in fairy tales. Taking note of this as a potentially significant omission could lead to a series of analytical questions, the first being How might this common denominator of certain kinds of children's stories be explained?

Here's another example of a case in which a writer might want to pursue the implications of something being left out. Consider what you might make of a cigarette advertisement that includes a line of laughing young men and women in unisex attire holding one of their number across their outstretched arms but no cigarettes or any sign of smoking. What might the omission of smoking in the picture mean, since its sponsor no doubt wishes to encourage the activity? What does this omission imply about the nature of the advertisement's message and its means of influencing viewers?

CHARGE 3: "SOME SUBJECTS WEREN'T MEANT TO BE ANALYZED"

The preceding example raises the argument that it is foolish to analyze subjects that were meant only to entertain (like science-fiction movies) or to serve some practical need (like shopping malls or blue jeans). Should analytical thinkers steer clear of subjects that supposedly weren't meant to be analyzed, like bowling and Barbie dolls and late-night television? This is a more complex question because it runs into people's prejudices about so-called "highbrow" and "lowbrow" activities. If asked to name highbrow subjects, most of us would come up with the same kind of list—Mozart's string quartets, for example, or foreign movies with subtitles. To the extent that analytical thinking is labeled a highbrow activity, highbrows are meant to stick to their own turf. Take your Mozart but leave my romance novels and fast-food favorites alone.

The question of *intention*—what was and what wasn't "meant" to be analyzed— is, at least in part, an extension of the highbrow/lowbrow divide. Barbie dolls, for example, and Saturday morning cartoon shows are made for children. But the fact that the creators of Barbie were trying to make money by entertaining children rather than trying to create a cultural artifact doesn't rule out analysis of Barbie's characteristics (built-in earrings, high-heeled feet), marketing, and appeal as a cultural phenomenon. Similarly, the makers of tough-guy movies may not have intended to produce propaganda on the value of rugged individualism and may even have produced completely different statements of their intentions. What the makers of a particular product or idea intend, however, is only a part of what their work means; intention does not finally control the implications that a work possesses. In sum, the attempt to cordon off certain subjects as too lowbrow for analysis is, ironically, the elitist (in-group and exclusionary) position. Analysis knows no brow. Take any subject about which we want to understand more, and analysis will help.

DISTINGUISHING ANALYSIS FROM
EXPRESSIVE WRITING AND ARGUMENT

How does analysis differ from other kinds of thinking and writing? A common way of answering this question is to think of communication as having three possible centers of emphasis—the *writer,* the *subject,* and the *audience.* Communication, of course, involves all three of these components, but some kinds of writing concentrate more on one than on the others. Autobiographical writing, such as diaries or memoirs or stories about personal experience, centers on the writer and his or her desire for self-expression. Argument, in which the writer either advocates or challenges a policy or attitude, is reader centered; its goal is to bring about a change in readers' actions and beliefs. Analytical writing is more concerned with arriving at an understanding of a subject than it is with either self-expression or changing readers' views.

These three categories of writing are not mutually exclusive. So, for example, expressive (writer-centered) writing is also analytical in its attempts to define and explain a writer's feelings, reactions, and experiences. And analysis is a form of self-expression, since it inevitably reflects the ways a writer's experiences have taught him or her to think about the world. But even though expressive writing and analysis overlap, they also differ significantly in method and aim. In expressive writing, your primary subject is yourself, with other subjects serving as a means of evoking greater self-understanding. In analytical writing, your reasoning may derive from personal experience, but it is your reasoning and not you or your experiences that matters. Analysis asks not just "What do I think?" but "How good is my thinking? How well does it fit the subject I am trying to explain?"

In its emphasis on logic and the dispassionate scrutiny of ideas ("What do I think about what I think?"), analysis is a close cousin of argument. But analysis and argument are not the same. Analytical writers are frequently more concerned with persuading themselves, with discovering what they believe about a subject, than they are with persuading others. While the writer of an argument often goes into the writing process with some certainty about the position he or she supports, the writer of an analysis is more likely to begin with the details of a subject he or she wishes to better understand.

Accordingly, argument and analysis often differ in the kind of thesis statements they formulate. The thesis of an argument is usually some kind of *should statement:* readers should or shouldn't vote for bans on smoking in public buildings, or they should or shouldn't believe that gays can function effectively in the military. The thesis of an analysis is usually a tentative answer to a *what, how,* or *why* question; it seeks to explain why people watch professional wrestling, or what a rising number of sexual harassment cases might mean, or how certain features of government health care policy are designed to allay the fears of the middle class. The writer of an analysis is less concerned with convincing readers to approve or disapprove of professional wrestling or legal intervention into the sexual politics of the workplace or government control of health care than with discovering how each of these complex subjects might be defined and explained. As should be obvious, though, the best arguments are built upon careful analysis: the better you understand a subject, the more likely you will be to find valid positions to argue about it.

ANALYSIS VERSUS ARGUMENT IN WRITING ASSIGNMENTS

It is not always easy to determine which kind of writing an assignment asks for, but making these distinctions can matter a lot. As a case in point, let's consider the kinds of directions that were given to students for writing essays in an actual standardized placement exam. As you will see, focusing on this language of directions will reveal key differences between argument and analysis and offer a useful means of further defining these two kinds of writing. (To maintain this focus we have omitted the passages on which the essay topics were based.) As you read the assignment below, ask yourself what kind of writing it asks you to do.

> The writer of the following passage (from Thomas Carlyle's *Past and Present*) expresses an attitude toward work and in so doing makes certain assumptions about human nature. In a well-written essay, define precisely what that attitude and those assumptions are and analyze how the writer uses language to convince the reader of the rightness of his position.

Like many essay questions, this one uses the word *analyze* and assumes you know how it should direct your writing. But other language in the question could cause you to misread what you are being asked to do. The phrase "to convince the reader of the rightness of his position" contains the language of argument—*convince, rightness, position*. Notice, however, that you are *not* being asked to take a stand on the position the passage promotes. The phrase *analyze how* ("analyze how the writer uses language") is a clue that your essay should be primarily analytical rather than argumentative. An extended discussion of what seems to you to be right or wrong about Carlyle's argument might be intelligent and interesting, but it would not provide the analysis the assignment calls for. It would, in fact, be largely irrelevant to the question posed by the assignment, which concerns how the passage accomplishes certain ends rather than what your opinion of those ends might be.

Here are three more essay questions. One clearly asks for an argument, one for analysis, and one for a combination of the two. As you read, look for language that seems most clearly to direct you toward one of these kinds of writing or the other. (We have again omitted the passages to which the questions apply.)

> (a) Each of the two passages below offers a definition of freedom. In a well-written essay, describe the concept of freedom embodied in each and discuss the differences between the two.

> (b) The study described in the passage below draws certain conclusions about the present state of television in the United States and implies that television should reflect the real world. Consider whether you agree with these conclusions and this implication. Then write an essay in which you take and defend a position on one or more of the issues raised in the passage.

> (c) In a well-written essay, evaluate the truth of the following assertion: "It is human nature to want patterns, standards, and a structure of behavior. A pattern to conform to is a kind of shelter." Use evidence and examples from your reading or experience to make your argument convincing.

Example *a* uses the words *describe* and *discuss*. Although these words are sufficiently vague to give you some leeway, describing two concepts and differentiating them is primarily an analytical task. Although you might agree with one of the concepts more than the other, arguing for this preference could distract you from the more analytical role (interpretive and explanatory) you've been asked to play—providing your ideas on the concepts' meaning and implications rather than passing judgment on them.

The language of example *b* offers as overt a request for argument as you are likely to get: "should," "issues," "whether you agree," "take and defend a position." Even the word *consider,* which invites the more tentative and exploratory manner of analysis, is limited to "whether you agree." The question asks primarily for your judgments. To write the essay, however, you would need to analyze the passage (as well as the question) to decide what it means and to draw out implications that might affect your response.

Essay question *c* is tricky in its blending of language calling for argument and for analysis. The first part of the question asks you to "evaluate the truth of the assertion." The word *evaluate,* like the word *consider,* invites the sort of open weighing and balancing of various possibilities that characterizes analysis. But the word *truth* and the direction "make your argument convincing" invoke the true/false, right/wrong decision making typical of argument, along with argument's emphasis on persuasion.

Despite the question's apparent request for argument, the quotation it asks you to argue about first requires analysis: "It is human nature to want patterns, standards, and a structure of behavior. A pattern to conform to is a kind of shelter." Your first response to this assertion would necessarily be analytical—an answer to the question "what does it mean?" Since the assertion could mean more than one thing, you would need to propose the various possibilities (an aim of analysis) before you could go on to argue for the truth or falsehood of one of them.

What are the implications of the word *shelter,* for example? Is it a hiding place wherein one could complacently exclude standards and patterns that differed from his or her own? Or are we to read *shelter* more positively, as a haven wherein one could accumulate enough confidence and stability to deal effectively with the world? And what is the meaning of the phrase "a structure of behavior"? Only after you had used analysis to make decisions on these questions of meaning (not to mention what is meant by "human nature") could you go on to presenting your views on the truth of the assertion. A key part of any kind of writing is defining your terms. And a key part of responding to any question is analyzing the question. In this case, a large part of your essay would necessarily be devoted to working out the meaning of the assertion that you are meant to evaluate—a primarily analytical task.

ANALYSIS AND SUMMARY

One of the most common kinds of writing you'll be asked to do in college, other than analysis, is summary. Summary differs from analysis, because the aim of summary is to recount, in effect, to reproduce someone else's ideas. But summary and analysis, like analysis and argument, are clearly related, each depending on the other. Summary is important to analysis, since you can't analyze a subject without laying out its important parts for your reader. Similarly, analysis is important to

Figure 1.1 *Arrangement in Black and Grey: The Artist's Mother* by James Abbott McNeill Whistler, 1871. How would an analysis of this painting differ from a summary of it?

summary, because summarizing is more than just copying someone else's words. To write an accurate summary you have to ask analytical questions. Which of the ideas in the reading are most significant? Why? How do these ideas fit together? What do the key passages in the reading mean? Like analysis, summary requires you to gain perspective on your subject as a whole by explaining the meaning and function of each of that subject's parts.

So, summary, like analysis, is a tool of understanding and not just a mechanical task. But a summary stops short of analysis because summary typically makes much smaller interpretive leaps. A summary of the painting popularly known as *Whistler's Mother,* for example, would tell readers what the painting includes, which details are the most prominent, and even what the overall effect of the painting seems to be. An analysis would go further. It might tell us, for instance, that the painter's choice to portray his subject in profile contributes to our sense of her separateness from us and of her nonconfrontational passivity. We look at her, but she does not look back at us. Her black dress and the fitted lace cap that obscures her hair are not only emblems of her self-effacement, shrouds disguising her identity like her expressionless face, but also the tools of her self-containment and thus of her power to remain aloof from prying eyes.

What is the attraction of this painting (this being one of the questions that an analysis might ask)? What might draw a viewer to the sight of this austere, drably attired woman, sitting alone in the center of a mostly blank space? Perhaps it is the very starkness of the painting, and the mystery of self-sufficiency at its center, that attracts us.

ANALYSIS AND PERSONAL ASSOCIATION

Observations like these go beyond description, but, it is important to notice, they stay with the task of explaining the painting, rather than moving to private associations that the painting might prompt, such as effusions about old age, or rocking chairs, or the character and situation of the writer's own grandmother. Such associations could well be valuable unto themselves as a means of prompting a searching piece of personal writing. They might also help you to interpret some feature of the painting that you are working to understand, but such *associative* leaps are not the interpretive moves appropriate to analysis.

Analysis is a creative activity, a fairly open form of inquiry, but its imaginative scope is governed by logic. The hypothetical analysis we have offered is not the only reading of the painting that a viewer might make, since the same pattern of details might lead to different conclusions. But a viewer would not be free to conclude anything he or she wished, such as that the woman is mourning the death of a son or is patiently waiting to die. Such conclusions would be unfounded speculations, since the black dress is not sufficient to support them. Analysis often operates in areas where there is no one right answer, but, like summary and argument, it requires the writer to reason from evidence.

As we said at the beginning of this chapter, analysis is a form of detective work. It can surprise us with ideas that our experiences produce once we take the time to listen to ourselves thinking. But analysis is also a discipline; it has rules that govern how we proceed and that enable others to judge the validity of our ideas. A good analytical thinker needs to be the attentive Dr. Watson to his or her own Sherlock Holmes. That is what the remainder of this book will teach you to do.

GUIDELINES FOR WRITING ANALYTICALLY

1. Divide the subject into its defining parts, its main elements or ingredients, and consider how these parts are related, both to one another and to the subject as a whole.
2. When you analyze a subject, ask not just "What is it made of?" but also "How do these parts help me to understand the meaning of the subject as a whole?"
3. Seek to understand the subject you are analyzing before moving to a judgment about it.
4. Analytical writing makes explicit (overtly stated) what is implicit (suggested) in both your subject and your own thinking.

5. The thesis of an argument is usually some kind of *should* statement. The thesis of an analysis is usually a tentative answer to a *what, how,* or *why* question.

6. A key part of any kind of writing is defining your terms. A key part of responding to any question is to analyze the question.

7. Like analysis, summary requires you to gain perspective on your subject as a whole by explaining the meaning and function of each of that subject's parts. But a summary stops short of analysis, because a summary typically makes much smaller interpretive leaps.

8. Analysis often operates in areas where there is no one right answer. Like summary and argument, however, it requires the writer to reason from evidence.

CHAPTER 2

CONSTRUCTING EFFECTIVE TOPICS

THIS CHAPTER ADDRESSES THE methods and aims of analytical writing from the perspective of what you are expected to write about. Often thought of as a prelude to writing, the construction and interpretation of topics is, in fact, an essential part of the writing process.

ASSIGNED VERSUS OPEN TOPICS

Most of the analytical writing you do for your college courses will be in response to one of two situations: (1) you are given a topic to write about, with varying degrees of specificity about how you should proceed, or (2) you are asked to locate a topic of your own within guidelines that also vary in their specificity. There are obviously some big differences between having a topic assigned to you and coming up with one on your own. Ultimately, though, assigned and open (self-designed) topics share underlying similarities that outweigh these differences.

Perhaps the most important thing to recognize in your treatment of topics is that the effectiveness of your response to the topic will depend on your ability to interpret the directions and recognize the kind of writing being called for. Consider, for example, an assignment to "discuss how a supply-side economist might respond to the idea of eliminating most tariffs on imported goods." How do you interpret the word *discuss*? Should you confine your response to summarizing (restating) the reading you've done on the subject? Should you analyze the reading, by drawing out its unstated assumptions or pointing to inconsistencies in its position? Should you write an argument about the reading, revealing the extent to which you agree or disagree with the supply-side view?

Such questions, of course, are usually resolved best by consulting your professor, but often you will find that he or she does not have only one kind of response to the topic in mind. A major aim of most topics is to challenge you to focus further within the assigned boundaries: the professor constructs a topic that you construct some more. In this respect, virtually all assigned topics are, to some extent, open.

By the same token, virtually all open or self-designed topics contain invisible limits. When you are told to "write a paper" on tariff legislation or the novel *Moby Dick* or the Franco-Prussian War, you recognize that you aren't really free in all sorts of fundamental ways. You know not to discuss the war in terms of last Sunday's football game, or the novel in terms of the *Classics Illustrated* comic book version, or the tariff in terms of biblical laws about usury. As you gain experience in a particular discipline, you come to know the more specific rules that govern how a given kind of topic may be approached in that discipline. An English major knows, for example, that biographical information on an author may be used in an analysis of that author's work as an informing context but not as proof of the author's intentions. A psychology major knows that a hypothesis must be subjected to empirical testing.

In assigned topics, a discipline's methodology and ways of limiting and defining evidence are often prescribed overtly. In open topics, these prescriptions are more often assumed or implied; the professor assumes that you either already know the rules of the game or will learn them by having to design the topic. In both cases, formulating and interpreting topics are crucial parts of the writing process, not just preludes to it.

MAKING A TOPIC ANALYTICAL: LOCATING AN AREA OF UNCERTAINTY

Although disciplines vary in the kinds of questions they characteristically ask, every discipline is concerned with asking questions, exploring areas of uncertainty, and attempting to solve or at least clarify problems. As a general rule, you should seek out *live questions over inert answers*. Rather than leading you to a single or obvious answer, an analytical topic involves you in locating and exploring the questions in the information you have been studying. Its aim is to define a space in which you can have ideas about what you've been learning.

Finding a space in which you can have an idea doesn't mean that you should pursue your own ideas while ignoring all other information, nor does it mean that you should merely report information with no reference to your own thinking. Instead, you need to find ways of formulating and interpreting topics that locate a middle ground between these two extremes.

WHAT IT MEANS TO HAVE AN IDEA

What does it mean to have an idea? This question lies at the heart of your role in topic construction. In order to get beyond summary, must you have an idea that is entirely "original"? And, if you are to actively engage rather than just react to your subject, must you have an idea that revolutionizes your self-understanding and your stance toward the world?

Both of these expectations are unreasonably grand. Clearly, a writer in the early stages of learning about a subject can't be expected to arrive at an idea so original that, like a Ph.D. thesis, it radically revises complex concepts in a discipline. Nor should you count as ideas only those that lead to some kind of self-revelation.

What, then, does it mean to have an idea? You can probably best understand what it means by considering what ideas do and where they can be found. Here is a partial list:

- An idea answers a question; it explains something that needs to be explained.

- An idea usually starts with an observation that is puzzling, with something that you want to figure out rather than something that you think you already understand.

- An idea may be the discovery of a question where there seemed not to be one.

- An idea may make explicit and explore the meaning of something implicit—an unstated assumption upon which an argument rests or a logical consequence of a given position.

- An idea may connect elements of a subject and explain the significance of that connection.

- An idea often accounts for some dissonance, something that seems not to fit together.

Most analytical topics aim at getting you to locate questions like these, or they raise them for you, suggesting problems to resolve and competing ideas for you to bring into some kind of alignment. In other words—and this is the primary trait that most analytical topics share—they deliberately locate you in an area of *uncertainty*. They put you in a position where there is something to negotiate, where you are required not just to list answers but also to ask questions, make choices, and engage in reasoning about the meaning and significance of your evidence.

SEVEN RULES OF THUMB
FOR HANDLING COMPLEXITY

As the section above suggests, an analytical response to a topic involves you in explaining something that is not overtly explained for you in the subject matter you are studying. Such topics call on you, in other words, to deliberately situate yourself among sites of potential ambiguity or conflict, so that your writing can explore the complexity of your subject. In order to learn how to enter this uncertain space, you will first have to get over the fear that you are doing something wrong if you cannot arrive quickly at a clear and obvious answer. Many inexperienced writers deliberately avoid complexity—rejecting positions, for example, for which there is a possible counterargument—because of this fear.

If you want your education to teach you analytical skills and not just information, you need to resist the temptation to bail out when you encounter uncertainty and complexity. Although repeating material from lectures and readings will teach you ideas, it cannot teach you how to arrive at ideas. You can't learn to deduce the implications of former president John F. Kennedy's foreign policy, for example, only by paraphrasing how someone else has drawn out those implications.

Virtually all writers feel uncomfortable when encountering complexity. But discomfort need not lead to avoidance or to verbal paralysis. The following rules of thumb can help you respond to the complexities of the topics that you encounter rather than oversimplifying or evading them.

RULE 1: REDUCE SCOPE

Whenever possible, reduce drastically the range of your inquiry. Resist the temptation to include too much information. Even when an assignment calls for broad coverage of a subject, an effective and usually acceptable strategy is for you to cover the ground up front and then analyze one or two key points in greater depth.

For example, if you were asked to write on former president Franklin Roosevelt's New Deal, you would obviously have to open with some general observations, such as what it was and why it arose. But if you tried to stay on this general level throughout, your paper would have little direction or focus. You could achieve a focus, though, by moving quickly from the general to some much smaller and more specific part of the subject, such as attacks on the New Deal. You would then be able to limit the enormous range of possible evidence to a few representative figures, such as Huey Long, Father Coughlin, and Alf Landon. Once you began to compare the terms and legitimacy of their opposition to the New Deal, you would be much more likely to manage a complex analysis of the subject than if you had remained at the level of broad generalization. If you are unsure about the amount of focusing you can do with the topic, you should, of course, ask your professor. Typically you will find that some mixing of wide-angle coverage with more narrowly focused (and thus more in-depth) discussion is appropriate.

RULE 2: STUDY THE WORDING OF TOPICS FOR UNSTATED QUESTIONS

Nearly all formulations of a topic, whether the professor's or your own, contain a number of questions that will emerge when you ponder the wording. Framing these questions overtly is often the first step to having an idea. Take a topic question such as "Is feminism good for Judaism?" It seems to invite you simply to argue yes or no, but it actually requires you to set up and answer a number of implied questions. For example, what does "good for Judaism" mean? That which allows the religion to evolve? That which conserves its tradition? The same kinds of questions, defining and contextualizing and laying out implications, might be asked of the term *feminism*. And what of the possibility that feminism has no significant effect whatsoever?

As this example illustrates, even an apparently limited and straightforward question presses writers to make choices about how to engage it. So don't leap from the topic question to your plan of attack too quickly. One of the best tricks of the trade lies in smoking out and addressing the unstated questions implied by the wording of the topic.

RULE 3: SUSPECT YOUR FIRST RESPONSES

If you settle for your first, instinctive response, the result is likely to be superficial, obvious, and overly general. A better strategy is to examine your first responses for ways in which they are inaccurate and then develop the implications of these overstatements (or errors) into a new formulation. In many cases, writers go through this process of proposing and rejecting ideas ten times or more before they arrive at an angle or approach that will sustain an essay.

A first response is okay for a start, as long as you don't stop there. For example, most of us would agree, *at first glance,* that no one should be denied health care, or that a given film or novel that concludes with a marriage is a happy ending, or that the American government should not pass trade laws that might cause Americans to lose their jobs. On closer inspection, however, each of these responses begins to reveal its limitations. Given that there is a limited amount of money available, should everyone, regardless of age or physical condition, be accorded every medical treatment that might prolong life? And might not a novel or film that concludes in marriage signal that the society depicted offers too few options, or more cynically, that the author is feeding the audience an implausible fantasy to blanket over problems raised earlier in the work? And couldn't trade laws resulting in short-term loss of jobs ultimately produce more jobs and a healthier economy? As these examples suggest, first responses—usually pieces of conventional wisdom—can blind you to rival explanations. Try not to decide on an answer to questions you're given—or those of your own making—too quickly.

RULE 4: BEGIN WITH QUESTIONS, NOT ANSWERS

Whether you are focusing on an assigned topic or devising one of your own, you are usually better off to begin with something that you don't understand very well and want to understand better. Begin by asking what kinds of questions the material poses. So, for example, if you are convinced that Robinson Crusoe changes throughout Defoe's novel and you write a paper cataloguing those changes, you will essentially be composing a selective plot summary. If, by contrast, you wonder *why* Crusoe walls himself within a fortress after he discovers a footprint in the sand, you will be more likely to interpret the significance of events than just to report them.

RULE 5: FOCUS ON UNEXPECTED SIMILARITIES AND DIFFERENCES

The typical move when you are asked to compare two subjects is to collect a number of parallel examples and show how they are parallel. In the case of obvious similarities, you should move quickly to *significant differences within the similarity* and the implications of these differences. For example, both the Carolingian and Burgundian Renaissances share an emphasis on education, but if you were asked to compare them, you could reveal the character of these two historical periods more effectively by concentrating on the different purposes and origins of this interest in education. A corollary of this tip is that you should focus on *unexpected similarity rather than obvious difference*. It is no surprise that President Bill Clinton's economic package differed from former president Ronald Reagan's, but much could be written about the way that Clinton "out-Reaganed Bush" (as one political commentator put it) by appealing to voters with Reagan's brand of populist optimism.

RULE 6: WRITE ALL OF THE TIME ABOUT WHAT YOU ARE STUDYING

Writing about what you are studying while you are studying it is probably the single best preparation for developing interesting topics. Don't wait to start writing until you think you have an idea you can organize a paper around. Ideally, you should be formulating possible topics long before an actual topic is assigned. By writing informally—as a matter of routine—about what you are studying, you can acquire the habits of mind necessary to having and developing ideas. Similarly, by reading as often and as attentively as you can, and by writing spontaneously about what you read, you will accustom yourself to being a less passive consumer of ideas and information, and you will have more ideas and information available to think actively with and about. The various forms of informal writing go under the general heading of *prewriting*. We will discuss the most prevalent of these forms shortly.

RULE 7: EXPECT TO *BECOME* INTERESTED

Writing gives you the opportunity to cultivate your curiosity by thinking exploratively. Rather than approaching topics in a mechanical way or putting them off to the last possible moment and doing the assignment grudgingly, try giving yourself and the topic the benefit of the doubt. If you can suspend judgment and start writing, you will often find yourself uncovering interests where you had not seen them before. In other words, accept the idea that interest is a product of writing—not a prerequisite.

USING PREWRITING
TO FIND AND INTERPRET TOPICS

In general, prewriting aims to help you practice thinking about course materials before committing yourself to more sustained and formal writing. For most writers, prewriting offers the best antidote to superficial writing—and to writer's block. With prewriting you will be better able to deal with complexity because you will be less likely to cling doggedly to the first topic or response to a topic that occurs to you. And you will find yourself better able to develop and organize your ideas when you begin work on your more nearly finished drafts because you already will have explored some of the possible paths you might travel, and you already will have discovered and left behind potential dead ends.

There are many forms of prewriting, but they are all premised on the belief that the act of writing is not just a way of recording what you think but of discovering what you think. As the novelist E. M. Forster put it, "How can I tell what I think till I see what I say?" Unlike a finished essay, in which the sentences follow logically as you unfold your central idea, prewriting encourages you to leap *associatively* from idea to idea as these arise. One of the advantages of this less structured, less sequential kind of writing is that it reduces anxiety. Rather than worrying about what you can find to say, you start saying things. Not everything you come up with will be worthy of developing into a paper, but you will often be surprised at the connections you make and the workable starting points you discover when prewriting.

FREEWRITING

Freewrites are the loosest form of prewriting, requiring only that you write more or less continuously—and usually without much premeditation—for a specified period of time (usually between ten and twenty minutes). Try to keep moving. Don't pause to edit or correct or bite your pen or stare into space; just write. The pressure of writing continuously will reduce your anxiety about being wrong and encourage you to switch tracks when you hit a dead end or when a new idea springs up. Although some freewrites unfold along a single line, more often they allow you to survey the range of your thinking on a subject. Whenever you feel yourself getting stuck, try finishing the sentence "What I'm really trying to say is. . . ." Try finishing this sentence not just once but a half dozen times or more, and see what happens.

FOCUSED FREEWRITING

Focused freewrites follow the same procedure as freewrites, except that you attempt to stay within a more narrowly defined subject. Often you will take your best idea from a previous freewrite and then explore it on the page for ten minutes or so without stopping. Or you might put a single word or idea at the top of the page and write continuously about that. (By the way, this exercise is fun to try with common objects, so that you might freewrite about a piece of chalk, for example, as well as about a word, question, or concept.)

Focused freewrites are an especially useful way to move from a broad topic to a more carefully—which almost always means more narrowly—focused one. Focused freewrites can also help you notice more in your reading and be better prepared for class discussion. Try preparing for class by doing one or more focused freewrites on a single question or passage from the reading. You can locate passages for yourself by asking yourself questions like "Which part of the reading did I find the most interesting or significant or revealing or useful or unexpected or challenging?" Also try doing some open or more focused freewrites as soon as possible after a lecture or discussion, as this practice can greatly improve your ability to retain, and thus to build on and think about what you hear. Try starting points like "What I now understand about the subject is. . . ." Remember that you can include questions, as these occur to you, as well as statements. Then try various ways of answering your own questions. This essentially is what the process of constructing topics—and thus of writing—is all about: formulating and responding to questions.

JOURNALS

Unlike a personal diary in which you keep track of your days' activities and recount the feelings these occasioned, journals are for generating and collecting ideas and for keeping track of your interactions with course materials. A journal can be, in effect, a collection of focused freewrites that you develop in response to the reading and lectures in a course.

The best way to get a journal to work for you is to experiment. You might try, for example, copying and commenting on statements from your reading or class meetings that you found potentially illuminating. Use the journal to write down the ideas, reactions, and germs of ideas you had during a class discussion or that you found running around in your head after a late night's reading. Use the journal to retain your first impressions of books or films or music or performances, so that you can look back and trace the development of your thinking.

If possible, write in your journal every day. As with freewriting, the best way to get started is just to start, see what happens, and take it from there. Also as with freewriting, the more you write, the more you'll find yourself noticing, and thus the more you'll have to say.

MAKING YOUR RESPONSE
TO TOPICS MORE ANALYTICAL

By the time you reach college, you will have learned to recognize certain kinds of instructions that topics characteristically contain: compare and contrast, define, agree or disagree. The key words of a topic, both in topics of your own making and those that are assigned to you, trigger different kinds of writing. As we discussed in Chapter 1, analysis, although it appears in most other kinds of writing, has its own characteristic methods and aims. An analytical topic, one asking you to consider what some feature of a subject means or how it functions, requires a different approach from a topic asking you to take a firm and persuasive stand, as you might in a debate.

Much of the writing and thinking you will be asked to do in college is analytical. If you are not accustomed to writing analytically, you will need to learn how to see when a topic calls for analysis and how to design such topics for yourself. The following discussion will show you how to make more analytical responses to five common kinds of topics. These topics are

1. Summary
2. Personal response
3. Binaries (either/or questions)
4. Comparison and contrast
5. Definition

THE SUMMARY TOPIC

Advantages of Summary

All analytical topics require a blend of two components: a thinking component and an information component. Summary provides the information component. Summarizing is basically a translation process, and, as such, it is an essential part of learning. It is the way that not just facts and figures but also other people's theories and observations enter your writing. An effective summary requires significant analytical skill. Although summaries at their worst may merely present a list of sentences paraphrased or quoted randomly from a reading, summarizing effectively (as we suggested in the "Analysis and Summary" section of Chapter 1) requires you to determine what parts of the information are important, as well as figure out and articulate how these parts connect.

There are two contexts in which summary is particularly valuable: (1) as a preliminary or prewriting assignment designed to help you assimilate information and (2) as part of a larger analysis, providing information blended with or juxtaposed to your thinking about it.

How does summary function as part of a larger analysis? In focusing a topic, you are trying to discover the significance of a particular feature of your subject. It is essential when doing so to *contextualize* your subject accurately—to create a fair picture of what's there. If you don't take the time to get your whole subject in perspective, you are more prone to misrepresenting it in your analysis. Summary performs this contextualizing function.

Problems with Summary

Effective analytical topics, then, generally require a certain amount of summarizing but also require you to do more than give back what you've been given. They guide you to an area of uncertainty, giving you something to negotiate. Too often, however, summarizing becomes a way of avoiding active analytical involvement with your subject. Summarizing becomes a major problem in topic construction when you interpret the wording of the topic as a call to summarize when in fact it intends for you to analyze. In particular, the direction to "discuss" a topic creates the most ambiguity on the summarize/analyze borderline; consulting your professor is the easiest way to dispel this ambiguity.

Strategies for Using Summaries Analytically

Strategy 1: Rank the Items in Your List

The best way to get beyond passive summary is by selecting the information that you wish to discuss on some basis other than general *coverage* of the material. Most summaries are lists, and the standard ones simply follow the order established by the original text. The easiest way to free yourself from the listing mentality is to experiment with *ranking* the items on the list in various ways.

Let's say that you are assigned a paper on major changes in the tax law or on recent developments in U.S. policy toward Eastern Europe. Rather than simply collecting the information, try to arrange it into *hierarchies*. What are the least or most significant changes or developments, and why? Which are most overlooked or most overrated or most controversial or most practical, and why? This list of adjectives is virtually endless: many topics allow you the freedom to choose the principle you want to use for your ranking, so long as it is pertinent to contexts supplied by the course and remains within the guidelines given for the assignment. As always, if you fear that such a ranking violates the guidelines, you need only consult the professor.

A ranking goes beyond a summary because you are having to supply something that is not already evident in the reading—a series of decisions about the material and your rationales for them. And, unlike summary, ranking encourages you to ask questions. Say, for example, that you selected one of three changes in U.S. foreign policy toward Eastern Europe as the most overlooked. You would then be prompted not only to provide your reasons for making this claim but also to consider why and by whom this policy change has been overlooked, as well as what the significance of its being overlooked might be. As a result of ranking, perhaps three-quarters of your paper on policy changes toward Eastern Europe might center on the significance of one change. Rather than covering the entire field of policy changes by listing them all, you would be able to reduce the scope drastically and narrow your summary into a good topic.

Strategy 2: Shift the Focus from *What?* to *How?* and *Why?*

Admittedly, it is more difficult to get beyond summary in some subjects than in others. The nature of course content sometimes seems to leave space for little more than the summary question. A useful strategy, in such cases, is to revise topics that respond to "what" questions so that they lead you to "how" questions.

For example, if you were trying to get beyond the passive listing that would result from a question such as "Discuss the major discoveries that Darwin made on *The Beagle*," you might shift the critical focus from what Darwin says to how he proceeds. You could choose to focus on Darwin's use of the scientific method, in which case you would locate passages where Darwin expresses uncertainty, examining *how* he builds and, in some cases, discards hypotheses. Alternatively, you might focus on the theory of evolution itself, in which case you could select several passages that illustrate *how* Darwin proceeded from evidence to conclusion, and then rank them in order of importance to the overall theory, arguing for that ranking.

Strategy 3: Pursue Only Selected Features of Your Subject

If your construction of or response to a topic can be organized into a list that arranges its elements in no particular order, then your topic is still too broad—that is, it still includes too much summary. A question such as "What makes Chaucer's *Canterbury Tales* funny?" is likely to invite plot summary precisely because it is so general. But a revised question such as "How does Chaucer's use of religious commentary contribute to the humor of 'The Wife of Bath's Tale'?" narrows the *Tales* to a single tale and the humor to a single aspect of humor, which offers you a manageable space within which to analyze.

Similarly, an essay might address not why the American colonies rebelled against England but how American and British history textbooks differ in their treatment of the Boston Tea Party. The broader version of this subject invites passive summary—a list of standard generalizations about the American Revolution. The narrower version creates a space for you to enter, analyze, and arrive at a formulation not contained in the text you are studying. Notice that it also addresses, though in much more focused form, the larger question of why the colonies rebelled.

Although the suggestions we've offered here for making a summary more analytical will inevitably involve some loss of breadth—you won't be able to cover everything—this is usually a trade-off worth making. It is essential, however, in implementing this particular remedy to the passive summary that you check with your professor about whether you can refocus questions calling for broad coverage. You may be surprised to find that in many cases professors expect you to use this focusing strategy. For, as our examples illustrate, revising summary questions in order to make them more analytical does not slight the importance of information. Your ability to rank parts of your subject or choose a particularly revealing feature to focus on should indicate that you are in control of the material, more than if you just reproduced what was in the text. Before narrowing the focus, you can still begin with a brief survey of major points to contextualize your topic.

THE PERSONAL RESPONSE TOPIC

Advantages of Personal Response

How do you know when you are being asked for a personal response? And what does it mean to respond personally? When asked for your reactions to a particular subject, or for what you think is most important or interesting or revealing in it, you are being asked to select your own starting point for discussion, for the initial impressions that you will later analyze more systematically. You will often discover in such reactions the germ of an idea about the subject.

The biggest advantage of personal response topics is that they give you the freedom to explore where and how to engage your subject. Such topics often bring to the surface your emotional or intuitive response, allowing you to experiment with placing the subject in various contexts. You might, for example, offer your personal response to an article on the abuses of hazing in fraternity and sorority life in the context of your own experience. Or you might think about it in connection to some idea about in-groups and out-groups that you read about in a sociology course, or as it relates to what you read about cultural rituals in an anthropology course.

Another advantage of personal response questions is that they often allow you to get some distance on your first impressions, which can often be deceiving. If, as you reexamine your first reactions, you look for ways that they might *not* be accurate, you will often find places where you now disagree with yourself, in effect, stimulating you to think in new ways about the subject. In such cases, the first reaction has helped to clear the way to a second, and better, response.

Problems with Personal Response

Personal response becomes a problem when it distracts you from analyzing the subject. In most cases, you will be misinterpreting the intent of a personal response topic if you

1. View it as an invitation either to assert your personal opinions unreflectingly, or
2. Substitute narratives of your own experience for careful consideration of the subject

In a sense, all analysis involves your opinions, insofar as you are choosing what particular evidence and arguments to focus upon. But, at least in an academic setting, an opinion is more than simply an expression of your beliefs—it's a conclusion that you earn the rights to through a careful examination of evidence.

In most cases, when you are asked to respond personally, the professor is looking for more than your endorsement, appreciation, or denouncement of the subject. If you find yourself constructing a virtual list—"I agree with this point" or "I disagree with that point"—you are probably doing little more than matching your opinions with the points of view encountered in a reading. In such cases, rather than exploring the viewpoints in the material, you are simply reporting how well they fit with your own worldview.

Similarly, when you substitute personal narrative for analysis, your own experiences and prejudices tend to become an unquestioned standard of value. Your own disastrous experience with a health maintenance organization (HMO) may predispose you to dismiss a plan for nationalized health care, but your writing needs to examine in detail the holes in the plan, not evoke the three hours you lingered in some doctor's waiting room. It is, however, okay to integrate some personal experience into a topic, provided that you have also analyzed the subject past the anecdotal stage to the point where you have become aware of the argument that is exemplified by your narrative.

Strategies for Using Personal Responses Analytically

Strategy 1: Trace Your Responses Back to Their Causes

As the preceding discussion of problems with personal response topics suggests, you need to bring your reactions back to the subject so that you can identify and analyze exactly *what* in the reading has produced your reaction, *how*, and *why*. If you find an aspect of your subject irritating or interesting, disappointing or funny, you will be able to use rather than simply indulge such responses if you then examine a particular piece of evidence that has provoked them.

Let's say, for example, that you are assigned to respond to an article on ways of increasing the numbers of registered voters in urban precincts. You find the article irritating; your personal experience working with political campaigns has taught you that getting out the vote is not as easy as this writer makes it seem. From that starting point, you might analyze one (to you) overly enthusiastic passage, concentrating on how the writer has not only overestimated what campaign workers can actually do but also condescended to those who don't register—assuming, perhaps, that they are ignorant rather than indifferent or disillusioned.

Once you get down to analyzing evidence, you will often find that you no longer agree with your original response. The attack you planned on the article for its naïveté might instead become an explanation for the differences between the article's and your point of view. Perhaps the writer's enthusiasm was not founded so much on an oversimplification of the problem of getting out the vote as on another way of viewing the situation. Having opened this possibility, you might discover that the writer has in mind a much more long-term effect, or that urban models differ significantly from the suburban ones of your experience. A common result of tracing your responses back to their causes is a revision of your responses—not surprisingly, since you will inevitably be shifting the focus from your reactions to the material itself.

Another example: say that you are assigned to respond to a play that you found funny, such as J. M. Synge's *The Playboy of the Western World*. Your best strategy would be to locate one line that made you laugh—such as the playboy's declaration at the end of Act I that if he had known how popular with the women he would become by killing his father, he'd have done it long ago. You could then ask yourself where the humor lies in this remark, what it suggests (for example) about the attitudes of rural Irish culture toward fathers, and the significance of the fact that the playwright uses the line to end the act on a comic note.

Strategy 2: Assume That You May Have Missed the Point

It's difficult to see the logic of someone else's position if you are too preoccupied with your own. Similarly, it is hard to see the logic, or illogic, of your own position if you already assume it to be true. Because you have assumed that something is obviously true or false, you cease to think about it and quickly forget where your view came from in the first place.

Although an evaluative response (approve/disapprove) can sometimes spur analysis, it can also lead you to prejudge the case. If, however, you question the validity of your own point of view as a matter of course, you will sometimes recognize the possibility of an alternative point of view, as was the case in the voter registration example above. (See Figure 2.1.)

Strategy 3: Achieve Critical Detachment

Especially in cases where your primary response is emotional (anger, moral indignation, fear), you run the risk of getting so caught up in expressing how you feel

Figure 2.1   MAKING PERSONAL RESPONSE MORE ANALYTICAL

Evaluative Personal Response: "The article was irritating." This response is too broad and dismissively judgmental. Make it more analytical by tracing the response back to the evidence that triggered it.

A More Analytical Evaluative Response: "The author of the article over-simplifies the problem by assuming the cause of low voter registration to be voters' ignorance rather than voters' indifference." Although still primarily an evaluative response, this observation is more analytical. It takes the writer's initial response ("irritating") to a specific cause.

A Non-Evaluative Analytical Response: "The author's emphasis on in-creased coverage of city politics in local/neighborhood forums such as the churches suggests that the author is interested in long-term ef-fects of voter registration drives and not just in immediate increases." Rather than simply reacting ("irritating") or leaping to evaluation ("oversimplifies the problem"), the writer here formulates a possible explanation for the difference between her point of view on voter registration drives and the article's.

---

that you will not get around to examining the subject analytically. Paying too much attention to how a subject makes you feel or fits your experience of life can seduce you away from paying attention to how the subject itself operates. This problem is compounded in areas where there are few or no arguments in favor of an opposing point of view. Except in very limited cases, for example, you could not achieve critical detachment on the subject of racism by considering that it might be a good thing. In such cases, the aim of achieving critical detachment is not to get you to change your mind or even to assess the value of alternative points of view but rather to allow you to disengage your emotions enough for you to look closely at your subject and, in so doing, come to understand more about it.

In this context, consider how you might write about two vastly different treatments of racism, the charter of the Ku Klux Klan (KKK) and *Black Boy,* Richard Wright's autobiographical account of racist brutality during his boyhood in the American South. If the racism in both documents left you so morally out-raged that all you did was list examples of it and voice your disapproval, you would be able to write virtually the same personal response essay to both documents! In this respect, the documents themselves have become irrelevant.

How do you achieve critical detachment from your first responses in order to transform them into analysis? In the case of the KKK charter and *Black Boy,* for example, you could locate passages that provoked your reaction and carefully study their specific language. Question it. How do the passages you've selected re-veal the writers' assumptions about the nature or causes of racism? Or you might focus on a part of the larger subject, such as the language of racism or the psy-chological effects of racism. What are the apparent intentions of the authors, and how does their use of language define or manipulate their intended audience?

Whatever questions you ask, so long as they focus on the material rather than just your reactions to it, they can provide a very useful way of redirecting you from the merely personal and toward some more public and generalizable understanding.

Strategy 4: Locate the Topic within a Limiting Context

Suppose you are asked to write about the topic "Define your religious beliefs." Although this question would naturally lead you to think about your own experiences and beliefs, you would probably do best to approach the question in some more limiting context. The reading in the course could provide this limit. Let's say that thus far you have read two modern religious thinkers, Martin Buber and Paul Tillich. Reflecting on these thinkers' ideas would not necessarily push you and your convictions out of your essay but could give you a means of bringing your own beliefs into clearer view. "What do I believe?" would become "How does my response to Buber and Tillich illuminate my own assumptions about the nature of religious faith?" An advantage of this move, beyond making your argument less general, is that it would help you to get perspective on your own position.

Another way of limiting your context is to consider how one author or recognizable point of view that you have encountered in the course might respond to a single statement from another author or point of view. If you used this strategy to respond to the topic "Does God exist?" you might arrive at a formulation such as "How would Martin Buber critique Paul Tillich's definition of God?" Although this topic appears to exclude personal response entirely, it in fact does not. Your opinion would necessarily enter because you would be actively formulating something that is not already evident in the reading (how Buber might respond to Tillich).

BINARIES: EITHER/OR QUESTIONS

Advantages of Binaries

In human—and computerized—thinking, a binary is a pair of elements, usually in opposition to each other, as in off/on, yes/no, right/wrong, agree/disagree, and so on. Many ideas begin with a writer's noticing some kind of opposition or tension or choice within a subject—capital punishment *either* does *or* does not deter crime; a character in a novel is *either* a courageous rebel *or* a fool; a new environmental policy is *either* visionary *or* hopelessly impractical. A major advantage of looking for and using binaries is that they help you determine what issues are at stake in your subject, since binaries position you among competing choices. Thus, it is not surprising that binaries appear in so many topics.

Problems with Binaries

Creating opposing categories is fundamental to defining things. As the philosopher Herbert Marcuse says, "We understand that which is in terms of that which is not": light is that which is not dark; masculine is that which is not feminine; civilized is that which is not primitive. But as these examples may suggest, binaries are also dangerous because they can perpetuate what is called *reductive thinking,* especially if applied uncritically.

Reductive thinking oversimplifies a subject, eliminating alternatives between two extremes—that, for example, women are *either* virgins *or* whores, that teachers *either* instill a love of learning in students *or* alienate them from their feelings. As these examples suggest, if you restrict yourself to thinking in binary terms, you can run into two problems. First, most subjects cannot be adequately considered in terms of only two options—either this or that, with nothing in between. Second, binaries often conceal value judgments: the category "primitive," as opposed to "civilized," is not a neutral description but a devaluation.

In sum, it is useful to begin by constructing binaries but dangerous to stay with them too long, since you run the risk of ignoring the more complex gray area in between. Often there are more than two alternatives, or both alternatives have some truth to them, as in the question "Was the Civil War fought over slavery or economics?" We have all encountered paper topics framed in this way, but you should keep in mind that such questions often seek to stimulate your thinking—they are not necessarily pressing you to choose one side of the binary over the other as the absolute answer (that economics caused the war, and slavery had nothing to do with it, or vice versa).

Another common kind of topic that is related to both either/or and personal response questions is the agree/disagree question. Like either/or, the agree/disagree binary can lead to reductive thinking. And, like the personal response question, the agree/disagree question discourages critical detachment. Let us briefly consider two agree/disagree topics: (a) "Do you agree or disagree with the way that Charles Bovary treats his wife in the novel *Madame Bovary?*" (b) "Do you agree or disagree with Eisenhower's foreign policy decisions during the Cold War?" The problem with both questions is that they tend to open up the writer rather than the subject, and they invite oversimplified good/bad or yes/no responses that don't respect the complexity of the subject.

A writer's feelings about a fictional character (Bovary) will be important in an analysis only when connected to an argument about the meaning of the novel; the writer would do better to focus on the question "*How* does the novel predispose readers to judge Bovary's treatment of his wife—and *why?*" The wording of the question about Eisenhower's foreign policy similarly invites quick and overly broad judgment (consulting one's prejudices): the writer's task is not to approve or disapprove of Eisenhower but to analyze his decisions.

Strategies for Using Binaries Analytically

Strategy 1: Locate a Range of Opposing Categories

The first step in using binaries analytically is to locate and distinguish them carefully. Examine the topic thoroughly for binaries that are both *overtly specified* and *implied* by the topic's wording. Consider, for example, the binaries contained in the following topic: "Does the model of management known as total quality management (TQM) that is widely used in Japan work in the American automotive industry?" The most obvious binary in this question is *work* versus *not work.* But there are also other binaries in the question—Japanese versus American, for example, and TQM versus more traditional and more traditionally American models of management. These binaries, overtly named by the topic question, imply further binaries. Insofar as TQM is acknowledged to be a team-oriented, collaborative management model, the topic requires a writer to consider the accuracy and relative suitability of particular traits commonly ascribed to Japanese versus American workers, such as communal and cooperative versus individualistic and competitive.

Strategy 2: Analyze and Define the Opposing Terms

Having located the various binaries specified and implied by your topic, you should begin to analyze and define terms. What, for example, does it mean to ask whether TQM *works* in the American automotive industry? Does *work* mean "make a substantial profit"? Does *work* mean "produce more cars more quickly"? Does *work* mean "improve employee morale"? You would probably find yourself drowning in vagueness unless you carefully argued for the appropriateness of your definition of this key term.

Strategy 3: Question the Accuracy of the Binary

Having begun to analyze and define your terms, you would next need to determine how accurately they define the issues raised by your subject. You might consider, for example, the extent to which American management styles actually differ from the Japanese version of TQM. In the process of trying to determine if there are significant differences, you could start to locate particular traits in these management styles and in Japanese versus American culture that might help you to formulate your binary more precisely. Think of the binary as a starting point— a kind of deliberate overgeneralization—that allows you to set up positions you can then test in order to refine.

Strategy 4: Change "Either/or" to "The Extent to Which"

The best strategy in using binaries analytically is usually to locate arguments on both sides of the either/or choice that the binary poses. So, in answer to the question we mentioned earlier, "Was the Civil War fought over slavery or economics?" you would attempt to determine *the extent to which* each side of the binary—slavery *and* economics—could reasonably be credited as the cause of the war.

Making this move would not release you from the responsibility of taking a stand and arguing for it. But, by analyzing the terms of the binary, you would come to question it and ultimately to arrive at a more complex and qualified position to write about. For example, you might argue that economics rather than slavery was the primary cause of the Civil War, but your analysis might lead you to see that slavery is an economic issue as well as a moral one.

Admittedly, in reorienting your thinking from the obvious and clear-cut choices that either/or formulations provide to the murkier waters of "the extent to which," your decision process will be made more difficult. The gain, however, is that "the extent to which" mind-set, by predisposing you to assess multiple and potentially conflicting points of view, will enable you to address more fairly and accurately the issues raised by your subject.

Where might you end up if you approached our earlier sample topic (whether or not TQM works in the American automotive industry) by asking *the extent to which* one side of the binary better suits available evidence, rather than arguing that one side is clearly the right choice and the other entirely wrong? You would still be arguing that one position on TQM in American industry is more accurate than the other, but you would inevitably arrive at more carefully qualified conclusions than the question might otherwise have led you to. You would most likely take care, for example, to suggest the danger of assuming that all American workers are rugged individualists while all Japanese workers are communal bees.

COMPARISON/CONTRAST AND DEFINITION TOPICS

Advantages of Comparison/Contrast and Definition Topics

Among the most common topics are those that ask you to compare and/or contrast parts of a subject or to define its key concepts or terms. Like summary topics, these also call upon you to assemble and organize the information you have been acquiring in a course. We have chosen to treat comparison/contrast and definition topics together because both (1) organize the information into categories and (2) proceed on the basis of similarity and difference. At first glance, the comparative nature of definitions may appear less obvious, but, in defining, you first classify something as part of a group or category of comparable things, and then you differentiate it from those other things. A chair, for example, is a piece of furniture (classification) that one person can sit on, which differentiates it from other furniture, such as tables, which no one sits on, and from sofas, which several people can sit on.

The biggest advantage of comparison/contrast and definition topics, and the reason they get assigned so frequently, is that they press you to understand different parts of your subject *in relation to* one another. As a result, you can

1. Understand each part more clearly, since you will be considering what it has that another part does not and what it lacks that another part contains
2. Understand how the various parts of your subject are divided or connected

Earlier in this chapter, we suggested that an idea may connect elements and explain the significance of the connection and that it may account for some dissonance, something that seems not to fit together. The tasks that comparison/contrast and definition topics ask you to do lead in these directions: the fundamental assumption from which they spring is that you can usually discover ideas about a subject much more easily when you are not viewing it in isolation.

Problems with Comparison/Contrast and Definition

The fundamental problem of responding to comparison/contrast and definition topics unanalytically is *pointlessness*. Comparison/contrast and definition topics are not by nature pointless, but they often produce results that, quite literally, lack any controlling purpose or point. The problem arises because such topics sometimes appear to invite you simply to present inert information. Although these topics are meant to invite analysis, they are too often treated as ends in themselves.

Comparison/contrast topics produce pointless essays if you allow them to turn into matching exercises—that is, if you match different parts of the subject or common features of two subjects but don't get beyond the equation stage *(a, b, c = x, y, z)*. Writers fall into this trap when they have no larger question or issue to explore and perhaps resolve by making the comparison. If, for example, you were to pursue the comparison of the representations of the Boston Tea Party in British and American history texts, you would begin by identifying similarities and differences. But simply presenting these and concluding that the two versions resembled and differed from each other in some ways would be pointless.

Like comparison/contrast topics, *definition topics can produce pointless essays when you get no further than assembling pertinent information.* In other words, definition is meaningful only within some context: you define "rhythm and blues" because it is essential to any further discussion of the evolution of rock-and-roll music; or because you need that definition in order to discuss the British Invasion spearheaded by groups such as the Beatles, the Rolling Stones, and the Yardbirds in the late 1960s; or because you cannot classify John Lennon or Mick Jagger or Eric Clapton without it. Moreover, when you construct a summary of existing definitions with no clear sense of purpose, you tend to juxtapose definitions indiscriminately. As a result, you are likely to overlook conflicts among the various definitions and overemphasize their surface similarities.

Strategies for Using Comparison/Contrast Analytically

Given that your response to comparison topics can suffer from an essential underlying problem—pointlessness—it is not surprising that there is a single underlying solution: *give the comparison a point.* In most cases, you can provide this remedy by *ranking the information, focusing it, and then asking and answering the question "so what?"* All of the more specific strategies that follow develop from this starting point. Insofar as they also involve you in interpreting (that is, further constructing) the topic that has been assigned to you, a brief consultation with your professor will eliminate the risk that you might change the topic in a way that would not fulfill the intentions of the assignment.

Strategy 1: Discuss Revealing Similarities and Differences

Perhaps the best way to press yourself beyond the pointless comparison is to look at the categories you have assembled and ask yourself "So what?" In comparing the textbook treatments of the Boston Tea Party, you would probably first need to focus on particular matches that seem especially revealing—for example, that British and American texts trace the economic background of the incident in different ways. Then, in response to the "so what?" question, you would attempt to develop some explanation of what these differences reveal and why they are significant. You might, for example, decide that the British texts view the matter from a more global economic perspective, while American texts emphasize nationalism.

Strategy 2: Argue for the Significance of a Key Comparison

Rather than simply covering a range of comparisons, focus on a key comparison. This narrower focus might seem to eliminate other important areas of consideration. You will usually find, however, that you are not significantly reducing the scope, because this focusing will usually allow you to incorporate at least some of these other areas in a more tightly connected, less listlike fashion. So, for example, a comparison of the burial rites of two cultures will probably reveal more about them than a much broader but more superficial list of cultural similarities and differences. And in developing this comparison, you would probably be able to bring in cultural attitudes toward religion, gender, family structure, the land, and so forth. *In the majority of cases, covering less is covering more.*

Implicit in this way of fixing the comparison topic is the method of *ranking* introduced in the advice for fixing summary topics. You are ranking whenever you designate one part of your topic as especially important or revealing. As a critical move, ranking induces you to convert summary into analysis. Let's consider one more example. Suppose you are asked to compare General Norman Schwarzkopf's conduct of the Persian Gulf War with General Douglas MacArthur's strategy in World War II. As a first move, you could limit the comparison to some revealing parallel, such as the way each man dealt with the press, and then argue for its significance above other similarities or differences. You might, for instance, claim that in their treatment of the press we get an especially clear or telling vantage point on the two generals' strategies. At this point you are on your way to an analytical point—for example, that because MacArthur was more effectively shielded from the press at a time when the press was a virtual instrument of propaganda, he could make choices that Schwarzkopf might have wanted to make but couldn't.

Strategy 3: Use One Side of the Comparison to Illuminate the Other

Usually it is not necessary to treat each part of the comparison equally. It's a common misconception that each side must be given equal space. In fact, *the purpose of your comparison governs the amount of space you'll need to give to each part.* Often, you will be using one side of the comparison primarily to illuminate the other. For example, in a course on contemporary military policy, the ratio between the two parts would probably be roughly 70 percent on Schwarzkopf to 30 percent on MacArthur rather than 50 percent on each.

Strategy 4: Imagine How One Side of Your Comparison Might Respond to the Other

This strategy, a variant of the preceding one, is a particularly useful way of helping you to respond to comparison/contrast topics more purposefully. This model can be adapted to a wide variety of subjects. If you were asked to compare Sigmund Freud with one of his most important followers, Jacques Lacan, you would probably be better off focusing the broad question of how Lacan revises Freud by considering how and why he might critique Freud's interpretation of a particular dream in *The Interpretation of Dreams.* Similarly, in the case of the Gulf War example, you could ask yourself how MacArthur might have handled some key decision in the Gulf War and why. Or you might consider how he would have critiqued Schwarzkopf's handling of that decision and why.

Strategies for Using Definition Analytically

As with interpreting comparison topics, so with revising definition topics: the key is to give them a point, which is usually a matter of examining and using definitions rather than simply including them. As with comparison topics, if you are worried that you are changing the topic, simply check with your professor.

Strategy 1: Test the Definition against Evidence

One common form of the definition topic asks you to apply a definition to a body of information. It is rare to find a perfect fit. Therefore, you should, as a general rule, use the data to assess the accuracy and the limitations of the definition, rather than simply imposing it on your data and ignoring or playing down the ways in which it does not fit.

Suppose you were given the assignment "Define capitalism in the context of Third World economies." You might begin by matching some standard definition of capitalism with specific examples from one or two Third World economies, with the express purpose of detecting where the definition does and does not apply. In other words, you would respond to the topic by assaying *the extent to which* the definition provides an adequate tool for making sense of the subject.

Strategy 2: Explore Competing Parts of the Definition

Another common form of the definition topic focuses on the term itself—such as "What is capitalism?" Such topics generally aim to get you to achieve some perspective on the term, to understand its richness of implication. In such cases, you can avoid passive summary—simply listing a range of definitions from a range of sources—by exploring competing parts or versions of the definition.

The definition of capitalism that you might take from Karl Marx, for example, will differ in its emphases from Adam Smith's. In this case, you would not only isolate the most important of these differences but also try to account for the fact that Marx's villain is Smith's hero. Such an accounting would probably lead you to consider how the definition has been shaped by each of these writers' political philosophies or by the culture in which each theory was composed.

When you respond to a definition topic by exploring competing parts of the definition, you are, in effect, focusing on the significance of the difficulties of definition. That is, your analysis achieves direction and purpose by *problematizing* the term—locating and then exploring the significance of the uncertainties and conflicts of definition.

Strategy 3: Use a Definition from One Source to Critique Another

As a general rule, you should attempt to identify the points of view of the sources from which you take your definitions, rather than accepting them as uncontextualized "answers." If you can distinguish the particular slant, your treatment of definition topics will usually move beyond simply synthesizing lists of defining characteristics from your sources. Such synthesis is often a problem, since it tends to overlook the conflicting elements among various definitions of a key term.

A paper on alcoholism, for example, will lose focus if you use all of the definitions available. If, instead, you convert the definition topic into a comparison and contrast of competing definitions, you can more easily generate a point and purpose for your definition. By querying, for example, whether a given source's definition of alcoholism is moral or physiological or psychological, you can more easily problematize the issue of definition.

Strategy 4: Shift from *What?* Questions to *How?* and *Why?* Questions

It is no accident that we earlier offered virtually the same strategy for making summary topics more analytical: like all productive analytical topics, those that require definition finally depend on *why* or *how* questions, not *what* questions. Because, like summary topics, definition topics appear at first glance to be asking a *what* question, you need to be especially vigilant in resisting the temptation to do little more than gather information (in this case, uses of the term to be defined).

If, for example, you were confronted with the assignment to define the meaning of "darkness" in Joseph Conrad's *Heart of Darkness* and any two other modern British novels, you would do better to ask *why* the writers find darkness such a fertile term than simply to accumulate various examples of the term in the three books. You might start by isolating the single best example from each of the works, preferably one that reveals important differences as well as similarities. Then, in analyzing *how* each writer uses the term, you could work toward some larger point that would unify the essay. You might show how Conrad's metaphor evolves historically, gets reshaped by woman novelists, changes after World War I, and so forth.

GUIDELINES FOR CONSTRUCTING EFFECTIVE TOPICS

1. Start with questions rather than preconceived or obvious answers. Don't settle for your first response or idea.
2. Experiment with prewriting. Find out what you think by seeing what you say.
3. Use your interest to open up the subject, not yourself.
4. Analyze the topic by uncovering unstated assumptions and questioning key terms. What, for example, does *good* mean in the question "Is feminism good for Judaism?"
5. Seek out uncertainty and complexity. Look for multiple and competing possibilities to negotiate, rather than a single "right" answer.
6. Find ways to move beyond passive summary *(what* questions). Use information to develop some idea *(how* and *why* questions) rather than just repackaging what others have written.
7. Drastically reduce scope. Concentrate on what seems the most important or revealing part of your subject (ranking) rather than trying to cover everything.
8. Develop your observations by asking yourself "so what?" Why is what you have noticed significant?
9. Complicate binaries: get past either/or formulations. Explore the gray areas in between by determining "the extent to which" each side of the binary is true.

10. Avoid turning comparisons into pointless matching exercises. Set up similarities and differences only to discuss the significance of that comparison.
11. You needn't devote equal space to both sides of a comparison. If one side is used primarily to illuminate the other, a 30/70 ratio (or 20/80 or 40/60) makes more sense than 50/50.
12. Rather than answering a question of definition with inert summary, test the definition against evidence and/or explore its competing parts.

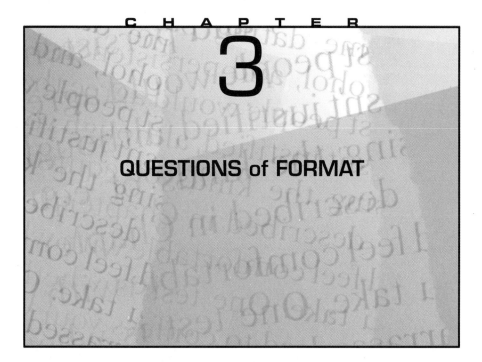

CHAPTER
3
QUESTIONS of FORMAT

THIS IS A CHAPTER about form, about the way writers structure their ideas. We have used the word *format*, however, rather than *form*, to indicate an emphasis on prescribed forms, such as those that members of the various academic disciplines conform to in their scholarly and professional writing. In many cases, you will be expected to conform to these formats in courses aiming at initiating you into a particular discipline. We will also use the term *format* for organizational schemes that are not discipline specific. These include standard patterns of thought (such as problem/solution or induction and deduction, which are often treated as formats in writing assignments) and other schemes that lay out the form of prospective papers in a series of steps.

The most explicit advice many students receive about writing in college has to do with the formats that govern how ideas and information may be presented in particular disciplines. In some disciplines, such as biology and psychology, all formal papers and reports must conform to an explicitly prescribed pattern of presentation. Other disciplines are less uniform and less explicit about their reliance on formats, but writers in these fields (English, for example, or history) usually operate within established forms. While knowing the required steps of a discipline's writing format won't write your papers for you, not knowing how writers in that discipline characteristically proceed can keep you from being read.

A "Voices from Across the Curriculum" section later in this chapter provides advice from faculty members in disciplines that typically require most or all formal writing to be done in a particular format. That section offers commentary from a biologist and a psychologist on the report format that is the staple of writing in the natural and some of the social sciences. This chapter is less concerned, however, with teaching you particular formats (a matter on which your professors are your best resource) than with teaching you ways of thinking about and putting to the best use whatever formats you are asked to write in.

THE TWO FUNCTIONS
OF FORMATS: PROCESS AND PRODUCT

A problem for many writers when learning to use formats is that they see only the emphasis on the form of a final product and remain too little aware of the underlying logic that allows formats to function as a means of finding and exploring ideas. Thus, the first step in learning to use formats productively is to recognize that they have two related but separate functions: product and process.

- *As sets of rules for organizing a final product,* formats make communication among members of a discipline easier and more efficient. By standardizing the means of displaying thinking in a discipline, the format enables readers to compare more readily one writer's work to that of others in the field, since readers will know where to look for particular kinds of information—the writer's methodology, for example, or his or her hypothesis or conclusions.

- *As guides and stimulants to the writing process,* formats offer writers a means of finding and exploring ideas. The procedures that formats contain seek to guide the writer's thinking process in a disciplined manner, prompting systematic and efficient examination of a subject. The notion of formats functioning as aids to invention—idea generation—goes at least as far back as Aristotle, whose *Rhetoric* defined twenty-eight general "topics" (such as considering causes and effects or dividing a subject into parts) that speakers might pursue in order to invent arguments.

Many beginning writers fear, however, that formats will interfere with their freedom of thought, rendering them less rather than more able to figure out what they want to say. This fear arises partly from a false assumption about the relationship between form and content—that content is somehow separate from and precedes form, and thus that following a format will stunt their thinking. According to this theory, form should be "applied" to content (rather like the mold into which one pours liquid Jell-O) only after the essentially mysterious creative process has done its work.

There is, of course, some truth to this conception and thus to the fear that concentrating on the form of the finished paper may be inhibiting. Writing is a complex mix of conscious activity and less conscious activities that do not respond readily or consistently to our demands. As any writer can attest, good ideas often occur when we least expect them to, frequently after we've stopped pursuing them. On other occasions, nothing worthwhile seems to come up, in spite of our most concentrated efforts.

Writing a paper, in other words, is not like assembling a piece of furniture by following the instructions on the package, but it is equally naive to believe that writers write in the absence of any instructions. Most of the thinking we do is generated by some kind of format, even if we are not aware of it. Many of the formats that you will encounter are not strictly prescriptive (sets of artificial rules to be imposed on the skittish creative process). Rather, they are descriptive accounts of the various *heuristics*—sets of questions and categories—that humans typically use to guide and stimulate their thinking.

Poets, for example, have continued to write sonnets, one of the most highly structured poetic formats, for hundreds of years because the form has *heuristic value*. It guides the writer down certain pathways that stimulate thought. The sonnet form itself—fourteen lines of rhymed iambic pentameter, typically moving in one logical and/or emotional direction for eight lines and then shifting direction in the final six—lends itself to the production of certain kinds of thinking, such as putting ideas into dialogue with each other, establishing complex logical relationships. Similarly, the conventional format of the scientific paper stimulates rather than merely contains thought. For example, by stipulating the inclusion of a review of prior research, this format induces the writer to arrive at thoughtful connections between his or her work and earlier experiments.

A problem is that the concept of formats as lines of inquiry (Aristotle's topics of invention) has become partially lost in the concept of formats as methods of arranging a finished piece of writing, that is, as imposing shape on a final product. Clearly, formats can both stimulate the writing process and organize the final product, but not when writers think of formats primarily as packaging and thus concern themselves with rigid adherence to form at the expense of more thoughtful exploration of content. Such writers tend to pay more attention to filling the required slots in the format than to what they fill them with: "Do I have a thesis?" "Yes." "Did I include examples?" "Yes." "Have I footnoted two sources?" "Yes."

At its worst, the slot-filler approach to thinking closes down avenues worthy of consideration with a premature attempt to hammer one option (usually the first one that springs to mind) into a prescribed form. Rather than encouraging a writer to examine and reexamine the thesis, the slot-filler approach can incline a writer only to make sure that some thesis is there. Nor is a writer likely to develop a lively sense of what evidence is and how it should be used, as long as he or she is more concerned with merely including it rather than analyzing it.

There is no easy answer to why writers oversimplify the function of formats, but we suspect that, at least to an extent, it comes from many writers having concluded early in their schooling that writing was largely a matter of following specified steps. This view is especially common among those who have been taught to write in the rudimentary format called *five-paragraph form,* which, in the name of clear organization, actually impedes the ability to write analytically.

The remainder of this chapter proceeds on the conviction that although formats are a necessary and useful aspect of academic writing, using them effectively requires writers to first overcome the slot-filler mentality that is the legacy of organizational schemes such as five-paragraph form. Accordingly, we move next to an analysis of this form and then to a discussion of formats across the curriculum—their rationale as structures for organizing a finished product and as structures for generating thought.

WHAT'S WRONG WITH FIVE-PARAGRAPH FORM?

Perhaps the best introduction to what's wrong with five-paragraph form can be found in Greek mythology. On his way to Athens, the hero Theseus encounters a particularly surly host, Procrustes, who offers wayfarers a bed for the night, but with a catch. If they do not fit his bed exactly, he either stretches them or lops off their extremities until they do. This story has given us the word *procrustean,* which the dictionary defines as "tending to produce conformity by violent or arbitrary means."

Five-paragraph form is a procrustean formula that most students learn in high school. While it has the advantage of providing a mechanical format that will give virtually any subject the appearance of order, it usually lops off a writer's ideas before they have the chance to form or stretches a single idea to the breaking point. In other words, this simplistic scheme blocks writers' ability to think deeply or logically, restricting rather than encouraging the development of complex ideas.

A complex idea is one that has many sides. To treat such ideas intelligently, writers need a form that will not require them to cut off all of those sides except the one that most easily fits the bed. Most of you will find the basic five-paragraph form familiar:

1. An introduction that announces the writer's main idea, about which he or she will make three points.
2. A paragraph on each of the three points.
3. A conclusion beginning "Thus, we see" or "In conclusion" that essentially repeats the introduction.

Here is an example in outline form:

Intro: *The food in the school cafeteria is bad. It lacks variety, it's unhealthy, and it is always overcooked. In this essay I will discuss these three characteristics.*

Paragraph 2: *The first reason cafeteria food is bad is that there is no variety.* (Plus one or two examples—no salad bar, mostly fried food, etc.)

Paragraph 3: *Another reason cafeteria food is bad is that it is not healthy.* (Plus a few reasons—high cholesterol, too many hot dogs, too much sugar, etc.)

Paragraph 4: *In addition, the food is always overcooked.* (Plus some examples—the vegetables are mushy, the "mystery" meat is tough to recognize, etc.)

Conclusion: *Thus, we see* . . . (Plus a restatement of the introductory paragraph.)

Most high school students write dozens of themes using this basic formula. They are taught to use five-paragraph form because it seems to provide the greatest good—a certain minimal clarity—for the greatest number of students. But the form does not promote logically tight and intellectually aggressive writing. It is a meat grinder that can turn any content into sausage. The two major problems it typically creates are easy to see.

1. The introduction reduces the remainder of the essay to *redundancy:* paragraph one tells the readers, in an overly general and listlike way, what they're going to hear; the succeeding three paragraphs tell the readers the same thing again in more detail, carrying the overly general main idea along inertly; and the conclusion repeats what the readers have just been told (twice). The first cause of all this redundancy lies with the thesis. As in the example, the thesis (cafeteria food is "bad") is too broad—an unqualified and obvious generalization—and substitutes a simple list of predictable points for a complex statement of idea.

2. The form *arbitrarily* divides content: why are there three points (or examples or reasons) instead of five or one? A quick look at the three categories in our example reveals how arbitrarily the form has divided the subject. Isn't overcooked food unhealthy? Isn't a lack of variety unhealthy? The format invites writers to list rather than analyze, to plug supporting examples into categories without examining them or how they are related. Five-paragraph form, as is evident in our sample's transitions ("first," "second," "in addition"), counts things off but doesn't make logical connections. At its worst, the form prompts the writer to simply append evidence to generalizations without saying anything about it.

The subject, on the other hand, is not as unpromising as the format makes it appear. It could easily be redirected along a more productive pathway. (If the food is bad, what are the underlying causes of the problem? Are students getting what they ask for? Is the problem one of cost? Is the faculty cafeteria better? Why or why not?)

Now let's look briefly at the introductory paragraph from a student's essay on a more academic subject. Here we can see a remarkable feature of five-paragraph form—its capacity to produce the same kind of say–nothing prose on almost any subject.

> Throughout the film, *The Tempest,* a version of Shakespeare's play, *The Tempest,* there were a total of nine characters. These characters were Calibano, Alonso, Antonio, Aretha, Freddy, the doctor, and Dolores. Each character in the film represented a person in Shakespeare's play, but there were four people who were greatly similar to those in Shakespeare who played a role in symbolizing aspects of forgiveness, love, and power.

The final sentence of the paragraph reveals the writer's addiction to five-paragraph form. It signals that the writer will proceed in a purely mechanical and superficial way, producing a paragraph on forgiveness, a paragraph on love, a paragraph on power, and a conclusion stating again that the film's characters resemble

Shakespeare's in these three aspects. The writer is so busy demonstrating that the characters are concerned with forgiveness, love, and power that she misses the opportunity to *analyze* the significance of her own observations. Instead, readers are drawn wearily to a conclusion; they get no place except back where they began. Further, the demonstration mode prevents her from analyzing connections among the categories. The writer might consider, for example, how the play and the film differ in resolving the conflict between power and forgiveness. Or she might ask herself, to what extent do the film and the play agree about which is the most important of the three aspects?

These more analytical approaches lie concealed in the writer's introduction, but they never get discovered because the five-paragraph form militates against analytical thinking. Its division of the subject into parts (only one aspect of analysis) has become an end unto itself. The procrustean formula insists upon a tripartite list in which each of the three parts is separate, equal, and, above all, *inert.*

FORMATS IN COLLEGE WRITING

What's the relationship between five-paragraph form and the formats that one encounters in college? And how can you recognize the difference between a limiting (procrustean) format and a useful one? Unlike five-paragraph form, most of the formats you encounter in college are roomier. They are not as rigidly overspecified, and they usually leave the writer space for more complex development of ideas. And, while five-paragraph form is a device created almost exclusively for beginning writers, a way of writing you are unlikely to encounter anywhere except in the classroom, most of the formats you encounter in college are used by novices and experts alike.

Formats are generally taught in college as part of the student's initiation into what is called a *discourse community.* A discourse community is a group of people bound together by certain habitual ways of communicating with one another. Lawyers, for example, constitute a discourse community. They share a common language (a discourse) and common ways of presenting information. Similarly, biologists or political scientists or actors or baseball players or even a group of friends can function as discourse communities. The formats used by academic disciplines help those disciplines function as discourse communities. Formats make communication among members of a discipline easier and more efficient.

Generally speaking, formats provide a logic for dividing a subject into manageable parts and a logical order for dealing with each of these parts. To develop ideas in depth, writers need some means of deciding what to talk about when. Unlike more mechanical organizational schemes, good formats help you to order your thinking *sequentially,* according to relatively distinct phases.

| *Voices from Across the Curriculum* |

FORMATS IN THE NATURAL AND SOCIAL SCIENCES

In some disciplines—especially in the natural sciences and psychology—the pattern of presentation for formal papers and reports is explicitly prescribed and usually mandatory. The American Psychological Association (APA), for example, issues a disciplinary style guide (now in its fourth edition) to which all writers seeking to publish in the field must adhere. In other disciplines, especially in the humanities and most of the social sciences, the accepted patterns of organization are less rigidly defined. Nonetheless, writers in these fields also operate to a significant extent within established forms, such as those set forth by the Modern Language Association (MLA) handbook. See Appendix A for a guide to citation and reference lists in APA, MLA, and number-reference styles.

The following is a summary by a professor of biology of the format writers use to report the results of experiments and other kinds of studies in his discipline.

There are firm rules in organizing scientific writing. Papers are usually divided into four major sections:

1. Introduction: provides context and states the question asked and the hypothesis tested in the study.
2. Methodology: accurately describes experimental procedure.
3. Results: states the results obtained.
4. Discussion: analyzes and interprets results with respect to the original hypothesis; discusses implications of the results.

As this organizational model should make clear, scientific papers are largely deductive, with a shift to inductive reasoning in the discussion when the writer usually attempts to generalize or extend conclusions to broader circumstances.

Scientific papers also include an *abstract,* which is placed on the page following the title page. The abstract summarizes the question being investigated in the paper, the methods used in the experiment, the results, and the conclusions drawn. The reader should be able to determine the major topics in the paper without reading the entire paper. Compose the abstract *after* the paper is completed.

—*R. Niesenbaum, Professor of Biology*

Writing in psychology, as the following summary from a psychology professor shows, is typically organized in the same way as papers in the natural sciences:

In writing in the social sciences, there is a standard plot, with three alternative endings. The *Introduction* (a standard section of APA style) sets forth the

continued

problem, which the *Methods* section promises to address. The *Results* section "factually" reports the outcome of the study, with the *Discussion* section interpreting the results. "The Data" are given the starring role in determining which ending is discussed in the Discussion: hypothesis confirmed, hypothesis rejected, or hard to say. (I would say "which ending the author chooses" versus "which ending is discussed," but the data are supposed to be determinative, and the role of the author/investigator neutral.) Analytic thinking comes in setting up the problem and making sense of the results in conjunction with existing literature on the subject.

—A. Tjeltveit, Professor of Psychology

Not all disciplines will provide a standard recipe for finished papers, and, even in disciplines in which writing typically conforms to a particular organizational scheme, the form of writing often changes according to purpose and audience. The following observations, from an economics professor, suggest that you will often find yourself in situations in which there are various loose guidelines about form rather than a single format.

It is important to state that the economics profession, unlike other disciplines such as psychology, has no generally accepted guidelines for how economists should write. There are books and articles on the subject by economists, yet it would be a mistake to take these as evidence of widely accepted standards of writing. I have approached my economics colleagues, and their impressions are roughly the same as mine. No graduate student has ever been treated to a reading of the "ten commandments" of good writing in economics. Style and format vary greatly in economics; they are a function of the type of piece being written. Is it theoretical? empirical? historical? biographical? Or is it a critical commentary? Again, while these considerations may influence the general shape of a paper, the rules are loose at best. If anything, I see my job, admittedly in a very small way, as attempting to change the way economics is written. Perhaps, I am saying, there should be only one rule: engage the reader.

—J. Marshall, Professor of Economics

Because formats offer a means not only of displaying thinking in a discipline but also of shaping (in the sense of creating) it, the format that a discipline tacitly or overtly requires conditions its members to think in particular ways. Learning to use the format that scientists use predisposes you to think like a scientist. Learning the differences among the various disciplines' formats can help you recognize differences in *epistemology* (ways of knowing). As we stress elsewhere in this book, how you say something is always a part of what you say; the two can't be easily separated.

But, by concentrating on apparent differences in the surface features of writing in the disciplines, it is possible to overemphasize difference and to

continued

underestimate the amount of common ground that the disciplines share. The various formats across the disciplines, the skeletons that both shape and display thinking in those disciplines, are actually quite similar. They usually contain most of the same elements, although they might call these elements by different names and prefer that they occur in slightly different orders. A science paper and a history paper, for example, both advance a hypothesis, provide context for it, specify methodology, and support their claims by carefully weighing the evidence.

USING FORMATS IN EXPLORATORY DRAFTS

As we observed in our discussion of formats as process and product, it is possible to lose sight of the heuristic value of formats and instead become concerned with formats primarily as disciplinary etiquette. When this happens, the valuable function that formats can serve in analytical writing—their capacity to encourage certain kinds of investigation—is lost.

The solution to this problem probably sounds easier than it is: you need to find the space in a format that will allow it to work as a heuristic. Consider how you might go about using even a highly specified organizational scheme like the following:

1. State the problem.
2. Develop criteria of adequacy for a solution.
3. Explore at least two inadequate solutions.
4. Explicate the proposed solution.
5. Evaluate the proposed solution.
6. Reply to anticipated criticisms.

The comforting feature of this format is that it appears to tell you exactly what to do. Thinking, however, especially in the early stages of the writing process, is rarely as linear as the six numbered steps in the example above imply. Only by testing the adequacy of various solutions (step 3), for example, is one likely to arrive at a clear statement of the problem (step 1). And what if the problem has no solution or has several possible solutions, depending on the details of the problem? And couldn't the exploration of inadequate solutions (step 3) be the best means of discovering criteria of adequacy (standards for determining the acceptability of a solution in step 2)? As we observed earlier in the chapter, the problem with step-by-step assignment formats is that they can lead you to confuse matters of presentation—ways of organizing a finished product, with matters of invention—ways of stimulating the discovery of ideas.

Our questions about the format, however, also reveal your best means of using one like it:

- In the early stages of drafting, allow yourself to move freely among the steps in the order that best sparks your thinking. There will be time later to reassemble your results in the required order.

- Recognize that few formats insist on the writer's devoting exactly the same amount of space and attention to each of its steps or phases. If, for example, the relative inadequacy of any solution seems to you the most pressing thing you have to say, you should be able to place your emphasis accordingly.

This advice doesn't mean that you can select from the format the steps you wish to attend to and ignore the others. You can, however, lean more heavily on one of the steps and build your paper around it.

The best reason not to ignore any of the six steps in this problem/solution format we've been looking at is that the format does have a logic, although it leaves that logic unstated. The purpose of including at least two inadequate solutions (step 3), for example, is to protect the writer against moving to a conclusion too quickly on the basis of too little evidence. The requirements that the writer evaluate the solution and reply to criticisms are there to press the writer toward complexity, to prevent a one-sided and uncritical answer. In short, heuristic value in the format is there for a writer to use if he or she doesn't allow a premature concern with matters of form to take precedence over thinking.

COMMON THOUGHT PATTERNS: INDUCTION AND DEDUCTION

Organizational schemes vary according to whether a paper is largely inductive or deductive. A deductive paper will state at or near its beginning the general principle governing its examination of evidence. It is important to note that the general principle stated at the beginning of the paper and the idea stated as the paper's conclusion are usually not the same. Rather, the conclusion presents the idea that the writer has arrived at through the application of the principle.

The standard definition of deduction is "based on inference from accepted principles" or "the process of drawing a conclusion from something known or assumed." A deductive argument draws out the implications—infers the consequences—of a position you already agree to. As a thought process, deduction reasons from the general to the particular. For example, a deductive paper might state in its first paragraph that attitudes toward and rules governing sexuality in a given culture can be seen, at least in part, to have economic causes. The paper might then apply this principle, already assumed to be true, to the codes governing sexual behavior in several cultures, or several kinds of sexual behavior in a single culture. The writer's aim would be to use the general principle as a means of explaining selected features of particular cases.

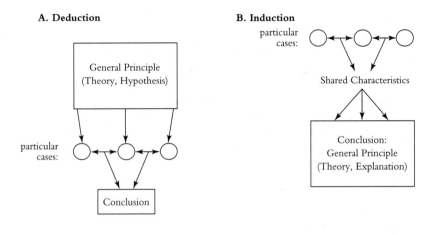

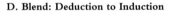

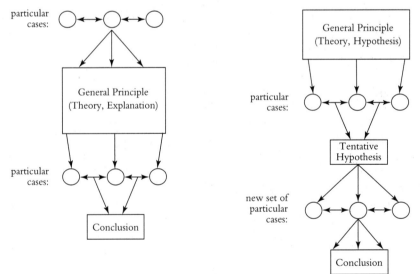

Figure 3.1 Deduction and Induction. Deductive reasoning (A) uses particular cases to exemplify general principles and analyze their implications. Inductive reasoning (B) constructs general principles from the analysis of particular cases. In practice, analytical thinking and writing blend deduction and induction, starting either with particular cases (C) or a general principle (D).

An inductively organized paper typically begins not with a principle already assumed to be true but with particular data for which it seeks to generate some explanatory principle. While deduction moves by applying a generalization to particular cases in point, induction moves from the observation of individual cases to the formation of a general principle. (See Appendix B for further discussion.)

Ideally, the principle arrived at through inductive reasoning is not deemed a workable theory until the writer has examined all possible instances (every left-handed person, for example, if you wish to theorize that left-handed people are better at spatial thinking than right-handers). But since this comprehensiveness is usually impossible, the thesis of an inductive paper (principle or theory arrived at through the examination of particulars) is generally deemed acceptable if a writer can demonstrate that the theory is based on a reasonably sized sampling of representative instances. This matter of a writer's establishing the representativeness of his or her examples is taken up in more detail in Chapter 7, "Analyzing Evidence." For present purposes, suffice it to say that a child who arrives at the thesis that all orange food tastes bad on the basis of squash and carrots has not based that theory on an adequate sampling of available evidence.

In practice, most writing evolves through a blend of induction and deduction. The examination of particular cases may illustrate the accuracy and usefulness of the general principle that generated the examination (deduction), but the writer's conclusions about the particular cases may also modify the generating principle (induction). The aim of analysis is usually to test the validity of a hypothetical (tentative) conclusion or to generate a theory that might plausibly explain a given set of data. In Chapter 4, "Finding and Developing a Thesis," we demonstrate in much more detail these methods of evolving ideas. We argue that no matter which pattern of organization—and thus of thought—a paper uses, its governing idea evolves through successive confrontations with evidence. (See Figure 3.1.)

GUIDELINES FOR USING FORMATS IN ANALYTICAL WRITING

The traditional organizational schemes that have been with us since Aristotle—problem/solution, comparison/contrast, classification, cause/effect, and so on—are attempts to describe some of the characteristic shapes, or patterns of movement, that thinking typically takes. Chapter 2, "Constructing Effective Topics," discusses some of these patterns. As a conclusion to this chapter, we recommend an all-purpose pattern, one that describes a standard working procedure in many kinds of analytical writing. The patterns of thought recommended in the rest of this book are all based on this thought template.

1. Begin analytical papers by defining some issue, question, problem, or phenomenon that the paper will address. The initial version of your thesis, which usually appears somewhere in the paper's first or second paragraph (depending on the conventions of the discipline you are writing in), should offer a tentative explanation, answer, or solution that the body of your paper will go on to apply and develop (clarify, extend, substantiate, qualify, and so on).

2. Move into the body of your paper by querying your tentative thesis and other opening observations with the question "So what?" which is shorthand for questions like "What does this observation mean?" and "Where does this thesis get me in my attempts to explain my subject?"

3. Test the adequacy of your initial claim (tentative thesis) by seeing how much of the available evidence it can honestly account for. Expect to encounter evidence that doesn't fit your initial formulation of the thesis.

4. When you encounter obstacles, try other ways of responding to your subject and other terms for talking about it. This is how a thesis evolves, by assimilating obstacles and refining terms.

5. Arrive at a conclusion in which you reflect on and reformulate your paper's opening position in light of the thinking your analysis of evidence has caused you to do. Culminate rather than merely restate your paper's main idea in the concluding paragraph. Do this by getting your conclusion to answer the question "So what?" which, in the conclusion, is shorthand for questions like "Where does it get us to view the subject in this way?" or "What are the possible implications or consequences of the position the paper has arrived at?"

C H A P T E R
4

FINDING and DEVELOPING
a THESIS

T HE *THESIS* OF AN analytical paper is an idea about your subject, a theory that explains what some feature or features of your subject mean. A *strong thesis* comes from carefully examining and questioning your subject in order to arrive at some point about its meaning and significance that would not have been immediately obvious to your readers. A *weak thesis* either makes no claim or makes a claim that does not need proving, such as a statement of fact or an opinion with which virtually all of your readers would most likely agree before reading your paper (for example, "Exercise is good for you").

In Chapter 5 we will explain in more detail what a thesis is by showing you how to convert several kinds of weak thesis statements into stronger ones. In this chapter, we focus not so much on what a thesis is but on what a thesis *does* and how writers go about finding one.

DEVELOPING A THESIS
IS MORE THAN REPEATING AN IDEA

It is important to note that the way a thesis functions in a paper—how fully it must be stated at the outset, for example, and what happens to it between the beginning of the paper and the end—is not the same for all disciplines. Disciplinary differences appear largest as you move back and forth between courses in the humanities and courses in the natural and certain of the social sciences. The most obvious difference is that the social and natural sciences generally use a pair of terms, *hypothesis* and *conclusion,* for our single term *thesis* (more on this in the first "Voices from Across the Curriculum" section). In the humanities and some social sciences, a writer's conclusions about his or her initial formulation of the thesis (hypothesis) usually appear through recasting of that formulation into a statement that more accurately and precisely explains the evidence. The thesis develops, as we will illustrate, through successive reformulations. In the sciences, successive reformulations of the thesis are less likely to be recorded in the final draft of the paper; however, the primary analytical activity in the sciences, as in all disciplines, is to repeatedly reconsider the assumptions upon which a conclusion is based.

Perhaps the most common misunderstanding about the thesis is that it must appear throughout the paper in essentially the same form—fixed and unchanging. In fact, it is only a weakly developed thesis that, like an inert (unreactive) material, neither makes anything happen nor undergoes any change itself. In contrast, in nearly all good writing the thesis gains in complexity as well as precision and accuracy as the paper progresses. Developing a thesis, in other words, means making it *evolve*, pruning and shaping it in response to evidence. In cases where the thesis itself cannot evolve, as, for example, in the report format of the natural and social sciences where the initial hypothesis must be either confirmed or denied, there is still movement (conceptual development) between the beginning of the paper and the end rather than repeated reassertion of one idea.

Weak thesis statements (poorly formulated and inadequately developed) are most easily detected by their repetitiveness and predictability. The writer says the same thing again and again, drawing the same overgeneralized conclusion from each piece of evidence ("and so, once again we see that . . ."). The problem with a thesis that functions as an inert formula is that it closes down a writer's thinking rather than guiding and stimulating it.

Inert thesis statements are, at least in part, products of a writer's adhering to an overly rigid and mechanical organizational scheme wherein any data that do not clearly conform to some single, oversimplified unifying point (such as Marlowe's *Doctor Faustus* is a play about greed, or government welfare programs stifle initiative) remain unnoticed or are studiously ignored. A quick check of whether a paper of yours has closed down your thinking in this way is to look at paragraph openings. If these read like a list, each beginning with an additive transition like "another" followed by a more or less exact repetition of your central point ("another example is . . . ," "yet another example is . . ."), you should suspect that you are not adequately developing your ideas.

This is not to say that all repetition is bad or that a writer's concluding paragraph should have no reference to the way the paper began. One function of the thesis is to provide the connective tissue, so to speak, that holds together a paper's three main parts—beginning, middle, and end. Periodic reminders of your paper's thesis, its unifying idea, are essential for keeping both you and your readers on track. As we demonstrate throughout this chapter, however, there is a big difference between developing and just repeating an idea.

MAKING A THESIS EVOLVE: THE THESIS AS CAMERA LENS

It is in establishing this key difference between development and repetition that the analogy of thesis as connective tissue breaks down. A better way of envisioning how a thesis operates is to think of it as a camera lens. This analogy more accurately describes the relationship between the thesis and the subject it seeks to explain: while the lens affects how we see the subject (what evidence we select, what questions we ask about that evidence), the subject we are looking at affects how we adjust the lens. The relationship between thesis and subject is, in other words, *reciprocal*. In good analytical writing, especially in the early, investigatory stages of writing and thinking, the thesis not only directs the writer's way of looking at evidence, but the analysis of evidence should also direct and redirect (bring about revision of) the thesis. Even in a final draft, writers are usually fine-tuning their governing idea in response to their analysis of evidence.

The enemy of good analytical writing is the fuzzy lens—imprecisely worded thesis statements. Very broad thesis statements, those that are made up of imprecise (fuzzy) terms, make bad camera lenses. They blur everything together and muddy important distinctions. If your lens is insufficiently sharp, you are not likely to see much in your evidence. If you say, for example, that the economic situation today is bad, you will at least have some sense of direction, but the imprecise terms "bad" and "economic situation" don't provide you with a focus clear enough to distinguish significant detail in your evidence. Without significant detail to analyze, you can't develop your thesis, either by showing readers what the thesis is good for (what it allows us to understand and explain) or by clarifying its terms.

A writer's thesis is usually fuzzier in a paper's opening than it is in the conclusion. Generally speaking, you should suspect that a paper ending with a claim worded almost exactly as it was in the beginning has not made its thesis adequately responsive to evidence. The body of the paper should not only substantiate the thesis by demonstrating its value in selecting and explaining evidence but also bring the opening version of the thesis into better focus.

MAKING A THESIS EVOLVE: A BRIEF EXAMPLE

Consider what might happen to the thesis "tax laws benefit the wealthy" between the beginning and end of a paper. If you were to start out with this rather fuzzy but not hopelessly overgeneral thesis, you would soon encounter evidence that would press you to make some distinctions that the initial formulation of your thesis leaves obscure. You would need, for example, to distinguish different sources of wealth and then to determine whether all or just some wealthy taxpayers are benefited by tax laws. Do people whose wealth comes primarily from investments benefit less (or more) than those whose wealth comes from high wages? Evidence might also lead you to consider whether tax laws by benefiting the wealthy also benefit other people indirectly. Both of these considerations would necessitate some reformulation of the thesis. By the end of the paper, the claim that tax laws benefit

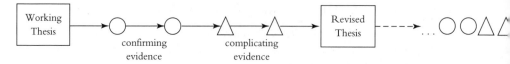

Figure 4.1 The Evolving Thesis. A strong thesis evolves as it confronts and assimilates evidence. Depending on the evidence, the evolved thesis may expand or restrict the original claim. The dotted line after the revised thesis indicates that the process may need to be repeated a number of times.

the wealthy should have evolved into a more carefully defined and qualified statement that reflects the thinking you have done in your analysis of evidence. This, by and large, is what good concluding paragraphs do—they reflect back on and reformulate your paper's initial position in light of the thinking you have done about it.

As this example demonstrates, rather than avoiding interpretations of evidence that conflict with the original formulation of your thesis, you should allow such evidence to complicate your thesis so that it more accurately reflects the complexity of the subject you are analyzing. Discovering complications is a goal, not a problem.

But, you might ask, isn't this reformulating of the thesis something a writer does before he or she writes the essay? Certainly some of it is accomplished in your prewriting phase—the exploratory drafting and note taking you do before you begin to compose the first draft of the essay. But your finished paper will necessarily be more than a list of conclusions. To an extent, all good writing reenacts the chains of thought that led you to your conclusions. Your revision process will have weeded out various false starts and dead ends that you may have wandered into on the way to your finished ideas, but the main routes of your movement from a tentative idea to a refined and substantiated theory should remain visible for readers to follow. (See Figure 4.1)

Voices from Across the Curriculum

THE EVOLVING THESIS AS HYPOTHESIS AND CONCLUSION

Because writing in the sciences is patterned according to the scientific method, writers in disciplines such as biology and psychology and other of the so-called hard sciences must report how the original thesis (hypothesis) was tested against empirical evidence and then conclude on this basis whether or not the hypothesis was confirmed. On this matter, an economics professor writes:

Economists do make pretense to follow scientific methodology. Thus we are careful not to mix hypothesis and conclusion. I think it's important to distinguish between what is conjectured, the working hypothesis, and what ultimately

continued

emerges as a result of an examination of the evidence. Conclusions come only after some test has been passed.

—*J. Marshall, Professor of Economics*

This professor goes on to observe that regardless of the qualifications a writer might add to the thesis in the course of writing a paper, he or she would still have to be sure to arrive at a conclusion about the validity of the paper's original assertion. He suggests some risks in conceptualizing the thesis as an idea that gets shaped and developed throughout a paper:

Questions are put into sharper focus when a working hypothesis is clearly stated, and the evidence is marshalled to either confirm or disconfirm it. If in the course of a paper a claim is refined and extended in response to evidence, is not the original assertion left untested? Have you not modified what you originally set out to test? I am not opposed to such modifications, but do fear that what the paper set out to address could become lost. So FDR was an experimenter; he cared deeply about the disadvantaged; he had little formal training in economic reasoning. Great, wonderful. I'm glad to know all this. But hey, you were going to tell me whether or not he was a Keynesian.

—*J. Marshall, Professor of Economics*

The gap between this way of thinking about the thesis and the concept of an evolving thesis that we are developing in this chapter is not as large as it may seem. In fact, one of the chapter's main points—if not *the* main point—is that something must happen to the thesis between the introduction and the conclusion so that the conclusion does more than just reassert what had already been asserted in the beginning. To put this concept in the language of the sciences, the paper's hypothesis needs to be carefully tested against evidence, the results of which allow the writer to draw conclusions about the hypothesis's validity. So, in the sciences, although the hypothesis itself does not change, the testing of it and subsequent interpretation of those results produce commentary on and, often, qualifications of the paper's central claim.

It should go without saying that if the empirical evidence doesn't confirm your hypothesis, you rethink your hypothesis, but it's a complex issue. Researchers whose hypotheses are not confirmed in fact often question their *method* ("if I had more subjects," or "a better manipulation of the experimental group," or "a better test of intelligence," etc.) as much as their hypothesis. And that's often legitimate. Part of the challenge of psychological research is its reliance on a long array of assumptions. Failure to confirm a hypothesis could mean a problem in any of that long array of assumptions. So failure to confirm your hypothesis is often difficult to interpret.

—*A. Tjeltveit, Professor of Psychology*

OVERVIEW OF THE CHAPTER'S EXAMPLES

The remainder of this chapter offers extended analyses of three examples, illustrating the evolution of three theses at different stages in the writing process. The first example illustrates how prewriting (an exploratory draft) can be used to locate and focus a workable thesis. The second example shows how the initial formulation of a thesis might evolve—through a series of complications—over the course of a more finished draft. The final example, a published essay, illustrates the way a thesis develops in a finished draft, with emphasis on how a writer reasons forward to conclusions by reasoning back to premises.

FINDING A THESIS IN AN EXPLORATORY DRAFT

Although the forms of final products in the various disciplines differ, the thinking process that allows a writer to arrive at and substantiate a supportable idea (thesis) about the meaning of evidence is markedly similar from discipline to discipline. The governing principle is that *the thesis evolves through a series of careful reformulations in light of the writer's analysis of evidence.*

Because the writing process is a way not just of recording but of discovering ideas, writers often set out with one idea or direction in mind and then, in the process of writing, happen upon a potentially better idea that emerges in the draft. These emerging thoughts may lead to a markedly different thesis, or they may provide the means of extending your paper's original thesis well beyond the point you'd settled for in your exploratory draft.

Different writers undertake this kind of conceptual revision—locating and defining the thesis—in different ways. Some, after varying amounts of prewriting, rely on repeated revisions as they work their way through a first draft (which, when finished, will be close to a final draft). Others move quickly through the first draft without much revision and then comprehensively rethink and restructure this draft (sometimes two, three, or more times). Whatever mode of revision (or combination of them) works best for you, the thinking processes we here define and demonstrate are central. They are the common denominators of the various stages of the drafting process.

Extended Analysis

VELÁZQUEZ'S INTENTIONS IN *LAS MENINAS*

Our method of demonstrating how writers use prewriting to find and focus a workable thesis is to take you through the steps a writer would follow in revising an exploratory draft of an actual paper, in this case a student paper on a painting, *Las Meninas* (Spanish for "the ladies in waiting"), by the seventeenth-century painter Diego Velázquez. As you read the draft, watch how the writer develops the claim made at the end of her first paragraph—that, despite the painting's

Figure 4.2 Diego Velázquez, *Las Meninas,* 1656. Approximately 10'5" x 9'. Museo del Prado, Madrid.

complexity, it clearly reveals at least some of the painter's intentions (referred to elsewhere in the paper as what the painting is saying, what it suggests, or what the painter wants). We have boldfaced each appearance of this claim in the text of the paper to make the writer's development of her central idea easier to follow.

VELÁZQUEZ'S INTENTIONS IN *LAS MENINAS*

1 Velázquez has been noted as being one of the best Spanish artists of all time. It seems that as Velázquez got older, his paintings became better. Towards the end of his life, he painted his masterpiece, *Las Meninas*. Out of all of his works, *Las Meninas* is the only known self-portrait of Velázquez. There is much to be said about *Las Meninas*. **The painting is very complex, but some of the intentions that Velázquez had in painting *Las Meninas* are very clear.**

2 First, we must look at the painting as a whole. The question which must be answered is, who is in the painting? The people are all members of the Royal Court of the Spanish monarch, Philip IV. In the center is the daughter of the king who would eventually become Empress of Spain. Around her are her *meninas* or ladies in waiting. These *meninas* are all daughters of influential men. To the right of the *meninas* are dwarfs who are servants, and the family dog who looks fierce but is easily tamed by the foot of the little dwarf. The more unique people in the painting are Velázquez himself who stands to the left in front of a large canvas, the king and queen whose faces are captured in the obscure mirror, the man in the doorway, and the nun and man behind the *meninas*. **To analyze this painting further, the relationship between characters must be understood.**

3 Where is this scene occurring? Well, most likely it is in the palace. But, why is there no visible furniture? **Is it because Velázquez didn't want the viewers to become distracted from his true intentions? I believe it is to show that this is not just a painting of an actual event.** This is an event out of his imagination.

4 Now, let us become better acquainted with the characters. The child in the center is the most visible. All the light is shining on her. **Maybe Velázquez is suggesting that she is the next light for Spain and that even God has approved her** by shining all the available light on her. Back in those days there was a belief in the divine right of kings, so this just might be what Velázquez is saying.

5 The next people of interest are the ones behind the *meninas.* The woman in the habit might be a nun and the man a priest.

6 The king and queen are the next group of interesting people. They are in the mirror which is to suggest they are present, but they are not as visible as they might be. Velázquez suggests that they are not always at the center where everyone would expect them to be.

7 The last person and the most interesting is Velázquez. He dominates the painting along with the little girl. He takes up the whole left side along with his gigantic easel. But what is he painting? As I previously said, he might be painting the king and queen. But I also think he could be pretending to paint us, the viewers. The easel really gives this portrait an air of mystery because Velázquez knows that we, the viewers, want to know what he is painting.

8 The appearance of Velázquez is also interesting. His eyes are focused out here. They are not focused on what is going on around him. It is a steady stare. Also interesting is his confident stance. He was confident enough to place himself in the painting of the royal court. **I think that Velázquez wants the king to give him the recognition he deserves by including him in the "family."** And the symbol on his vest is the symbol given to a painter by the king to **show that his status and brilliance have been appreciated by the monarch.** It is unknown how it got there. It is unlikely that Velázquez put it there himself. That would be too outright and Velázquez was the type to give his messages subtly. Some say that after Velázquez's death, King Philip IV himself painted it to finally give Velázquez **the credit he deserved for being a loyal friend and servant.**

9   I believe that Velázquez was very ingenious by putting his thoughts and feelings into a painting. He didn't want to offend the king who had done so much for him. It paid off for Velázquez because he did finally get what he wanted, even if it was after he died.

Although its thinking is still underdeveloped, this version of the student's paper is a good exploratory draft. The writer has begun to interpret details and draw conclusions from what she sees, rather than just describing (summarizing) the scene depicted on the canvas or responding loosely to it with her unanalyzed impressions. Theorizing about her evidence—details of the painting—has taken her to several relatively specific and plausible ideas about the meaning of the painting that readers viewing the same evidence would be likely to accept as reasonable.

Typical of an early draft, this one is written more for the writer—as a form of inquiry—than for readers. The writer reports her thoughts as they occur, but she doesn't always explain how she arrived at them. As is also characteristic of exploratory drafts, the thesis doesn't emerge until near the end (in paragraph 8), probably at the point where the writer first recognized and thus became able to formulate the idea her evidence has directed her to. Of the several possible thesis statements that appear near the paper's end, the one the writer seems to settle on is: "I think that Velázquez wants the king to give him the recognition he deserves by including him in the 'family.'"

The discovery of a thesis is one of the primary aims of an exploratory draft, but getting a potentially workable thesis articulated is not the end of the process. Having arrived at a workable thesis, the writer now needs to *use* it, trying to re-see the evidence from the perspective it provides and to specify (qualify, clarify) the thesis on the basis of this reseeing. Making the thesis more fully responsive to evidence, either by formulating a mostly new thesis and beginning again or by modifying the existing thesis, is the primary activity of conceptual revision (as opposed to correcting and editing). Your aim here is not to go around and around forever but to go back and forth between thesis and evidence, allowing each to adjust how you see the other, until you find the best possible fit between the two.

STRATEGIES FOR FINDING A THESIS IN AN EXPLORATORY DRAFT

Strategy 1: Check for Competing or Multiple Theses

In the *Las Meninas* paper, as is often the case in early drafts, no single idea emerges clearly as the thesis. Instead, we get three related but not entirely compatible ideas vying for control of the paper. As previously noted, the one that seems to have emerged most prominently as the thesis is "I think that Velázquez wants the king to give him the recognition he deserves by including him in the 'family.'" But we could easily have chosen two other ideas from near the end of the draft as potential theses: that the painter wished "the king to show that his [the painter's] status and brilliance have been appreciated" and that the painting was a bid for "the credit he deserved for being a loyal friend and servant." These three ideas about the painter's intentions could be made to work together, but at present the writer is left with an uneasy fit among them.

Strategy 2: Check for Evidence That Does Not Seem to Be Adequately Accounted for by Your Thesis

The process of revising for ideas begins in earnest when you start checking to make sure that the thesis you have formulated accounts for as much of your evidence as possible, or, at least, that the thesis is not contradicted by some of that evidence. In other words, you need to actively test your thesis by asking yourself whether any features of your subject do not seem to fit with this idea.

What happens when the writer begins to search for evidence that doesn't seem to be adequately accounted for by her various thesis formulations? One of her potential theses (that the painter uses the painting as a bid for recognition of his status and brilliance) accounts for at least some of her evidence—the painter's prominent easel and brush, for example, as well as his own prominence in the painting. But this version of the thesis fails to account for some of the writer's other evidence, such as the prominence of other servants in the painting, the painting's title ("The Ladies in Waiting"), and the domestic scene created by the inclusion of king, queen, and princess. The theses to which this evidence seems to point—that the painter wishes to be included in the family and/or be given credit for being a loyal friend and servant—don't adequately account for evidence like the painter's prominence (second only in prominence to the princess), his confident stare, and the apparent decentering of the king and queen. And what about the large dwarf, presumably another servant to the court, who dominates the right-hand side of the painting? Do any of the paper's tentative theses account for his inclusion and his positioning, staring at viewers from the right-hand foreground as the painter does from the left?

Having noticed various mismatches of this sort in your draft—between thesis and evidence as well as among possible theses—your key revision strategy should be to view these inconsistencies as opportunities rather than faults. In an exploratory draft, varying interpretations of evidence are your raw material, records of your thinking that can be refined and developed in the next draft. The challenge is to recognize when an idea you've arrived at is a starting point rather than an end to the writing process.

Strategy 3: Use Conflicting Evidence to Evolve Your Thesis

When you've found conflicting or inadequately explained evidence, try using it to evolve your existing thesis rather than beating a too-hasty retreat. If there are features of your subject that your thesis seems not to adequately account for, you need not conclude that you should immediately throw out your thesis and start over. Although such radical revision sometimes may turn out to be what is needed, you should first try to use evidence that is not accounted for by your current thesis as a means of further evolving that idea.

To an extent, the writer of the *Las Meninas* paper has already begun the process of testing her thesis against evidence that seems not to fit and then using that evidence to reformulate her thesis. In paragraph 4, for example, the writer comes up with a thought that might have become her thesis—that the painting was

Velázquez's way of endorsing the divine right of kings. But evidence that the writer includes in paragraphs 6 and 7 (the decentering of the king and queen as well as the prominence and confident stare of the painter) apparently caused her to drop the divine-right idea. The position to which she shifts—that the painting asks that someone's strengths be recognized—is not an entirely new start, however. The shift is from the painting as showcase of royal power to the painting as showcase of the painter's own power. Although a careful reader can infer this chain of thought, the writer needs to make it more explicit so that readers can more easily participate in and evaluate the thinking that caused the writer's thesis to evolve.

Strategy 4: Develop the Implications of Your Evidence and of Your Own Observations as Fully as You Can by Repeatedly Asking "So What?"

The uneasy fit between thesis and evidence and among competing versions of the thesis can be recognized and addressed as the writer more tenaciously pursues implications. Pursuing implications means that you need to make explicit something that is suggested but not overtly articulated by your evidence and by your own statements about that evidence.

The writer of this paper has a tendency to end paragraphs with promising observations and then walk away, leaving the observations undeveloped. Rather than draw out the implications of her observations, she halts her thinking too soon in order to move on to the next piece of evidence. It is worth noting that this is partly an organizational problem. The writer's repeated return to the unchanging paragraph opening, "Another interesting feature . . . another interesting feature," traps her into listing parallel examples rather than building connections among them.

The best way to pursue implications is to spell out the questions suggested by the evidence and your own observations. The writer should be asking herself: "What am I getting at here?" or "What might I conclude about this feature of my evidence?" The shorthand version of such questions—one especially likely to prompt analysis—is *"So what?"*

There are a significant number of "So what?" questions left dangling in this draft of the *Las Meninas* paper. The statement that concludes paragraph 6, for example, contains two points that require further analysis. *So what* that the king and queen are diminished and decentered? *So what* that the painter violates conventional expectations by not placing the king and queen "at the center where everyone would expect them to be"? To what conclusions, the writer should say to herself, do these observations lead me?

The writer has, of course, made some of her thinking about implications overt. She asserts that "the relationship between characters must be understood" (end of paragraph 2). From here she might have gone on to a potential answer to her "So what?" questions: that perhaps the relative size and/or prominence of figures in the painting can be read as indicators of their importance, or of what the painter wants to say about their importance.

Following this line of thinking, the writer could begin proposing and testing various more specific answers to her "So what?" questions about the size and placement of the king and queen relative to other figures in the painting.

Proposed answer: Perhaps the king and queen have been reduced so that Velázquez can showcase their daughter, the princess.

Test of this answer: The size and location of the princess (center foreground) seem to support this answer, as does the princess' being catered to by the ladies in waiting. But, if the painting is meant to showcase the princess, what is the point of the painter's having made himself so large?

Another possible answer: Perhaps the size and physical prominence of the king and queen are relatively unimportant. In that case, what matters is that they are a presence, always overseeing events (an idea implied but not developed by the writer in paragraph 6).

Test of this answer: Further support for this answer comes from the possibility that we are meant to see them as reflected in a mirror on the back wall of the painter's studio (an idea the writer mentions), in which case they would be standing in front of the scene depicted in the painting, literally overseeing events. There isn't much evidence against this answer, except, again, for the large size of the painter and the trivializing implications of the king and queen's diminution, but these are significant exceptions.

Another possible answer: Perhaps the painter is demonstrating his own ability to make the king and queen any size—any level of importance—he chooses. Although the writer does not overtly say so, the king and queen are among the smallest as well as the least visible figures.

Test: This answer might help make sense of the piece of evidence that has not fit comfortably with the other answers—the prominence and large size of the painter relative to other figures in the painting. But this answer suggests a reading of the painting that would make it unusual for an era in which most other court paintings flattered royal figures by portraying them as larger than life—powerful and heroic. The writer will need to pursue the next step in her thesis-hunting process with particular care: looking for other features of the painting that might corroborate her theory.

Strategy 5: Make Connections—Put the Evidence Together

In her revision, the writer would need to look for connections, both in her thinking and among her pieces of evidence. Only in this way would she be able to decide which explanation for the decentering of the king and queen makes most sense.

The writer has, in fact, already made a connection between two pieces of her evidence by noting in passing that the painter "dominates the painting along with the little girl" (paragraph 7). If the painter and the princess are parallel in prominence, what might the painter be saying to viewers (including his patrons, the king and queen) about his relationship to the royal family? Is this where part of the writer's thesis (painter asking to be accepted as member of the royal family) comes from, although she has not specifically told us so? And what kind of inclusion in the family might the writer (and the painter) have in mind? Might her implication through the word "family" be that the painter's desire is for status more equal with his royal patrons? If so, is the decentering and reduction of the king and queen a kind of loaded joke, a playful comment (or visual pun) in which the painter's stature at court is portrayed as "bigger" than that of his royal patrons?

STEP-BY-STEP SAMPLE REVISION

What follows is an outline version of our hypothetical revision, a more tightly structured summary of the discussion in the preceding section. It is organized according to the strategies we've been exemplifying, each followed by a recap of the thinking it might cause the writer to produce. The pursuit of implication, the "So what?" question, is not listed here as a separate step because it is now assumed as an integral part of each step in the revision process.

Step 1: Locate the draft's thesis (or various possible theses), and test this against evidence that doesn't clearly fit.

The writer might ask, for example, whether a painter who depicts himself as bigger than the king and queen and parallel in prominence with the princess is seeking only to be recognized as a loyal servant who deserves to be included in the family.

Step 2: Modify your thesis so that it more precisely and accurately accounts for your evidence.

If the painting says something to the king and queen, perhaps it is that artists are important and deserve to be recognized because they have their own kind of power.

Step 3: Evaluate the adequacy of the new thesis formulation by seeing what else in your evidence it might explain.

The thesis arrived at in step 2 would explain more of the writer's own observations than any of her earlier formulations. It would explain, for example, the painter's prominence and the relative insignificance of the monarchs: that he, in effect, creates their stature (size, power) in the world through his paintings. Framed in a mirror and appearing to hang on the wall, the king and queen are, arguably, suspended among the painter's paintings, mere reflections of themselves—or, rather, the painter's reflection of them.

Step 4: Continue to use the implications of evidence to modify your thesis until you arrive at a formulation that seems to offer the best explanation of as much of your evidence as possible.

If the painter is demonstrating that he can make the members of the royal family any size he wants, then the painting is a bid for recognition (as the writer has said), but it could also be seen as a playful though not so subtle threat: be aware of my power and treat me well or suffer the consequences. As artist, the painter decides how the royal family will be seen. The king and queen depend on the painter, as they do in a different way on the princess, with whom Velázquez makes himself equal in prominence, to extend and perpetuate their power.

We emphasize before leaving this example that the version of the thesis that we have just proposed is not necessarily the "right" answer. Looked at in a different context, the painting might have been explained primarily as a demonstration of the painter's mastery of the tools of his trade—light, for example, and perspective. But our proposed revision of the thesis for the *Las Meninas* paper does have the advantage of unifying the observations the writer has made, and it seems capable of accounting for a wide range of evidence. It offers, for example, a plausible explanation for the presence of that large dwarf in the right-hand foreground. Positioned in a way that links him with the painter, the dwarf arguably furthers the painting's message and does so, like much else in the painting, in the form of a loaded joke: the small ("dwarfed" by the power of others) are brought forward and made big.

Similarly, another of the writer's key observations—that the painter "plays" with viewers' expectations—fits with the thesis that the painting asks for recognition of the artist's power, not just his loyal service. In subverting viewers' expectations both by decentering the monarchs and concealing what is on the easel, the painter again emphasizes his power, in this case, over the viewers (among whom might be the king and queen if their images on the back wall are mirror reflections of them standing, like us, in front of the painting). He is not bound by their expectations and in fact appears to use those expectations to manipulate the viewers: he can make them wish to see something he has the power to withhold.

KNOWING WHEN TO STOP

How do you know when you've done enough reformulating of your thesis? You can't know for sure when you've arrived at the best possible idea about your evidence unless you are working in a field in which your thesis can be tested against irrefutable evidence (carefully controlled experiments and statistical data, for example—though even these are rarely irrefutable). Getting the thesis to account for (respond to) all rather than just some of your evidence does not mean that a writer needs to discuss every detail of the subject. Writers (rather like trial lawyers) must take care not to ignore important evidence, especially if it would alter their "case," but no analysis can address everything—nor should it. Your job as a writer is to select those features of your subject that seem most significant and to argue for their significance. An analysis says to readers, in effect, "These are the details that best reveal the nature and meaning of my subject, or at least the part of the subject that I am trying to address."

DEVELOPING A THESIS
THROUGH SUCCESSIVE COMPLICATIONS

As the previous example showed, the first step in finding a thesis is to recognize that one will not appear to you, ready-made, in the material you are analyzing. Summarizing may help you to find an analytical thesis, but a restatement of some idea that is already clearly stated in your subject is not a thesis. The process of finding a thesis—an idea about the facts and ideas in your subject—begins only when you start to ask questions about the material, deliberately looking for a place where you detect some kind of problem to be solved.

More often than not, when inexperienced writers face a situation in which evidence seems to be unclear or contradictory, they tend to make one of two unproductive moves: they either ignore the conflicting evidence, or they abandon the problem altogether and look for something more clear-cut to write about. But finding a problem is not a problem—it's an opportunity, as the following example shows.

Extended Analysis

EDUCATING RITA

Let's consider the stages you might go through within a more finished draft to evolve a thesis about a film. In *Educating Rita,* a working-class English hairdresser (Rita) wants to change her life by taking courses from a professor (Frank) at the local university, even though this move threatens her relationship with her husband (Denny), who burns her books and puts pressure on her to quit school and get pregnant. Frank, she discovers, has his own problems: he's a divorced alcoholic who is bored with his life, bored with his privileged and complacent students and bent on self-destruction. The film follows the growth of Frank and Rita's friendship and the changes it brings about in their lives. By the end of the film, each has left a limiting way of life behind and has set off in a seemingly more promising direction. She leaves her constricting marriage, passes her university examinations with honors, and begins to view her life in terms of choices; he stops drinking and sets off, determined but sad, to make a new start as a teacher in Australia.

Initial thesis: "Educating Rita *celebrates the liberating potential of education.*" Given the film's relatively happy ending and the presence of the word "educating" in the film's title, your first stab at composing a thesis about *Educating Rita* might be to say that it celebrates the liberating potential of education. You would next see how far you could make the thesis go in accounting for evidence. The tentative thesis seems compatible, for example, with Rita's achievement of greater self-awareness and independence. But other evidence troubles the adequacy of this thesis: Rita's education causes her to become alienated from her husband, her parents, and her social class; at the end of the film she is alone and unsure about her direction in life. In Frank's case, the thesis runs into even more problems. His boredom, drinking, and alienation seem to have been caused, at least in part, by his education rather than by his lack of it. He sees his book-lined study as a prison. Moreover, his profound knowledge of literature has not helped him to control his life: he comes to class drunk, fails to notice or care that his girlfriend is having an affair with one of his colleagues, and asks his classes whether it is worth gaining all of literature if it means losing one's soul.

Question: What are you to do? You cannot convincingly argue that the film celebrates the liberating potential of education, since that thesis ignores such a significant amount of the evidence. Nor can you "switch sides" and argue that the film attacks education as life denying and disabling, even though this thesis is also partially true.

Answer 1: What *not* to do. Faced with evidence that complicates your thesis, the one thing not to do is run away from the challenge of trying to figure out what the film has to say about education. The "problem" you have discovered offers an opportunity to modify your thesis rather than abandon it. After all, the thesis still fits some of the evidence. Rita is arguably better off at the end of the film than at the beginning: we are not left to believe that she should have remained resistant to education, like her husband, Denny, whose world doesn't extend much beyond the corner pub.

Answer 2: What to do. Recognize that the complications you've encountered are an opportunity to make your thesis evolve. Take advantage of this opportunity by making apparent complications—the film's seemingly contradictory attitudes about education—*explicit* and then modifying the wording of your thesis in a way that might resolve or explain these contradictions. You might, for example, be able to resolve an apparent contradiction between your initial thesis (the film celebrates the liberating potential of education) and the evidence by proposing that there is more than one version of education depicted in the film. In this case, you could divide education as represented by the film into two kinds, enabling and stultifying. Then the next step in the development of your thesis would be to elaborate on how the film seeks to distinguish true and enabling forms of education from false and debilitating ones (as represented by the self-satisfied and status-conscious behavior of the supposedly educated people at Frank's university).

Revised thesis: "Educating Rita *celebrates the liberating potential of enabling (in contrast to stultifying) education.*" Having refined your thesis in this way, you would then repeat the step of seeing what the new wording allows you to account for in your evidence. The new addition to your thesis might, for example, explain Frank's problems as being less a product of his education than of the cynical and pretentious versions of education that surround him in his university life. You could posit further that, with Rita as inspiration, Frank rediscovers at least some of his idealism about education.

What about Frank's emigration to Australia? If we can take Australia to stand for a newer world, one where education would be less likely to become the stale and exclusive property of a self-satisfied elite, then the refined version of the thesis would seem to be working well. In fact, given the possible thematic connection between Rita's working-class identity and Australia (associated, as a former frontier and English penal colony, with lower-class vitality as opposed to the complacency bred of class privilege), the thesis about the film's celebration of the contrast between enabling and stultifying forms of education could be sharpened further. You might propose, for example, that the film presents institutional education as desperately in need of frequent doses of "real life" (as represented by Rita and Australia)—infusions of lower-class pragmatism, energy, and optimism—if it is to remain healthy and open, as opposed to becoming the oppressive property of a privileged social class. This is to say that the film arguably exploits stereotypical assumptions about social class. *Revised thesis:* "Educating Rita *celebrates the liberating potential of enabling education, defined as that which remains open to healthy doses of working-class, real-world infusions."*

What our hypothetical development of this thesis should reveal is that the best way to make your thesis move forward (evolve) is to *acknowledge the questions* that each new formulation of it prompts you to ask. Allowing your thesis to run up against potentially conflicting evidence ("But what about this?") enables you to build upon your initial idea, extending the range of evidence it can accurately account for by clarifying and qualifying its key terms. Similarly, you can make your *supporting ideas* (those on which your thesis depends) more accurate and less susceptible to oversimplification by seeking evidence that might challenge their key terms.

Sharpening the language of your supporting assertions will help you develop your thesis. Consider, for example, the wording of the supporting idea that *Educating Rita* has a happy ending. Some qualification of this idea through consideration of possibly conflicting evidence could produce an adjustment in the first part of our hypothetical thesis, that the film celebrates education and presents it as liberating. At the end of the film, Frank and Rita walk off in opposite directions down long, empty airport corridors. Though promising to remain friends, the two do not become a couple. This closing emphasis on Frank and Rita's alienation from their respective cultures, and the film's apparent insistence on the necessity of their each going on alone, significantly qualifies the happiness of the "happy ending."

Once you have complicated your interpretation of the ending, you will again need to modify your thesis in accord with your new observations. Does the film simply celebrate education if it also presents it as being, to some degree, incompatible with conventional forms of happiness? By emphasizing the necessity of having Frank and Rita each go on alone, the film may be suggesting that in order to be truly liberating, education, as opposed to its less honest and more comfortable substitutes, inevitably produces and even requires a certain amount of loneliness and alienation. *Revised thesis:* "Educating Rita *celebrates the liberating potential of enabling education (kept open to real-world, working-class energy) but also acknowledges its potential costs in loneliness and alienation."* (See Figure 4.3.)

PLACING AND DEVELOPING THE THESIS IN A FINAL DRAFT

As this hypothetical evolution of a thesis has shown, thesis development means more than just piling up evidence in support of some single, unchanging idea. In most kinds of writing and in most academic disciplines, the thesis itself is developed (changed) by the evidence, usually through a series of complications. Although a certain amount of this development will not prove worth sharing with your readers in your final draft, much of it will and should remain. Readers need to see the shaping of the thesis as it comes into contact with different facets of your evidence. Final drafts often begin, in fact, by predicting the evolution of their theses; thus the

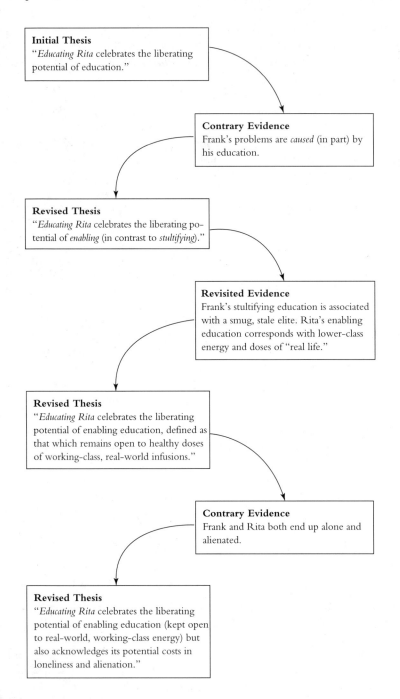

Initial Thesis
"*Educating Rita* celebrates the liberating potential of education."

Contrary Evidence
Frank's problems are *caused* (in part) by his education.

Revised Thesis
"*Educating Rita* celebrates the liberating potential of *enabling* (in contrast to *stultifying*)."

Revisited Evidence
Frank's stultifying education is associated with a smug, stale elite. Rita's enabling education corresponds with lower-class energy and doses of "real life."

Revised Thesis
"*Educating Rita* celebrates the liberating potential of enabling education, defined as that which remains open to healthy doses of working-class, real-world infusions."

Contrary Evidence
Frank and Rita both end up alone and alienated.

Revised Thesis
"*Educating Rita* celebrates the liberating potential of enabling education (kept open to real-world, working-class energy) but also acknowledges its potential costs in loneliness and alienation."

Figure 4.3 Successive Revisions of a Thesis. An initial thesis about *Educating Rita* evolves through successive complications as it reexamines evidence in the film.

Rita paper might open with the claim that *at first glance* the film seems to celebrate the liberating potential of education. You could then lay out the evidence for this view and proceed to complicate it in the ways we've discussed.

What typically happens is that you lead (usually at the end of the first paragraph or at the beginning of the second) with the best version of your thesis that you can come up with that will be understandable to your readers without a lengthy preamble. If you find yourself writing a page-long introductory paragraph in order to get to your initial statement of thesis, try settling for a simpler articulation of your central idea in its first appearance. As you move through the paper, keep yourself and your readers in mind of your purpose: to substantiate, elaborate on, test, and qualify your paper's opening gambit.

DEVELOPING A THESIS BY REASONING BACK TO PREMISES

As the preceding discussion has argued, a strong thesis evolves, but not haphazardly: it directs a chain of reasoning by which you analyze evidence. Good writing moves in two directions along this chain—forward to conclusions and backward to *premises* (assumptions that provide reasons for thinking that the conclusion is valid). While pressing your thesis forward, it is a good idea to *"update" your thesis periodically*, rehearsing for the reader and for yourself how this central claim is evolving. This practice will help keep your argument logically coherent and accessible to your reader.

In pressing a thesis backward, you need to locate and examine the premises that underlie it. Behind your assumptions rest further assumptions, ideas so deeply embedded in the roots of your argument that, if you can see them at all, they seem not to need defending. All arguments ultimately rest on fundamental assumptions called *givens*— positions not in need of argument because you assume the reader will "give" them to you as true. Often, however, these assumptions *do* need to be argued, or at least tested. The failure to examine these assumptions (premises) is the downfall of many essays. As the following example illustrates, it is crucial for you to reason backward in a chain far enough to recognize your premises and the givens that underlie them.

Reasoning Back to Premises: A Brief Example

For instance, no matter how you move forward from the initial thesis of our earlier example, "tax laws benefit the wealthy," you can get into trouble if you don't also move backward to consider the premises embedded in this thesis about the purpose of tax laws. In this case, the wording of the thesis seems to conceal an egalitarian premise: the assumption that tax laws should not benefit anyone or, at least, that they should benefit everyone equally. But what is the purpose of tax laws? Should they redress economic inequities? Should they spur the economy by

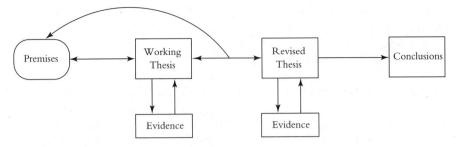

Figure 4.4 Reasoning Back to Premises. A writer makes the thesis evolve by reasoning not only forward to conclusions but also backward to underlying assumptions (premises).

rewarding those who generate capital? You might go to the U.S. Constitution and/or legal precedents to resolve such questions, but our point here is that you would need to move your thesis back to this point and test the validity of the assumptions upon which it rests. Regardless of how you evolved your thesis—attacking tax laws, defending them, showing how they actually benefit everyone, or whatever—you would risk arguing blindly if you failed to question what the purpose of tax law is in the first place. This testing of assumptions would, at the least, cause you to qualify and refine your thesis. (See Figure 4.4.)

Extended Analysis

A SAMPLE ESSAY: *PLAYING BY THE ANTIOCH RULES*

Because the following essay originally appeared as a newspaper editorial, it is less expository (explanatory) than much academic analytical writing. We have included it in this chapter on finding and using a thesis because it so clearly illustrates how a writer reasons forward to conclusions by reasoning backward to premises. The piece is also a useful reminder that fair and reasonable argument is supported by analysis.

As you read this editorial on the controversial rules established at Antioch College to govern sexual conduct among its students, try to focus not only on the content of the argument but also on its form—that is, how the writer moves from one phase of his thinking to the next. Toward this end, we have added our own summaries of what each paragraph of the editorial accomplishes. At the end of the editorial we sum up the writer's primary developmental strategies in a form you can apply to your own writing.

PLAYING BY THE ANTIOCH RULES
BY ERIC FASSIN

1   A good consensus is hard to find—especially on sexual politics. But the infamous rules instituted last year by Antioch College, which require students to obtain explicit verbal consent before so much as a kiss is exchanged, have created just that. They have provoked

indignation (this is a serious threat to individual freedom!) as well as ridicule (can this be serious?). Sexual correctness thus proves a worthy successor to political correctness as a target of public debate.

[Writer names the issue: the complaint that rules threaten individual freedom.]

2 Yet this consensus against the rules reveals shared assumptions among liberals, conservatives and even radicals about the nature of sex in our culture.

[Writer identifies members of unlikely consensus.]

3 The new definition of consent at Antioch is based on a "liberal" premise: it assumes that sexual partners are free agents and that they mean what they say—yes means yes, and no means no. But the initiator must now obtain prior consent, step by step, which in practice shifts the burden of clarification from the woman to the man. The question is no longer "Did she say no?" but "Did she say yes?" Silence does not indicate consent, and it becomes his responsibility to dispel any ambiguity.

[Writer identifies "freedom" premise underlying rules.]

4 The novelty of the rules, however, is not as great as it seems. Antioch will not exert more control over its students; there are no sexual police. In practice, you still do what you want—as long as your partner does not complain . . . the morning after. If this is censorship, it intervenes ex post facto, not a priori.

[Writer questions premise that rules will actually control individual freedom more than present norms.]

5 In fact, the "threat" to individual freedom for most critics is not the invasion of privacy through the imposition of sexual codes, but the very existence of rules. Hence the success of polemicists like Katie Roiphe or Camille Paglia, who argue that feminism in recent years has betrayed its origins by embracing old-style regulations, paradoxically choosing the rigid 1950s over the liberating 1960s. Their advice is simply to let women manage on their own, and individuals devise their own rules. This individualist critique of feminism finds resonance with liberals, but also, strangely, with conservatives, who belatedly discover the perils of regulating sexuality.

[Writer locates "anti-regulatory" (laissez-faire) premise beneath "freedom" premise.]

6 But sexual laissez-faire, with its own implicit set of rules, does not seem to have worked very well recently. Since the collapse of established social codes, people play the same game with different rules. If more women are complaining of sexual violence, while more men are worrying that their words and actions might be misconstrued, who benefits from the absence of regulation?

[Writer attacks "laissez-faire" premise for ineffectiveness.]

7 A laissez-faire philosophy toward relationships assumes that sexuality is a game that can (and must) be played without rules, or rather that the invention of rules should be left to individual spontaneity and creativity, despite rising evidence that the rule of one's own often leads to misunderstandings. When acted out, individual fantasy always plays within preordained social rules. These rules conflict with the assumption in this culture that sex is subject to the reign of nature, not artifice, that it is the province of the individual, not of society.

[Writer uncovers premise beneath "laissez-faire": that sex is "natural" and thus outside social rules.]

8   Those who believe that society's constraints should have nothing to do with sex also agree that sex should not be bound by the social conventions of language. Indeed, this rebellion against the idea of social constraints probably accounts for the controversy over explicit verbal consent—from George Will, deriding "sex amidst semicolons," to Camille Paglia railing "As if sex occurs in the verbal realm." As if sexuality were incompatible with words. As if the only language of sex were silence. For *The New Yorker,* "the [Antioch] rules don't get rid of the problem of unwanted sex at all; they just shift the advantage from the muscle-bound frat boy to the honey-tongued French major."

[Writer develops linguistic implications of "natural" premise and questions assumption that sex is incompatible with language.]

9   This is not very different from the radical feminist position, which holds that verbal persuasion is no better than physical coercion. In this view, sexuality cannot be entrusted to rhetoric. The seduction of words is inherently violent, and seduction itself is an object of suspicion. (If this is true, Marvell's invitation "To His Coy Mistress" is indeed a form of sexual harassment, as some campus feminists have claimed.)

[Writer develops further implications: attack on rules masks fear of language's power to seduce; writer questions equation of seduction with harassment.]

10   What the consensus against the Antioch rules betrays is a common vision of sexuality which crosses the lines dividing conservatives, liberals and radicals. So many of the arguments start from a conventional situation, perceived and presented as natural: a heterosexual encounter with the man as the initiator and the woman as gatekeeper—hence the focus on consent.

[Writer redefines *consensus* as sharing unacknowledged premise that conventional sex roles are natural.]

11   The outcry largely results from the fact that the rules undermine this traditional erotic model. Not so much by proscribing (legally), but by prescribing (socially). The new model, in which language becomes a normal form of erotic communication, underlines the conventional nature of the old one.

[Writer reformulates thesis about anti-rules consensus: rules undermine attempts to pass off traditional sex roles as natural.]

12   By encouraging women out of their "natural" reserve, these rules point to a new definition of sexual roles. "Yes" could be more than a way to make explicit the absence of "no"; "yes" can also be a cry of desire. Women may express demands, and not only grant favors. If the legal "yes" opened the ground for an erotic "yes," if the contract gave way to desire and if consent led to demand, we would indeed enter a brave new erotic world.

[Writer extends implications of thesis: rules could make sex more erotic rather than less free.]

13   New rules are like new shoes: they hurt a little at first, but they may fit tomorrow. The only question about the Antioch rules is not really whether we like them, but whether they improve the situation between men and women. All rules are artificial, but, in the absence of generally agreed-upon social conventions, any new prescription must feel artificial. And isn't regulation needed precisely when there is an absence of cultural consensus?

[Writer questions standard by which we evaluate rules; proposes shift in terms from artificial versus natural to whether or not rules will improve gender relations.]

14   Whether we support or oppose the Antioch rules, at least they force us to acknowledge that the choice is not between regulation and freedom, but between different sets of

rules, implicit or explicit. They help dispel the illusion that sexuality is a state of nature individuals must experience outside the social contract, and that eroticism cannot exist within the conventions of language. As Antioch reminds us, there is more in eroticism and sexuality than is dreamt of in this culture.

[Writer culminates thesis: rules are good because they force us to acknowledge as a harmful illusion the idea that sex operates outside social conventions.]

Despite its brevity, this editorial covers a daunting amount of ground—an examination of "shared assumptions among liberals, conservatives and even radicals about the nature of sex in our culture" (paragraph 2). The writer, given his audience (readers of the Sunday *New York Times),* allows himself more breadth in both his topic and his claims than he would if he were writing an article on the same subject in an academic setting, where he would narrow his focus in order to supply more analysis of issues and evidence. The aim of editorials like this one is not only to inform or persuade but also to provoke and entertain. Nevertheless, the strategies that direct the thinking in this piece are, with some minor exceptions, the same as they would be in a more extended analytical piece. They are central strategies that you can apply to many sorts of writing situations as a means of finding and developing your ideas.

STRATEGIES FOR DEVELOPING THE THESIS BY REASONING BACK TO PREMISES

1. *Set up a claim but delay passing judgment on it.* In the concluding sentence of paragraph 1, the word *target* suggests that the essay might attack Antioch's policy. In paragraph 2, however, the writer does not go on to demonstrate what is threatening and potentially ridiculous about Antioch's sexual contract, but neither does he yet offer his own conclusion on whether the views he has thus far described are right or wrong. Instead, he slows down the forward momentum toward judgment and begins to analyze what the consensus against the Antioch rules might *mean*— the "shared assumptions" it reveals "among liberals, conservatives and even radicals about the nature of sex in our culture." In fact, the author spends the first three-quarters of the essay trying on various answers to this question of meaning.

   (Note: A careful reader would recognize by tonal signals such as the exclamation mark after "serious threat to individual freedom!" that the opening paragraph has, in fact, begun to announce its position, albeit not overtly, by subtly overstating its opposite. It is not until later in the editorial, however, that we can clearly recognize that the writer is employing a common introductory strategy—defining the position you plan to argue against.)

2. *Decide what is really at issue by reasoning back to premises.* Rather than proceeding directly to a judgment on whether or not the rules threaten individual freedom, the writer carefully searches out the assumptions—the premises and givens—underlying the attacks on the rules. (This is a key step missing from most inadequately developed analyses and arguments.) He proposes, for example, that underneath the consensus' attack on the rules and its defense of individual freedom lies a basic

premise about sex and society, that sexuality should not be governed by rules because it is natural rather than cultural: "These rules conflict with the assumption in this culture that sex is subject to the reign of nature, not artifice, that it is the province of the individual, not of society."

3. *Be alert for terms that create false dichotomies.* A *false dichotomy* (sometimes called a *false binary*) inaccurately divides possible views on a subject into two opposing camps, forcing a choice between black and white, when some shade of gray might be fairer and more accurate. When reading or when writing an argument of your own, it is a good strategy to question any "either/or" dichotomy. Consider whether its opposing terms define the issue fairly and accurately before accepting an argument in favor of one side or the other.

Consider, too, how you might reject both choices offered by an either/or opposition in order to construct an alternative approach that is truer to the issues at hand. This is what the author of the editorial does. He outlines and then rejects as a false dichotomy the consensus view that sexual behavior is *either* a province of individual freedom *or* it is regulated by society:

false dichotomies	freedom versus regulation natural versus artifical no rules versus rules

The author argues instead that much of what we perceive to be natural is in fact governed by social rules and conventions, such as the notion of men as sexual initiators and women as no-sayers and gatekeepers. He proposes that what is really at stake is a different dichotomy, a choice between two sets of rules, one implicit and one explicit:

reformulated dichotomies	rules versus rules implicit versus explicit not working versus might work based on "no" versus based on "yes"

The editorial concludes that we need to decide questions of sexual behavior—at Antioch and in the culture at large—by recognizing and evaluating the relative merits of the two sets of rules rather than by creating a false dichotomy between rules and no rules, between regulation and freedom.

4. *In your conclusion, return to the position that you set out to explore, and restate it in the more carefully qualified way you arrived at in the body of your essay:* "The choice is not between regulation and freedom, but between different sets of rules. . . ."

Clearly, the essay's conclusion does not simply repeat the essay's introductory claims, but it does respond to the way in which the essay began. So why, one might ask, didn't the writer just offer the argument in his closing paragraph as his first paragraph and then prove it? One answer to this question has to do with the reader: the position articulated in the essay's closing paragraph is too complex and too dependent on the various considerations that preceded it to be stated intelligibly and concisely in the introduction. Another answer has to do with the writer: writing is a matter not just of communicating with and persuading readers but of communicating with and persuading yourself. The evolution of a thesis involves the discovery of new ways of thinking brought about by successive confrontations with evidence. The history of your various changes in thinking is, in many ways, the thesis of the essay.

By the time you get to drafting the final or close-to-final version of the essay, you will be writing with a reasonably secure sense of how you will conclude, but even then it is not always possible or desirable to try to encapsulate in a paper's first couple of sentences what it will actually take the whole paper to explain. The ultimate conclusion of an analytical essay often is not apparent at the outset even to the writer.

Voices from Across the Curriculum

REASONING BACK TO PREMISES

In the following "Voices" entry, an economics professor sets up a difference between issues that can be resolved by theorizing alone and those that require the collection of data. Notice, however, that the thinking move he describes is not only from one kind of evidence to another but also from a question to its underlying premises:

On some occasions, students find that they have confronted an issue which cannot be resolved by the deductive method. This can be exciting for them. Will cutting marginal tax rates cause people to work more? The answer is yes or no depending on the premises underlying the work–leisure preferences incorporated into your model. So theorizing gets us nowhere. We must discover those work–leisure preferences to reach a conclusion. Ultimately, we must appeal to the facts; theory is not enough.

—*J. Marshall, Professor of Economics*

Before one can find the necessary data, one needs to find the right question. This is the primary skill behind finding and developing a thesis.

GUIDELINES FOR FINDING AND DEVELOPING A THESIS

1. A thesis is an idea that you formulate and reformulate about your subject. It should offer a theory about the meaning of evidence that would not have been immediately obvious to your readers.
2. Look for a thesis by focusing on an area of your subject that is open to opposing viewpoints or multiple interpretations. Rather than attempting to locate a single right answer, search for something that raises questions.

3. The body of your paper should serve not only to substantiate the thesis by demonstrating its value in selecting and explaining evidence but also to bring the opening version of the thesis into better focus.

4. Evolve your thesis—move it forward—by seeing the questions that each new formulation of it prompts you to ask.

5. Develop the implications of your evidence and of your observations as fully as you can by repeatedly asking, "So what?"

6. When you encounter potentially conflicting evidence (or interpretations of that evidence), don't simply abandon your thesis. Take advantage of the complications to expand, qualify, and refine your thesis until you arrive at the most accurate explanation of the evidence that you can manage.

7. Reason forward to conclusions by reasoning backward to premises.

8. Arrive at the final version of your thesis by returning to your initial formulation—the position you set out to explore—and restating it in the more carefully qualified way you have arrived at through the body of your paper.

9. To check that your thesis has evolved, locate and compare the various versions of it throughout the draft. Have you done more than demonstrate the general validity of an unqualified claim?

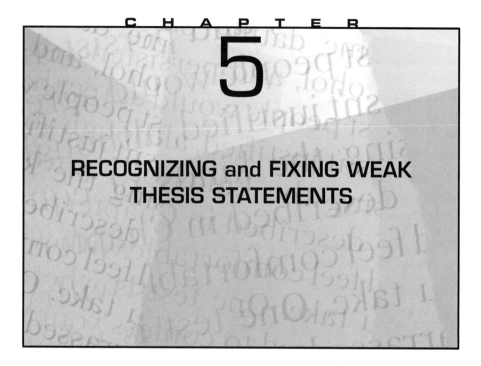

CHAPTER 5

RECOGNIZING and FIXING WEAK THESIS STATEMENTS

In Chapter 4 we illustrated how a thesis works and the thought process a writer goes through in formulating and using a thesis. In this chapter we show you how to recognize and fix the most common kinds of weak thesis statements—those most likely to obstruct effective analytical writing.

FIVE KINDS OF WEAK THESES AND HOW TO FIX THEM

Weak thesis statements take various forms. Often they contain clichéd, obvious, or overly general ideas and so don't need or are not worth proving. Other kinds of weak theses substitute for analysis either a global value judgment (for example, individualism is good) or a personal like or dislike (for example, shopping malls are wonderful places). To reiterate the definition we offered in Chapter 4: a *strong thesis* makes a claim that needs proving; a *weak thesis* either makes no claim or is an assertion that does not need proving.

We now turn to examples of five kinds of weak thesis statements—actual excerpts from student papers—and show how they can be reworded in ways that will lead to analysis.

Weak Thesis Type 1: The Thesis Makes No Claim

The following statements are not productive theses because they do not advance an idea about the topics the papers will explore.

Problem Examples

- I'm going to write about Darwin's concerns with evolution in *The Origin of Species.*

- This paper will address the characteristics of a good corporate manager.

The problem examples name a subject and link it to the intention to write about it, but they don't make any claim about that subject. As a result, they direct neither the writer nor the reader toward some position or plan of attack. The second problem example begins to move toward a point of view through the use of the value judgment "good," but there is still no assertion—no framework for analysis. The statement-of-intention thesis invites a list: one paragraph for each quality the writer chooses to call "good." Even if the thesis were rephrased as "This paper will address why a good corporate manager needs to learn to delegate responsibility," the thesis would not adequately suggest why such a claim would need to be argued or defended. There is, in short, nothing at stake—no issue to be resolved.

Solution

Raise specific issues for the essay to explore.

Solution Examples

- Darwin's concern with survival of the fittest in *The Origin of Species* leads him to neglect a potentially conflicting aspect of his theory of evolution—survival as a matter of interdependence.

- The very trait that makes for an effective corporate manager—the drive to succeed—can also make the leader domineering and therefore ineffective.

It should be noted that some disciplines expect writers to offer a statement of method and/or intention in their papers' openings. Generally, however, these openings also make a claim: for example, "In this paper I will examine how congressional Republicans undermined the attempts of the Democratic administration to legislate a fiscally responsible health care policy for the elderly," *not* "In this paper I will discuss America's treatment of the elderly."

Weak Thesis Type 2:
The Thesis Is Obviously True or Is a Statement of Fact

The following statements are not productive theses because they do not require proof. A thesis needs to be an assertion with which it would be possible for readers to disagree.

Problem Examples

- The jean industry targets its advertisements to appeal to young adults.

- The flight from teaching to research and publishing in higher education is a controversial issue in the academic world. I will show different views and aspects concerning this problem.

If few people would disagree with the claim that a thesis makes, there is no point in writing an analytical paper on it. Though one might deliver an inspirational speech on a position that virtually everyone would support (such as the value of tolerance), endorsements and appreciations don't lead to analysis; they merely invite people to feel good about their convictions.

In the second problem example above, few readers would disagree with the fact that the issue is "controversial." In the second sentence of that example, the writer has begun to identify a point of view—that the flight from teaching is a "problem"—but her next declaration, that she will "show different views and aspects," is a statement of fact, not an idea. The phrasing of the claim is noncommittal and so broad that it prevents the writer from formulating a workable thesis.

Solution

Find some avenue of *inquiry*—a question about the facts or an issue raised by them. Make an assertion with which it would be possible for readers to disagree.

Solution Examples

- By inventing new terms, such as "loose fit" and "relaxed fit," the jean industry has attempted to normalize, even glorify, its product for an older and fatter generation.

- The "flight from teaching" to research and publishing in higher education is a controversial issue in the academic world. As I will attempt to show, the controversy is based to a significant degree on a false assumption, that doing research necessarily leads teachers away from the classroom.

WEAK THESIS TYPE 3: THE THESIS RESTATES CONVENTIONAL WISDOM

Restatement of one of the many clichés that constitute a culture's conventional wisdom is not a productive thesis unless you have something to say about it that hasn't been said many times before.

Problem Examples

- An important part of one's college education is learning to better understand others' points of view.

- From cartoons in the morning to adventure shows at night, there is too much violence on television.

- *"I* was supposed to bring the coolers; *you* were supposed to bring the chips!" exclaimed ex-Beatle Ringo Starr, who appeared on TV commercials for Sun County Wine Coolers a few years ago. By using rock music to sell a wide range of products, the advertising agencies, in league with corporate giants such as Pepsi, Michelob, and Ford, have corrupted the spirit of rock and roll.

All of these examples say nothing worth proving because they are clichés. (Conventional wisdom is a polite term for clichés.) Most clichés were fresh ideas once, but over time they have become trite, prefabricated forms of nonthinking. Faced with a phenomenon that requires a response, many inexperienced writers rely on a knee-jerk reaction: they resort to a small set of culturally approved "answers." In this sense, clichés resemble statements of fact, but they usually aren't. So commonly accepted that most people nod to them without thinking, statements of conventional wisdom make people feel a comfortable sense of agreement with one another. The problem with this kind of packaged solution is that conventional wisdom is so general and so conventional that it doesn't teach anybody—including the writer—anything. Worse, since the cliché *appears* to be an idea, it prevents the writer from engaging in a fresh, open-minded exploration of his or her subject.

There is some truth in all of the problem examples, but none of them complicates its position. A thoughtful reader could, for example, respond to the claim that advertising has corrupted the spirit of rock and roll by suggesting that rock and roll was highly commercial long before it colonized the airwaves. The conventional wisdom that rock and roll is somehow pure and honest while advertising is phony and exploitative in fact invites the savvy writer to formulate a thesis that overturns these clichés. As our solution example demonstrates, one could argue that rock actually has improved advertising, not that ads have ruined rock— or alternatively, that rock has shrewdly marketed idealism to a gullible populace, at least since the love generation captured the national imagination in the late sixties. At the least, a writer deeply committed to the original thesis would do better to examine what it was that Ringo was selling—what he stands for in this particular case—than to discuss rock and advertising in such general terms.

Solution

Seek to complicate—see more than one point of view on—your subject. Avoid conventional wisdom unless you can qualify it or introduce a fresh perspective on it.

Solution Examples

- Although an important part of one's college education is learning to better understand others' points of view, a persistent danger is that the students will simply be required to substitute the teacher's answers for the ones they grew up uncritically believing.

- Although some might argue that the presence of rock and roll soundtracks in TV commercials has corrupted rock's spirit, this point of view not only falsifies the history of rock but also blinds us to the ways that the music has improved the quality of television advertising.

WEAK THESIS TYPE 4: THE THESIS MAKES AN OVERLY BROAD CLAIM

An overly general claim is not a productive thesis because it oversimplifies and is too broad to direct development. Such statements usually lead either to "say-nothing" theses or to reductive categorical thinking.

Problem Examples

- Violent revolutions have had both positive and negative results for humanity.
- There are many similarities and differences between the Carolingian and the Burgundian Renaissances.
- *Othello* is a play about love and jealousy.
- It is important to understand why leaders act in a leadership role. What is the driving force? Is it an internal drive for the business or group to succeed, or is it an internal drive for the leader to dominate over others?

Overly generalized theses avoid complexity. At their worst, as in our first three examples, they settle for assertions broad enough to fit almost any subject and thus say nothing in particular about the subject at hand. A writer in the early stages of his or her drafting process might begin working from a general idea, such as what is positive and negative about violent revolutions or how two historical periods are like and unlike, but these formulations are not specific enough to guide the development of a paper. Such broad categories are likely to generate listing, not thinking. We can, for example, predict that the third thesis above will prompt the writer to produce a couple of paragraphs demonstrating that *Othello* is about love and then a couple of paragraphs demonstrating that *Othello* is about jealousy, without analyzing what the play says about either.

The best way to avoid this trap is to sensitize yourself to the characteristic phrasing of such theses: "both positive and negative," "many similarities and differences," "both pros and cons." Virtually everything from meatloaf to taxes can be both positive and negative.

Solution

Convert broad categories and generic (fits anything) claims to more specific assertions; find ways to bring out the complexity of your subject.

Solution Examples

- The differences between the Carolingian and Burgundian Renaissances outweigh the similarities.
- Although *Othello* appears to attack jealousy, it also supports the skepticism of the jealous characters over the naïveté of the lovers.

A clear symptom of an overly generalized thesis can be found by looking at its grammar. Each of the first three problem examples, for example, relies mostly on nouns rather than verbs; the nouns announce a broad heading, but the verbs don't do anything with or to the nouns. In grammatical terms, these thesis statements don't *predicate* (affirm or assert something about the subject of a proposition). Instead, they rely on anemic verbs like *is* or *are,* which function as equal signs, linking general nouns with general adjectives, rather than specifying more complex relationships.

By replacing the equal sign with a more active verb, you can force yourself to advance some sort of claim, as in one of our solutions, for example: "The differences between the Carolingian and Burgundian Renaissances *outweigh* the similarities." Although this reformulation remains quite general, it at least begins to direct the writer along a more particular line of argument. Replacing the equal sign will usually impel you to rank ideas in some order of importance and to assert some conceptual relation among them.

In other words, the best way to remedy the problem of overgeneralization is to move toward *specificity* in word choice, in sentence structure, and in idea. If you find yourself writing "The economic situation is bad," consider revising it to "The tax policies of the current administration threaten to reduce the tax burden on the middle class by sacrificing education and health-care programs for everyone":

Broad Noun	+	Weak Verb	+ Vague, Evaluative Adjective
The economic situation		is	bad.

Specific Noun	+	Active Verb	+	Assertive Predicate
(The) tax policies (of the current administration)		threaten to reduce (the tax burden on the middle class)		by sacrificing education and health-care programs for everyone.

By eliminating the weak thesis formula—broad nouns + *is* + vague, evaluative adjective—a writer is compelled to *qualify,* or define carefully each of the terms in the original proposition, arriving at a more particular and conceptually richer assertion.

Our fourth problem example, inquiring into the motivation of leaders in business, demonstrates how the desire to generalize can drive writers into logical errors. Because this thesis overtly offers readers two possible answers to its central question, it appears to avoid the problem of oversimplifying a complex subject. But this appearance of complexity is deceptive because the writer has reduced the possibilities to only two answers—an either/or choice: is the driving force of leadership a desire for group success or a desire to dominate others? Readers can only be frustrated by being asked to choose between two such options when the more logical answer probably lies somewhere in between or somewhere else altogether.

WEAK THESIS TYPE 5:
THE THESIS ADVANCES UNSUBSTANTIATED OPINION

A statement of one's personal convictions or one's likes or dislikes does not alone supply sufficient grounds for a productive thesis.

Problem Examples

- The songs of the punk rock group Minor Threat relate to the feelings of individuals who dare to be different. Their songs are just composed of pure emotion. Pure emotion is very important in music, because it serves as a vehicle to convey the important message of individuality. Minor Threat's songs are meaningful to me because I can identify with them.

- Sir Thomas More's *Utopia* proposes an unworkable set of solutions to society's problems because, like communist Russia, it suppresses individualism.

- Although I agree with Jeane Kirkpatrick's argument that environmentalists and businesses should work together to ensure the ecological future of the world, and that this cooperation is beneficial for both sides, the indisputable fact is that environmental considerations should always be a part of any decision that is made. Any individual, if he looks deeply enough into his soul, knows what is right and what is wrong. The environment should be protected because it is the right thing to do, not because someone is forcing you to do it.

Like conventional wisdom, personal likes and dislikes can lead inexperienced writers into knee-jerk reactions of approval or disapproval, often expressed in a moralistic tone. The writers of the problem examples above assume that their primary job is to judge their subjects, not to evaluate them analytically. As a result, such writers lack critical detachment, not only from their topics, but, crucially, from their own assumptions and biases. They have taken personal opinions for self-evident truths.

The most blatant version of this tendency occurs in the third problem example, which asserts, "Any individual, if he looks deeply enough into his soul, knows what is right and what is wrong. The environment should be protected because it is the right thing to do." Translation (only slightly exaggerated): "Any individual who thinks about the subject will obviously agree with me because my feelings and convictions feel right to me, and therefore they must be universally and self-evidently true." The problem is that this writer is not distinguishing between his own likes and dislikes (or private convictions) and what he takes to be "right," "real," or "true" for everyone else. Testing an idea against your own feelings and experience is not an adequate means of establishing whether something is accurate or true.

Solution

Try on other points of view honestly and dispassionately; treat your ideas as hypotheses to be tested rather than obvious truths. In the following solution examples, we have replaced opinions (in the form of self-evident truths) with ideas—theories about the meaning and significance of their subjects that could be supported with evidence.

Solution Examples

- Sir Thomas More's *Utopia* treats individualism as a serious but remediable social problem. His radical treatment of what we might now call "socialization" attempts to redefine the meaning and origin of individual identity.

- Although I agree with Jeane Kirkpatrick's argument that environmentalists and businesses should work together to ensure the ecological future of the world, her argument undervalues the necessity of pressuring businesses to attend to environmental concerns that may not benefit them in the short run.

It is fine, of course, to write about what you believe and to consult your feelings as you formulate an idea. But the risk you run in arguing from your *unexamined* feelings and convictions is that you will prematurely dismiss from consideration anything that is unfamiliar or does not immediately conform to what you already believe. The less willing you are to test these established and habitual convictions, the less chance you will have to refine or expand the ways in which you think. You will continue to play the same small set of tunes in response to everything you hear. And without the ability to think from multiple perspectives, you will be less able to defend your convictions against the ideas that challenge them because you won't really have examined the logic of your own beliefs.

At the root of this problem lurks an anti-analytical bias that predisposes many writers to see any challenge to their habitual ways of thinking as the enemy and to view those who would raise this challenge as cynics who don't believe in anything. Such writers often feel personally attacked, when in fact the conviction they are defending is not really so personal after all. Consider, for example, the first two problem examples, in which both writers take individualism to be an incontestable value. Where does this conviction come from? Neither of the writers arrived at the thesis independent of the particular culture in which they were raised, permeated as it is by the "rugged individualism" of John Wayne and Sylvester Stallone movies.

In other words, individualism as an undefined blanket term verges on cultural cliché. That it is always "good" or "positive" is a piece of conventional wisdom. But part of becoming educated is to take a look at such global and undefined ideas that one has uncritically assimilated. Clearly, the needs and rights of the individual in contemporary American culture are consistently being weighed and balanced against the rights of other individuals and the necessity of cooperation in groups. Look at the recent nationwide concerns with health maintenance organizations (HMOs), which control health costs but constrain the individualism of the physician, or with the rights of crime victims who are banding together to seek support from a government they believe is protecting the individual rights of the criminal at the expense of the individual rights of the victim.

In light of these considerations, the writers of the first two problem examples would have to question the extent to which they can attack a book or support a rock band merely on the basis of whether or not each honors individualism. If the author of the second problem example had been willing to explore how Thomas More conceives of and critiques individualism, he or she might have been able to arrive at a revealing analysis of the tension between the individual and the collective rather than merely dismissing the entire book.

This is not to say that the first requirement of analytical writing is that you abandon all conviction or argue for a position that you do not believe. But we are

suggesting that the risk of remaining trapped within a limited set of culturally in-
herited opinions is greater than the risk that you will run by submerging your
personal likes or dislikes and instead honestly and dispassionately trying on different points of view. The energy of analytical writing comes not from rehearsing
your convictions but from treating them as hypotheses to be tested, as scientists
do—finding the boundaries of your ideas, reshaping parts of them, seeing connections you have not seen before.

THE DANGERS OF CATEGORICAL THINKING

Looking back over the examples in this section, you will notice that a number of them engage in what is called *categorical thinking.* That is, they are overly
global—inclined to all-or-nothing claims. Good analytical writing makes careful
distinctions; categorical thinking puts everything into big, undifferentiated categories, labeled all black or all white, with nothing in between.

Categorical thinking is an unavoidable and distinctive feature of how all
human beings go about analyzing a subject. In order to generalize from particular
experiences, we try to put those experiences into meaningful categories. But it
can be dangerous when these categories are not only too broad but also too simply connected, as in the either/or choices to which categorical thinking is prone:
approve/disapprove, real/unreal, accurate/inaccurate, believable/unbelievable.
Such thinking often comes down to a basic decision either to support the subject
or to denounce it. This rush to value judgment can so dominate a writer's attention that he or she fails to examine not only the values upon which the judgment
is based but also the subject itself. The writer who evaluates leadership in terms of
its selflessness/selfishness, for example, needs to pause to consider why we should
evaluate leadership in these terms in the first place.

TWO WAYS TO IMPROVE
THE LOGIC OF YOUR THESIS STATEMENTS

We will refer to the following two examples to illustrate how to strengthen
the logic of your thesis statements by *qualifying your claims* and *checking for the unstated assumptions upon which your claims depend.*

Example I

I think that there are many things shown on television that are damaging for people to see. But there is no need for censorship. No network is going to show violence without the approval of the public, obviously for financial reasons. What
must be remembered is that the public majority will see what it wants to see in our
mass society.

Example II

Some members of our society feel that [the televised cartoon series] *The Simpsons* promotes wrong morals and values for our society. Other members find it funny and entertaining. I feel that *The Simpsons* has a more positive effect than a negative one. In relation to a real-life marriage, Marge and Homer's marriage is pretty accurate. The problems they deal with are not very large or intense. As for the family relationships, the Simpsons are very close and love each other.

WAY 1: QUALIFY YOUR CLAIMS

The main problem with Example I is the writer's failure to qualify his ideas, a problem that causes him to generalize to the point of oversimplification. Note the writer's habit of stating his claims absolutely:

"there is *no* need for censorship"

"*no* network is going to show violence without"

"*obviously* for financial reasons"

"what *must* be remembered"

"the public majority *will* see"

We have italicized the words that make these claims unqualified.

Broad, pronouncement-like claims are difficult to support fairly. The solution is for the writer to more carefully *limit* his claims, especially his key premise about public approval. The assertion that a commercial television industry will, for financial reasons, give the public "what it wants" is true to an extent, but the writer needed to modify this claim as well as considering other possibilities. Couldn't it also be argued, for example, that, given the power of television to shape people's tastes and opinions, the public sees not just what it wants but what it has been taught to want? This necessary complication of the writer's argument about public approval seriously undermines the credibility of his global assertion that "there is *no* need for censorship." The remedy lies with qualifying his thesis. Simply reversing it to "there *is* a need for censorship" would not solve the problem, because the need for defining and limiting the writer's position will be just as great on the other side of the issue.

Example II would appear to be more qualified than Example I (since it acknowledges the possibility of at least two points of view). The writer opens by attempting to acknowledge the existence of more than one point of view on the show; and rather than broadly asserting that the show is positive and accurate, she tempers these claims (as italics show): "I *feel* that *The Simpsons* has a *more* positive effect *than* a negative one. . . ."; "Marge and Homer's marriage is *pretty* accurate." These qualifications, however, are superficial. Although "pretty" would seem to admit that the show is not entirely accurate, the statements that follow the accuracy claim do not pursue this qualification. The writer does not explore what *accuracy* means. Instead, she assumes the standard of accuracy (that an accurate show is a good show) as a given.

WAY 2: CHECK FOR UNSTATED ASSUMPTIONS

Before she could convince us to approve of *The Simpsons* for its accuracy in depicting marriage, the writer of Example II would have to convince us that accuracy is a *reasonable criterion* for evaluating television shows (especially cartoons) rather than simply accepting it as an unstated assumption. One could certainly argue against her unstated premise. Would an accurate depiction of the life of a serial killer, for example, necessarily make for a "positive" show? Similarly, if a fantasy show has no interest in accuracy, is it necessarily "negative" and without moral value?

When writers present a debatable premise as if it were self-evidently true, the conclusions built upon it cannot stand. At the least, the writer of Example II needs to recognize her debatable premise, articulate it, and make an argument in support of it. She also needs to precede her judgment about the show with more analysis. Before deciding that the show is "more positive than negative" and thus does not promote "wrong morals and values for our society," she needs to more deeply analyze what the show has to say about marriage, how it goes about making this statement, and why (in response to what).

Likewise, if the writer of Example I had looked at his own claims rather than rushing to argue an absolute position on censorship, he would have noticed how much of the thinking that underlies them remains unarticulated and thus unexamined. His argument that "there is no need for censorship," for example, depends on the validity of another of his assertions, that "no network is going to show violence without the approval of the public, obviously for financial reasons." The writer's argument depends on readers' accepting a position that he asserts ("obviously") as though it were too clearly true to need defending. Spelling out the issue of the network's financial dependence on public approval would help this writer clarify and qualify his thesis. It would also allow him to sort out the logical contradiction with his opening claim that "there are many things shown on televison that are damaging for people to see." If televison networks will only broadcast what the public approves of, then apparently the public must approve of being damaged or fail to notice that it is being damaged. If the public either fails to notice it is being damaged or approves of it, aren't these credible arguments for, rather than against censorship?

THE RELATIONSHIP BETWEEN ARGUMENT AND INTERPRETATION

In order to formulate an insightful idea—an effective thesis—you may have to alter some of your conceptions of what writing is supposed to do. The agree/disagree mode of writing and thinking that you often see in editorials, hear on radio or television, and even practice sometimes in school may incline you to focus all your energy on the bottom line—aggressively advancing a claim for or against some view—without first engaging in the exploratory interpretation of evidence that is so necessary to arriving at thoughtful arguments.

Writing, especially as it is used in school, is often divided into kinds. And clearly, the kind of writing this book addresses—analysis—does differ in both method and aim from, say, descriptive writing or narration. Those of you who have been taught to write arguments may find that some of the prescriptions we offer on analytical writing seem to run counter to what you've learned. Our aim in this section is to break down unnecessary divisions between argument and analysis, proposing that the interpretive skill called "close reading" is essential to both.

A close reading *explicates* (unfolds) an interpretation by making explicit selected features of your subject that otherwise might not be readily recognized or understood. A close reading moves beyond the obvious, but it does not leap to some hidden meaning that is unconnected to the evidence. Rather, it follows logically from the evidence; the meaning is implicit in the details, waiting to be brought out by the writer careful enough to look closely and questioningly.

It is a common misconception that interpretation (close reading) occurs only in art or literature courses and that science, social science, and philosophy courses require a different kind of writing called "argument." Many of you will have been introduced to writing arguments through the debate model—writing pro or con on a given position, with the aim of defeating an imagined opponent and convincing your readers of the rightness of your position. But as the *American College Dictionary* says, "to argue implies reasoning or trying to understand; it does not necessarily imply opposition." It is this more exploratory, tentative, and dispassionate mode of argument that this book encourages you to practice.

Adhering to the more restrictive, debate-style definition of argument can create a number of problems for careful analytical writers:

1. By requiring writers to be oppositional, it inclines them to discount or dismiss problems in the side or position they have chosen; they cling to the same static position rather than testing it as a way of allowing it to evolve.
2. It inclines writers toward either/or thinking rather than encouraging them to formulate more qualified positions that integrate apparently opposing viewpoints.
3. It overvalues convincing someone else at the expense of developing understanding.

Too often interpretation and argument are treated as essentially different kinds of writing, each with a particular purpose. In practice, interpretation and argument are inseparable. As our examples in Chapter 4 show, even the most tentative and cautiously evolving interpretation is ultimately an argument; it asks readers to accept a particular interpretation of a set of data. And like argument, interpretation carefully connects evidence with claims; it does not, as it is sometimes misconceived, incline the writer toward undirected and purposeless impressionism.

Similarly, even the most passionately committed argument is an interpretation. Its credibility rests on the plausibility of its reading of evidence. You cannot argue from evidence unless you are first sure that you know what that evidence means. Most illogical argument occurs when writers assume that the meaning of their data is self-evident. In other words, you need to analyze your subject dispassionately before you can fairly argue a position about it.

Analysis is an important corrective to narrow and needlessly oppositional thinking. A writer who is skeptical of global generalizations and of unexamined value judgments may sound timid and even confused compared with the insistent pronouncements of daytime talk shows and televised political debates. But the effort you put into carefully formulating your ideas by qualifying them, checking for unstated assumptions, and acknowledging rather than ignoring problems in your position will make you a stronger writer and thinker.

GUIDELINES FOR RECOGNIZING AND FIXING WEAK THESIS STATEMENTS

1. Your thesis should make a claim with which it would be possible for readers to disagree. Find some avenue of inquiry rather than defending statements your readers would accept as obviously true.
2. Be skeptical of your first (often semiautomatic) response to a subject. It will often be a cliché or too broad. Avoid conventional wisdom unless you can qualify it or introduce a fresh perspective on it.
3. Convert broad categories and generic (fits anything) claims to more specific assertions. Find ways to bring out the complexity of your subject.
4. Submit the wording of your thesis to this grammatical test: if it follows the "abstract noun + *is* + evaluative adjective" formula ("The economic situation is bad"), substitute a more specific noun and an active verb that will force you to *predicate* something about a focused subject ("Tax laws benefit the rich").
5. Treat your thesis as a hypothesis to be tested rather than an obvious truth. Examine and question your own terms and categories rather than simply accepting them.
6. Always work to uncover and make explicit the unstated assumptions (premises) underlying your thesis. Don't treat debatable premises as givens.
7. As a rule, be suspicious of thesis statements that depend on words such as *real, accurate, believable, right,* and *good.* These words frequently signal that you are offering personal opinions—what "feels" right to you—as self-evident truths for everybody.

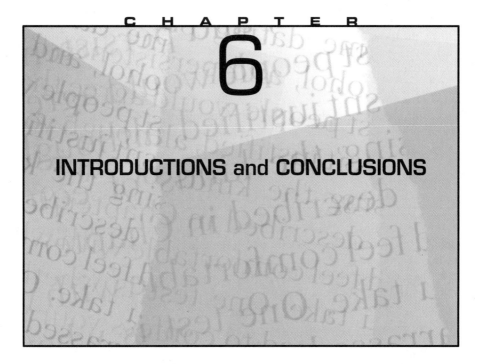

C H A P T E R

6

INTRODUCTIONS and CONCLUSIONS

YOU HAVE PROBABLY NOTICED that it is difficult to read attentively and do something else at the same time. Imagine, for instance, trying to read a book while playing a guitar. Depending on the difficulty of the reading matter and your powers of concentration, you might not be able even to listen to a guitar and read at the same time. When you read, you enter a world created of written language—a textual world—and to varying degrees, you leave the world "out there." Even if other people are around, we all read in relative isolation; our attention is diverted from the social and physical world upon which the full range of our senses normally operates.

In this context, now place yourself in the position of the writer, rather than a reader, and consider the functions of the introduction and conclusion in a piece of writing. Your introduction takes the reader from a sensory world and submerges him or her into a textual one. And your conclusion returns the reader to his or her nonwritten reality. Introductions and conclusions *mediate*—they carry the reader from one way of being to another. They function as the most *social* parts of any written communication, the passageways in which you need to be most keenly aware of your reader.

At both sites, there is a lot at stake. The introduction gives the reader his or her first impression, and we all know how indelible that can be. The conclusion leaves the reader with a last—and potentially lasting—impression of the written world you have constructed.

Most of the difficulties in composing introductions and conclusions arise in deciding how you should deal with the thesis. How much of it should you put into the introduction? Should your conclusion summarize the thesis or extend it? To an extent, the formats and conventions of a particular academic discipline may arbitrate such questions. For that reason, this chapter relies heavily on Voices from Across the Curriculum. It also indicates basic strategies for constructing introductions and conclusions, and it targets some of the most common problems. As with other aspects of writing analytically, there are no absolute rules for writing introductions and conclusions, but insofar as disciplinary conventions permit, *in introductions, play an ace but not your whole hand; and in conclusions, don't just summarize—culminate.*

THE FUNCTION OF INTRODUCTIONS

As its Latin roots suggest—*intro,* within + *ducere,* to lead or bring—an introduction brings the reader into a subject. Its length varies, depending on the scope of the writing project. An introduction may take a paragraph, a few paragraphs, a few pages, a chapter, or even a book. In most academic writing that you will do, one or two paragraphs is a standard length. In that space you should try to accomplish some or all of the following objectives:

- Define your topic—the issue, question, or problem—and say why it matters.
- Indicate your method of approach to the topic.
- Provide necessary background or context.
- Offer the working thesis (hypothesis) that your paper will develop.

An objective missing from this list that you might expect to find there is the admonition to engage the reader. Clearly, as our opening comments suggest, all introductions need to engage the reader, but this admonition is too often misinterpreted as a directive to be entertaining or cute. In academic writing, you don't need a gimmick to engage your readers; you can assume they care about the subject. You will engage them if you can articulate why your topic matters, doing so in terms of existing thinking in the field.

Especially in a first draft, the objectives listed above are not so easily achieved, which is why many writers defer writing a polished version of the introduction until they have completed at least one draft of the paper. At that point, you will usually have a clearer notion of why your subject matters and which aspect of your thesis to place first. Often the conclusion of a first draft becomes the introduction to the second draft. Other writers find that they can't proceed on a draft until they have arrived at an introduction that clearly defines the question or problem they plan to write about and its significance. For these writers, crafting an approach to the topic in the introduction is a key part of their planning phase, even though they also expect to revise the introduction based on what happens in their initial drafts.

In any case, the standard shape of an introduction is a *funnel*. It starts wide, providing background and generalization, and then narrows the subject to a particular issue or topic. Here is a typical example from a student paper:

People have a way of making the most important obligations perfunctory, even trivial, by the steps they take to observe them. For many people, traditions and rituals become actuality; the form overshadows the substance. They lose sight of the underlying truths and what these should mean in their lives, and they tend to believe that observing the formalities fulfills their obligation. This is true of professional ethics as they relate to the practice of examining and reporting on financial data—the primary role of the auditor.

The paragraph begins with a generalization in the first sentence (about making even important obligations perfunctory) and funnels it down in the last sentence to a working thesis (about the ethics of an auditor's report on financial data).

Voices from Across the Curriculum

PUTTING THE THESIS IN CONTEXT

In the following quotations, notice that implicit in all of the professors' accounts is some concept of the funnel. Rather than leaping immediately to the paper's issue, question, or problem, most effective introductions provide some broader context to indicate why the issue matters.

Although some expression of the main idea should find its way into the opening paragraph, that paragraph is also an opportunity to draw the reader in, to convince the reader to read on. What's the point of your paper? Why is the issue important? Is it a theoretical issue? A policy issue? What's the historical context? Is this a question that represents a part of a larger question?

—*J. Marshall, Professor of Economics*

As the above comment suggests, the introduction is a primary site for anticipating and answering the questions that readers will bring. The next comment, from a professor of political science, suggests one generally applicable way of focusing these questions of context down to a specific point of departure, setting the stage for the first statement of the thesis.

I think it is important to understand that an introduction is not simply the statement of a thesis but also the place where the student needs to set a context, a framework that makes such a thesis statement interesting, timely, or in some other way important. It is common to see papers in political science begin by pointing out a discrepancy between conventional wisdom (what the pundits say) and recent political developments, between popular opinion and empirical evidence, or between theoretical frameworks and particular test cases. Papers, in other words, often begin by presenting *anomalies*.

I encourage students to write opening paragraphs that attempt to elucidate such anomalies by (1) stating the specific point of departure: are they taking issue with a bit of conventional wisdom? popular opinions? a theoretical perspective? This provides the context in which a student is able to "frame" a particular problem,

continued

issue, etc. Students then need to indicate (2) why the above wisdom/opinion/theory has become problematic or controversial by focusing on a particular issue, event, test case, or empirical evidence. (Here the student's choice of topic becomes important since topics must be both relevant to the specific point of departure as well as to some degree controversial.) I would also expect in the opening paragraph(s) (3) a brief statement of the tentative thesis/position to be pursued in the paper. This can take several forms, including the revising of conventional wisdom/theory/opinions, discarding these in favor of alternative conceptions, or calling for redefinition of an issue and question. In papers directed towards current political practices (for instance, an analysis of a particular environmental policy or of a proposal to reform political parties), the thesis statement may be stated by indicating (a) hidden or flawed assumptions in current practices, or (b) alternative reforms and/or policy proposals.

—*G. Gambino, Professor of Political Science*

Especially in the hard sciences and psychology, the standard form for introductions is controlled fairly strictly by formats. (Also see Chapter 3, "Questions of Format.") Like the professors quoted here, however, the ones who follow also emphasize the importance of isolating a specific question or issue and locating it within a wider context.

Papers in psychology begin with an abstract, which summarizes the article. The abstract is followed by an introduction, in which the author introduces the problem under study, develops its background in terms of relevant literature, and states the purpose and rationale of the study (this is a very close paraphrasing of the *Publication Manual of the American Psychological Association*, 4th ed., 1994). The researcher wants to build the case that, given the research problem under investigation, and given the previous research investigating the problem, this study will advance scientific knowledge of the phenomenon.

—*A. Tjeltveit, Professor of Psychology*

Note how little the model for an introduction changes in moving from a social science, psychology, to the natural sciences of biology and physics:

A paper usually starts with some general observation or a description of known phenomena, and by providing the reader with some background information. The first paragraphs should illustrate an understanding of the issues at hand and should present an argument for why the research should be done. In other words, a context or framework is established for the entire paper. This background information must lead to a clear statement of the objectives of the paper and the hypothesis that will be experimentally tested. This movement from broad ideas and observations to a specific question or test starts the deductive scientific process.

—*R. Niesenbaum, Professor of Biology*

continued

This professor adds that most of the ideas in the introduction come from outside sources, such as scientific journals. The sources for this background information should be included in the References Cited section of the paper, but the introduction should be phrased in the writer's own words.

Even when regulated by a disciplinary format, the introduction may vary depending upon the context and audience, as in the following response from a physics professor.

I have my students write two distinctly different types of laboratory reports: one which is typical of a report submitted for publication, and one which is typical of an internal report written for a supervisor. The publishable paper typically represents a final report dealing with a completed study, while the internal report typically represents an interim report on a work-in-progress. These reports serve different purposes and are addressed to different audiences. Thus they will differ in their style, the amount of evidence which is presented to support a conclusion, and the degree of speculativeness of that conclusion.

The publishable paper in physics begins with an abstract, which briefly describes the experiment, gives the conclusion, and the significance of the work, all in three or four sentences. The internal report would probably not have an abstract. In the opening paragraph of the main body of the paper, the writer tries to put the work to be described into some larger context. This context might include reference to some or all of the following: similar experiments, which may, or may not, have shown similar results; theoretical work suggesting the importance of the experiment, the scientific or technological significance of the work. Such an opening is very important for the publishable paper, but less important for the internal report, since the supervisor is probably aware of the work's larger context. This opening usually results in mentioning and referencing many previously published papers.

—R. Milligan, Professor of Physics

Although the various models articulated here differ in small ways from discipline to discipline, the essential characteristics that they share suggest that most professors across the curriculum want the same things in an introduction: the locating of a problem or question within a context that provides background and rationale, culminating in a working thesis.

Voices from Across the Curriculum

USING PROCEDURAL OPENINGS

In the interests of clear organization, some professors require students to include in the introduction an explanation of how their paper will proceed.

continued

Such general statements of method and/or intention are known as *procedural openings.*

> I encourage students to provide a "road map" paragraph early in the paper, perhaps the second or third paragraph. (This is a common practice in the professional journals.) The "road map" tells the reader the basic outline of the argument. Something like the following: "In the first part of my paper I will present a brief history of the issue. . . . This will be followed by an account of the current controversy. . . . Part III will spell out my alternative account and evidence. . . . I then conclude. . . ." I think such a paragraph becomes more necessary with longer papers.
>
> —*G. Gambino, Professor of Political Science*

> I address the issue of an opening paragraph by having the students conceive of an opening section (or introduction) that tells the uninformed reader what's about to happen. I'll say, "Assume I know next to nothing about what lies ahead; so let me, the reader, know. 'My paper's about boom. In it, I'll do boom, boom. I chose this topic for the following reasons: boom, boom, boom.' Then get on with it."
>
> —*F. Norling, Professor of Business*

As the professor of political science observes, the procedural opening is particularly useful in longer papers, where it can provide a condensed version of what's to come as a guide for readers. Also note that he advises placing it early in the essay but not in the first paragraph, which, as seen in his earlier contribution to this chapter, he reserves for "presenting anomalies." In other words, he seems to value the introduction primarily as a site for the writer's idea, "stating the specific point of departure," and, that taken care of, only secondarily as a place for forecasting the plan of the paper. These priorities bear mentioning because they imply a potential danger in relying too heavily on procedural openings: that the writer will avoid making a claim at all.

As Chapter 5 ("Recognizing and Fixing Weak Thesis Statements") argued, the statement of a paper's plan is not the same thing as its thesis, because the plan need not contain an idea about the topic that the paper will explore and defend. Consider the deficiencies of the following procedural opening:

> In this paper I will first discuss the strong points and weak points in America's treatment of the elderly. Then I will compare this treatment with that in other industrial nations in the West. Finally, I will evaluate the various proposals for reform that have been advanced here and abroad.

continued

    As an introduction, this paragraph does not fare well in achieving the four objectives listed on page 96. It identifies the subject, but it neither addresses why the subject matters nor suggests the writer's approach. Nor does it provide background to the topic or suggest a hypothesis that the paper will pursue. Even though a procedural opening is built into the conventions of report writing, these conventions also stipulate that the writer include some clear statement of the hypothesis, counteracting the danger that the writer won't make any claim at all.

HOW MUCH TO INTRODUCE UP FRONT

    A big problem with introductions lies with the amount of work that needs to get done in a limited space. To specify a thesis and locate it within a larger context, to suggest the plan or outline of the entire paper, and to negotiate first relations with a reader—that's a lot to pack into a paragraph or two. In deciding how much to introduce up front, you must make a series of difficult choices. We list some of these choices below, phrased as questions you can ask yourself:

- How much can I assume that my readers know about my subject?
- Which parts of the research and/or the background are sufficiently pertinent to warrant inclusion?
- How much of my thesis do I include, and which particular part or parts should I begin with?
- What is the proper balance between background and foreground?
- Which are the essential parts of my plan or road map to include?

TYPICAL PROBLEMS THAT ARE SYMPTOMS OF DOING TOO MUCH

    If you consider the questions above, you can avoid writing introductions that try to do too much. When you try to do too much—to turn an introduction into a miniature essay—a variety of problems can result. In this context, consider the three problems discussed below as symptoms of overcompression, telltale signs that you need to reconceive and probably reduce your introduction.

Digression

    Digression results when you try to include too much background. If, for example, you plan to write about a recent innovation in video technology, you'll need to monitor the amount and kind of technical information you include in your opening paragraphs. You'll also want to avoid starting at a point that is too far away from your immediate concerns, as in "From the beginning of time humans have needed to communicate."

The standardized formats that govern procedural openings in some disciplines can help you to avoid digressing endlessly. There is a given sequence of steps to follow for a psychology report of an empirical study, for instance. Nonetheless, these disciplinary conventions still leave plenty of room for you to lose your focus. You still must choose which contexts are sufficiently relevant to be included up front.

In those disciplines that expect you to include context but do not stipulate a specific manner of doing so, the number of choices is greater, and so is the danger that you will get sidetracked into paragraphs of background that bury your thesis and frustrate your readers. One reason that many writers fall into this kind of digression in introductions is that they misjudge how much their audience needs to know. As a general rule in academic writing, *don't assume that your readers know little or nothing about the subject.* Instead, use the social potential of the introduction to negotiate your audience, setting up your relationship with your readers, and making clear what you are assuming they do and don't know.

Incoherence

Incoherence results when you try to preview too much of your conclusion. Incoherent introductions move in too many directions at once, usually because the writer is trying to conclude before going through the discussion that will make the conclusion comprehensible. The language you are compelled to use in such cases tends to be too dense, and the connections between the sentences tend to get left out, since there isn't enough room to include them. After having read the entire paper, your readers may be able to make sense of the introduction, but in that case, the introduction has not done its job.

The following introductory paragraph is incoherent, primarily because it tries to include too much. It neither adequately connects its ideas nor defines its terms.

> Twinship is a symbol in many religious traditions. The significance of twinship will be discussed and explored in the Native American, Japanese Shinto, and Christian religions. Twinship can be either in opposing or common forces in the form of deities or mortals. There are several forms of twinship which show duality of order versus chaos, good versus evil, and creation versus destruction. The significance of twinship is to set moral codes for society and to explain the inexplicable.

Prejudgment

Prejudgment results when you appear to have already settled the question to be pursued in the rest of the paper. The problem here is logical. In the effort to preview your conclusion at the outset, you risk appearing to assume something as true that your paper will in fact need to test. In most papers in the humanities and social sciences, where the thesis evolves in specificity and complexity between the introduction and conclusion, writers and readers can find such assumptions prejudicial. Opening in this way, at any event, can make the rest of the paper seem redundant. Even in the sciences, where a concise statement of objectives, plan of attack, and hypothesis are usually required up front, a separate Results section is reserved for the conclusion.

The following introductory paragraph prejudges, which is to say that it offers a series of conclusions already assumed to be true without introducing the necessary background issues and questions that would allow the writer to adequately explore these conclusions.

> Field hockey is a sport that can be played by either men or women. All sports should be made available for members of both sexes. As long as women are allowed to participate on male teams in sports such as football and wrestling, men should be allowed to participate on female teams in sports such as field hockey and lacrosse. If females press for and receive equal opportunity in all sports, then it is only fair that men be given the same opportunities. If women object to this type of equal opportunity, then they are promoting reverse discrimination.

Voices from Across the Curriculum

LIMITING INTRODUCTORY CLAIMS

The following cautionary advice addresses the problem of making strong claims too early:

I might be careful about how tentative conclusions should play in the opening paragraph because this can easily slide into a prejudging of the question at hand. I would be more comfortable with a clear statement of the prevailing views held by others. For example, a student could write on the question, "Was Franklin Delano Roosevelt a Keynesian?" What purpose would it serve in an opening paragraph to reveal without any supporting discussion that FDR was or was not a Keynesian? What might be better would be to say that in the public mind FDR is regarded as the original big spender, that some people commonly associate New Deal policies with general conceptions of Keynesianism, but that there may be some surprises in store as that common notion is examined.

In sum, I would discourage students from making strong claims at or near the beginning of a paper. Let's see the evidence first. We should all have respect for the evidence. Strong assertions, bordering on conclusions, too early on are inappropriate.

—*J. Marshall, Professor of Economics*

OPENING GAMBITS: A FEW SOLUTIONS

The primary challenge in writing introductions, it should now be evident, lies in occupying the middle ground between overasserted prejudgment and irresolute avoidance of taking any position. There are a number of fairly common opening gambits that can help you to achieve an effective middle ground.

Gambit 1: Challenge a Commonly Held View

One of the best opening gambits is to *challenge a commonly held view.* This is what the economics professor quoted previously advises when he suggests that rather than announcing up front the answer to the question at which the paper arrives, you convey that "there may be some surprises in store as that common notion is examined." This move has several advantages. Most important, it provides you with a framework *against* which to reply; it allows you to begin by *reacting.* Moreover, since you are responding to a known position, you have a ready way of integrating context into your paper. As the professor notes of the FDR example, until we understand why it matters whether or not FDR was a Keynesian, it is pointless to answer the question.

Gambit 2: Begin with a Definition

In the case of the FDR example, a writer would probably include another common introductory gambit, *defining* Keynesianism. Beginning with a definition is a reliable way to introduce a topic, so long as that definition has some significance for the discussion to follow. If the definition doesn't do any conceptual work in the introduction, the definition gambit becomes a pointless cliché.

Gambit 3: Offer a Working Hypothesis

But, you may be wondering, where is the thesis in the FDR example? As the economics professor suggests, you are often better off introducing a *working hypothesis*—an opening claim, sometimes in the form of a question, that stimulates the analytical process—instead of offering some full declaration of the conclusion. The introduction he envisions, for example, implies that the question of FDR's Keynesianism is not as simple as is commonly thought, further implying that the common association of "New Deal policies with general conceptions of Keynesianism" is, to some extent, false.

Gambit 4: Lead with Your Second-Best Example

Another versatile opening gambit, where disciplinary conventions allow, is to *use your second best example to set up the issue or question* that you later develop in depth with your best example. This gambit is especially useful in papers that proceed inductively on the strength of representative examples. As you are assembling evidence in the outlining and prewriting stage, in many cases you will accumulate a number of examples that illustrate the same basic point. For example, several battles might illustrate a particular general's military strategy; several primaries might exemplify how a particular candidate tailors his or her speeches to appeal to the religious right; several scenes might show how a particular playwright romanticizes the working class, and so on.

Save the best example to receive the most analytical attention in your paper. If you were to present this example in the introduction, you would risk making the rest of the essay vaguely repetitive. A quick close-up of another example will strengthen your argument or interpretation. By using a different example to raise the issues, you suggest that the phenomenon exemplified is not an isolated case and that the major example you will eventually concentrate upon is indeed representative.

What kind of example should you choose? By calling it "second best," we mean only to suggest that it should be another resonant instance of whatever issue or question you have chosen to focus upon. Given its location up front and its function to introduce the larger issues to which it points, you should handle it more simply than subsequent examples. That way your readers can get their bearings before you take them into a more in-depth analysis of your best example in the body of your paper.

Gambit 5: Exemplify the Topic with a Narrative

One more opening gambit that is common in the humanities and social sciences is the *narrative opening*. The narrative introduces a short, pertinent, and vivid story or anecdote that exemplifies a key aspect of your topic. Although generally not permissible in formal reports in the natural and social sciences, narrative openings are common across the curriculum in virtually all other kinds of writing. Here is an example from a student paper in psychology:

> In the past fifteen years, issues surrounding AIDS have incited many people to examine their thoughts and feelings about homosexuality. As a result, instances of prejudice and discrimination towards gays, lesbians, and bisexuals have risen recently (Herek, 1989). While some instances are sufficiently damaging to warrant criminal charges, other instances of prejudice occur everyday that are less serious. Nonetheless, they demonstrate a problem with our society that needs to be addressed. I witnessed one of these subtle demonstrations of prejudice in a social psychology class. The topic of the class was love and relationships, how they develop, endure, and deteriorate. Although the professor had not specifically stated it previously, the information being presented was relevant to homosexual relationships as well as heterosexual ones. At one point during her lecture, the professor was presenting an example using a hypothetical sorority member. The professor, in passing, referred to the sorority member's love relationship partner as a "she." This reference to a homosexual relationship did not seem intentional on the professor's part. However, many in the class noticed and reacted with silence at first, then glances at neighbors, which led finally to nervous laughter. After this disruption ended, a student explained to the professor what had been said that caused the disruption. And in response the professor promptly explained that the theories for love and relationships also applied to homosexual relationships.
>
> In that moment of nervous laughter, many in the class displayed prejudice against homosexual relationships. In particular, they were displaying a commonly held belief that homosexual relationships are not founded on the same emotions, thoughts, and feelings that heterosexual relationships are. The main causes of prejudice displayed in class against homosexuality include social categorization and social learning.

As this introduction funnels down to its thesis, the readers have received a graphic sense of the issue the writer will now develop nonnarratively. Such nonnarrative treatment is necessary, for, by itself, anecdotal evidence can be seen as merely personal. Storytelling is suggestive but can never constitute proof; it needs to be corroborated. In the previous paragraph the writer has strengthened his credibility by focusing not on his personal responses but on the lesson to be drawn from his experience—a lesson that other people might also draw from it.

Like challenging a commonly held view or using a second best example, a narrative opening will also help to safeguard you from trying to do too much up front. All three gambits enable you to play an ace, establishing your authority with your reader, without having to play your whole hand. In other words, when disciplinary conventions permit, introductions set up a starting position; they don't necessarily offer a miniature version of the essay. As a general rule, an effective introduction will pose one problem and offer one enigmatic example—seeking in some way to engage the reader in the thought process that the writer is beginning to unfold. *The introduction seeks to raise the issue, not settle it.*

THE FUNCTION OF CONCLUSIONS

Like introductions, conclusions have a key social function: they escort the readers out of the paper, just as the introduction has brought them in. What do readers want as they leave the textual world you have taken them through? Although the form and length of the conclusion depend on the purpose and disciplinary conventions of the particular paper, it is possible to generalize a set of shared expectations for conclusions across the curriculum. In some combination most readers want three things: a judgment, a culmination, and a send-off.

Judgment

The conclusion is the site for final judgment on whatever question or issue or problem the paper has focused upon. In most cases, this judgment occurs in overt connection with the introduction, often repeating some of its key terms. However tentatively, the conclusion reconsiders the opening hypothesis, and, if possible, rules yea or nay. It also revisits explicitly the introductory claim for why the topic matters.

Culmination

More than simply summarizing what has preceded or reasserting your main point, the conclusion needs to culminate. The word *culminate* is derived from the Latin *columen,* meaning top or summit. To culminate is to reach the highest point, and it implies a mountain (in this case, of information and analysis) that you have scaled. When you culminate a paper in a conclusion, you bring things together and ascend to one cumulative statement of your thinking.

Send-Off

The climactic effects of judgment and culmination provide the basis for the send-off. The send-off is both social and conceptual, a final opening out of the topic that leads the reader out of the paper with something further to think about.

As is suggested by most of the following Voices from Across the Curriculum, the conclusion needs to move beyond the close analysis of data that has occupied the body of the paper into a kind of speculation that the writer has earned the right to formulate.

Here is an example of a conclusion that contains a final judgment, a culmination, and a send-off. The paper, a student's account of what she learned about science from doing research in biology, opens with the claim that, to the apprentice, "science assumes an impressive air of complete reliability, especially to its distant human acquaintances." Having been attracted to science by the popular view that it proceeds infallibly, she arrives at quite a different final assessment:

> All I truly know from my research is that the infinite number of factors that can cause an experiment to go wrong make tinkering a lab skill just as necessary as reading a buret. A scientist can eventually figure out a way to collect the data she wants if she has the patience to repeatedly recombine her materials and tools in slightly different ways. A researcher's success, then, often depends largely on her being lucky enough to locate, among all the possibilities, the one procedure that works.
>
> Aided more by persistence and fortune than by formal training, I evolved a method that produced credible results. But, like the tests from which it derived, the success of that method is probably also highly specific to a certain experimental environment and so is valid only for research involving borosilicate melts treated with hydrofluoric and boric acids. I've discovered a principle, but it's hardly a universal one: reality is too complex to allow much scientific generalization. Science may appear to sit firmly on all-encompassing truths, but the bulk of its weight actually rests on countless little rules tailored for particular situations.

This writer deftly interweaves the original claim from her introduction—that "science assumes an impressive air of complete reliability"—into a final *judgment* of her topic, delivered in the last sentence. This judgment is also a *culmination,* as it moves from her account of doing borosilicate melts to the small but acute generalization that "little rules tailored for particular situations," rather than "all-encompassing truths," are the mainstay of scientific research. Notice that a culmination does not need to make a grand claim in order to be effective. In fact, the relative smallness of the final claim, especially in contrast to the sweeping introductory position about scientific infallibility, ultimately provides a *send-off* made effective by its unexpected understatement.

Voices from Across the Curriculum

WAYS OF CONCLUDING

The three professors quoted next all advise some version of the judgment/culmination/send-off combination. The first "Voice" stresses the send-off:

continued

I tell my students that too many papers "just end," as if the last page or so were missing. I tell them the importance of ending a work. One could summarize main points, but I tell them this is not heavy lifting. They could raise issues not addressed (but hinted at) in the main body: "given this, one could consider that." I tell them that a good place for reflection might be a concluding section in which they take the ball and run: react, critique, agree, disagree, recommend, suggest, or predict.

I help them by asking, "Where does the paper seem to go *after* it ends on paper"? That is, I want the paper to live on even though the five pages are filled. I don't want to suddenly stop thinking or reacting just because I've read the last word on the bottom of page five. I want an experience, as if the paper is still with me.

I believe the ending should be an expansion on or explosion of possibilities, sort of like an introduction to some much larger "mental" paper out there. I sometimes encourage students to see the concluding section as an option to introduce ideas that can't be dealt with now. Sort of a "Having done this, I would want to explore boom, boom, boom if I were to continue further." Here the students can critique and recommend ("Having seen 'this,' one wonders 'that'").

—*F. Norling, Professor of Business*

In contrast to these observations, the comment below emphasizes judgment—the need to answer clearly the primary question that the paper has addressed:

There must be a summation. What part did the Stock Market Crash of 1929 play in the onset of the Great Depression? Let's hear that conclusion one more time. Again, but now in an abbreviated form, what's the evidence? What are the main ambiguities that remain? Has your paper raised any new questions for future research? Are there any other broader ramifications following in the wake of your paper?

—*J. Marshall, Professor of Economics*

Although it is true that the conclusion is the place for "broader ramifications," this phrase should not be understood as a call for a global generalization. As the next quotation suggests, often the culmination represents a final limiting of a paper's original claim.

In the professional journals, conclusions typically appear as a refined version of a paper's thesis—that is, as a more qualified statement of the main claim. An author might take pains to point out how this claim is limited or problematic, given the adequacy of available evidence (particularly in the case of papers dependent on current empirical research, opinion polls, etc.). The conclusion also may indicate the implications of current or new evidence on conventional wisdom/theory—how the theory needs to be revised, discarded, etc. Conclusions of papers that deal with contemporary issues or trends usually consider the practical consequences or the expectations for the future.

continued

The conclusion does not appear simply as a restatement of a thesis, but as an attempt to draw out its implications and significance (the "so what?"). This is what I usually try to impress upon students. For instance, if a student is writing on a particular proposal for party reform, I would expect the concluding paragraph to consider both the significance of the reform and its practicality.

I should note that professional papers often indicate the tentativeness of their conclusions by stressing the need for future research and indicating what these research needs might be. While I haven't tried this, maybe it would be useful to have students conclude papers with a section called "For Further Consideration" in which they would indicate those things that they would have liked to have known but couldn't, given their time constraints, the availability of information, and lack of methodological sophistication. This would serve as a reminder of the tentativeness of conclusions and the need to revisit and revise arguments in the future (which, after all, is a good scholarly habit).

—*G. Gambino, Professor of Political Science*

Voices from Across the Curriculum

DISCUSSION SECTIONS OF REPORTS

As was the case with introductions, the conclusions of reports written in the natural sciences and psychology are regulated by formalized disciplinary formats. Conclusions, for example, occur in a section titled "Discussion." As the three "Voices" below demonstrate, the organization and contents of Discussion sections vary little from discipline to discipline. For that matter, the imperatives that guide Discussion sections share essential traits with conclusions across the curriculum. Look for the similarities in the following three comments.

The conclusion occurs in a section labelled "Discussion," and as quoted from the *Publication Manual of the American Psychological Association* (4th ed., Washington, D.C., 1994), is guided by the following questions:

- What have I contributed here?

- How has my study helped to resolve the original problem?

- What conclusions and theoretical implications can I draw from my study? (p. 19)

In a broad sense, one particular research report should be seen as but one moment in a broader research tradition that *preceded* the particular study being written about and that will *continue after* this study is published. And so the conclusion should tie this particular study into both previous research and future

continued

research. The author looks to the future in the Discussion section by considering implications for the theory guiding this study, and (when applicable) practical implications of this study. One of the great challenges of writing a research report is thus to place this particular study within that broader research tradition. That's an analytic task.

—*A. Tjeltveit, Professor of Psychology*

The writer should discuss the physical significance of what has been measured and concluded. A conclusion should be more than just a number. The main body of the publishable paper leads inexorably to the conclusion, with the conclusion based on the analysis of the evidence given in the paper. The conclusion is nearly always the result of inductive, rather than deductive, reasoning. It often suggests additional experiments, or ways to improve the current experiment, such as an alternative method of data analysis.

—*R. Milligan, Professor of Physics*

Papers are concluded with a Discussion section in which conclusions are analyzed, qualified, and ultimately their implications for the "bigger picture" are presented. The conclusion of the paper often represents the move from the deductive to the inductive aspect of science. The specific results first are interpreted (but not restated), and their implications and limitations are then discussed. The original question should be rephrased and discussed in light of the results presented. Conclusions should be qualified and alternative explanations should be considered. Finally, conservative generalizations and new questions are posed.

—*R. Niesenbaum, Professor of Biology*

The biology professor adds additional advice on the specific language to use in the Discussion section, cautioning against use of the word *prove:* results may *support, verify,* or *confirm* your hypothesis, or they may *negate, refute,* or *contradict* it.

There is striking overlap in the advice these cross–disciplinary "Voices" offer. All caution that the conclusion should provide more than a restatement of what you've already said. All suggest that the conclusion should, in effect, serve as the introduction to some "larger mental paper out there" (as one professor puts it), beyond the confines of your own paper. By consensus, the professors make three recommendations for conclusions:

1. *Pursue implications.* Reason inductively from your particular study to consider broader issues, such as the study's practical consequences or applica-

tions, or future-oriented issues, such as avenues for further research. To unfold implications in this way is to broaden the view from the here-and-now of your paper by looking outward to the wider world and forward to the future.

2. *Come full circle.* Unify your paper by interpreting the results of your analysis in light of the context you established in your introduction.

3. *Identify limitations.* Acknowledge restrictions of method or focus in your analysis, and qualify your conclusion (and its implications) accordingly.

Consider how the following example does the three things that the professors have recommended: unfolds implications, comes full circle, and limits claims. The example provides the concluding paragraphs to the paper from which we earlier quoted the introduction as an example of a narrative opening. That opening anecdote, you may recall, introduced the problems of social categorization and social learning as causes of homophobia in the academic environment.

> There are many other instances of prejudice, stereotyping, and discrimination against homosexuals. These range from beliefs that homosexual partners cannot be adequate parents, to exclusion from the military, to bias (hate) crimes resulting in murder. But in recent decades, attempts have been made to help end these discriminations. One of the first occurred in 1973 when the American Psychological Association changed its policy so that homosexuals were no longer regarded as mentally ill (Melton, 1989). Thus the stigma that homosexuals were not able to fully contribute to society was partially lifted.
>
> Other ways that have been suggested to reduce prejudice regarding homosexuals include increasing intergroup contact. In this way, each group may come to recognize similarities and encounter counter-stereotypical information. Herek (1989) also suggests that education in elementary through high schools about diversity and tolerance of it, for students as well as teachers, may help prevent stereotypes, prejudice, and hate crimes. And if they are made aware of their schemas and stereotypes, people may consider information they would have ignored based on their schemas. We may never be able to eliminate the process of social categorization, but perhaps we may be able to teach that all out-groups are not necessarily "bad."

In the first paragraph the writer adeptly shifts direction—"But in recent decades"—from cataloguing the range of homophobic responses to assessing the changes in the overall climate. In so doing, he comes full circle, returning implicitly to the original problem phrased in the introduction and referring again to the source (Herek) used there, but now in the context of what can be done to redress the problem. Note as well how carefully he has qualified the final summary of evidence, laying the foundation for the concluding claim: the stigma "was *partially* lifted" in 1973; "We *may* never be able to eliminate . . . but *perhaps* we *may* be able to teach"; and so forth (our italics). As a result of this careful qualification, the implications of the study are not overstated but modestly offered as a quiet hope.

SOLVING TYPICAL PROBLEMS IN CONCLUSIONS

The primary challenge in writing conclusions, it should now be evident, lies in finding a way to culminate your analysis without claiming either too little or too much. There are a number of fairly common problems to guard against if you are to avoid either of these two extremes.

Redundancy

In Chapter 3, "Questions of Format," we lampooned an exaggerated example of the five-paragraph form for constructing its conclusion by stating "Thus, we see" and then repeating the introduction verbatim. The result is *redundancy*. As you've seen, it's a good idea to refer back to the opening, but don't reinsert it mechanically. Instead, reevaluate what you said there in light of where you've ended up, repeating only key words or phrases from the introduction. This kind of *selective repetition* is a desirable way of achieving unity and will keep you from either of two opposite mistakes—either repeating too much or bringing up a totally new point in the conclusion.

Raising a Totally New Point

Raising a totally new point can distract or bewilder a reader. This problem often arises out of a writer's praiseworthy desire to avoid repetition. As a rule, you can guard against the problem by making sure that you have clearly expressed the conceptual link between your central conclusion and any implications you may draw. An implication is not a totally new point but one that follows from the position you have been analyzing.

Similarly, although a capping judgment or send-off may appear for the first time in your concluding paragraph, it should have been *anticipated* by the body of your paper. Conclusions often indicate where you think you (or an interested reader) may need to go next, but you don't actually go there. In a paper on the economist Milton Friedman, for example, if you think that another economist offers a useful way of critiquing him, you probably should not introduce this person for the first time in your conclusion.

Overstatement

Many writers are confused over how much they should claim in their conclusion. Out of the understandable desire for a grand culmination, writers sometimes *overstate* the case; that is, they assert more than their evidence has proven, or even suggested. Must a conclusion arrive at some comprehensive and final answer to the question that your paper has analyzed? Depending on the question and the disciplinary conventions, you may need to come down exclusively on one side or another. In a great many cases, however, the answers with which you conclude can be more moderate and modest. Especially in the humanities, good analytical writing seeks to unfold successive layers of implication, so it's not even reasonable for you to expect neat closure. In such cases, you are usually better off qualifying your final judgment, drawing the line at a point of relative stability.

Anticlimax

It makes a difference precisely where in the final paragraph(s) you qualify your concluding claim. The end of the conclusion is a "charged" site, since it gives the reader a last impression of your paper. If you end with a concession, on a note that detracts from your fundamental thesis, you risk leaving the reader unsettled and, possibly, confused. The term for this kind of letdown from the significant to the inconsequential is *anticlimax*. In most cases, you will flub the send-off if you depart the paper on an anticlimax.

There are many forms of anticlimax besides ending with a concession. If your conclusion peters out in a random list or an apparent afterthought or a last-minute qualification of your claims, the effect is anticlimactic. And for many readers, if your final answer comes from quoting an authority in place of establishing your own, that too is an anticlimax.

At the beginning of this chapter we suggested that a useful rule for introductions was to play an ace but not your whole hand. In the context of this card-game analogy, it is similarly effective to save an ace for the conclusion. In most cases, this high card will provide an answer to some culminating "so what?" question—a last view of the implications or consequences of your analysis.

GUIDELINES FOR INTRODUCTIONS AND CONCLUSIONS

Introductions

1. Disciplinary conventions permitting, the introduction seeks to raise the issue, not settle it.
2. Engage your readers by articulating why, in terms of existing thinking on the subject, your topic matters. Avoid "catchy" introductory gimmicks in academic writing.
3. Always introduce a working (hypo)thesis, frame it with background or other context, and indicate your method or angle of approach. Cite relevant sources.
4. Especially in longer papers, you can use a procedural opening to forecast the organization clearly, but don't let it distract you from also stating your claim.
5. Don't try to do too much. Offer only the most relevant context, the most essential parts of your road map, and (disciplinary conventions permitting) a first rather than last claim.
6. Experiment with opening gambits. Challenge a common view, use your second best example to set up the issue, or exemplify the problem with a narrative opening (disciplinary conventions permitting).

Conclusions

7. Don't just summarize; culminate. Offer your most qualified statement of the thesis or your final judgment on the question posed in the introduction.

8. Come full circle. Revisit the introductory hypothesis and context. This strategy will unify your paper and help locate it within scholarly conversation on your topic.
9. Acknowledge the limitations of your discussion or study. Don't assert more than your evidence has established.
10. Give your conclusion a send-off. Leave the reader with implications or speculations to think about further. Avoid closing the conclusion with a concession.
11. Let your conclusion gradually escort the reader out of the paper. Like the introduction, it is a social site, so leave the reader with a positive last impression.

C H A P T E R

7

ANALYZING EVIDENCE

LINKING EVIDENCE AND CLAIMS

THIS CHAPTER IS ABOUT evidence—what it is, what it is meant to do, and how you can recognize when you are using it well. The chapter's overall argument is that you should use evidence to test, refine, and develop your ideas, rather than just to prove that they are correct. The chapter begins by analyzing two common problems—claims without evidence *(unsubstantiated claims)* and evidence without claims *(pointless evidence)*. It then moves to a discussion of strategies for analyzing evidence in depth.

By way of definition, a *claim* is what you want to prove. It is a point that you make about the meaning of your subject—its function, its overlooked danger, its misunderstood benefit, or whatever. *Evidence* refers to the information that is used to support or corroborate a claim. There are many kinds of evidence, such as details, facts, examples, and statistics. As you will see, whether or not something qualifies as acceptable evidence, and what it is evidence of, are often debatable.

THE FUNCTION OF EVIDENCE

A common assumption about evidence is that it is "the stuff that proves I'm right." Although this way of thinking about evidence is not wrong, it is much too limited. Corroboration (proving the validity of a claim) is one of the functions of evidence, but not the only one.

It helps to remember that the word *prove* comes from a Latin verb meaning "to test." The noun form of *prove, proof,* has two meanings: (1) the *evidence* sufficient to establish a thing as true or believable and (2) the *act of testing* for truth or believability. When you operate on the first definition of *proof* alone, you are far more likely to seek out evidence that supports only your point of view, ignoring or dismissing other evidence that could lead to a different and possibly better idea. You might also assume that you can't begin writing until you have arrived at an idea you're convinced is right, since only then could you decide which evidence to include. Both of these practices close down your thinking instead of leading you to a more open process of formulating and testing ideas.

Beginning with the goal of establishing an idea as believable and true can interfere with the need to examine it. Moreover, this approach can lead to an unnecessarily combative style of argument in which the aim is to defeat one's opponents—a style in which convincing others that you're right is more important than arriving at a fair and accurate assessment of your subject. By contrast, the advantage to following the second definition of the word *proof*—in the sense of testing—is that you will be better able to negotiate among contesting points of view. In addition, this practice will predispose your readers to consider what you have to say, because you are offering them not only the thoughts a person has had but also a person in the act of thinking.

THE FALLACY THAT FACTS CAN SPEAK FOR THEMSELVES

The first step in learning to explain the connection between your evidence and your claims is to remember that *evidence rarely, if ever, can be left to speak for itself.* When you leave evidence to speak for itself, you are assuming that it can be interpreted in only one way and that others will think as you do.

Writers who think that evidence speaks for itself generally do very little with it. Sometimes they will present it without making any overt claims, stating, for example, "There was no alcohol at the party" and expecting the reader to understand this statement as a sign of approval or disapproval. Alternatively, they may simply place the evidence next to a claim. Such writers will say, for example, "The party was terrible: there was no alcohol" or "The party was great: there was no alcohol." Merely juxtaposing the evidence to the claim leaves out the thinking that connects them, thereby implying that the logic of the connection is obvious. But even for readers prone to agree with you, just pointing to the evidence—regardless of the particular discipline within which you are writing—is not enough.

It should be acknowledged, however, that particular disciplines do influence the way you use evidence and thus the way that you think. What counts as evidence in one discipline may not be acceptable in another. And while some disciplines—the natural sciences, for example—require you to present your evidence first and then interpret it, others (the humanities and some social sciences) will expect you to interpret your evidence as it is presented. Nonetheless, it is possible to talk about methods of using evidence that apply across the curriculum. These methods, which the rest of this chapter discusses, can be applied to virtually any writing situation. They form a basic repertoire upon which the particular ways of using evidence in each discipline can be built.

Unsubstantiated Claims

problem: *Making claims that lack supporting evidence*

solution: *Learn to recognize and support unsubstantiated assertions.*

Unsubstantiated claims occur when you concentrate only on your conclusions, omitting the evidence that led to them. At the opposite extreme, pointless evidence results when you offer a mass of detail attached to an overly general claim. To solve both of these problems, you need to remember two rules. Whenever you make a claim

1. Offer your readers the evidence that led you to it.
2. Explain how the evidence led you to that conclusion.

The word *unsubstantiated* means "without substance." An unsubstantiated claim is not necessarily false; it just offers none of the concrete "stuff" upon which the claim is based. There are two compelling reasons to avoid unsubstantiated claims:

- Making such a claim assumes that readers will believe you just because you say this or that.
- Unsubstantiated claims deprive you of details. Without details, you're left with nothing concrete to think about.

If you lack some actual "stuff" to analyze, you can easily get stuck in a set of abstractions, which tend to overstate your position, inhibit your thinking, and leave your readers wondering exactly what you mean. The further away your language gets from references to physical detail—things that you can see, hear, count, taste, smell, and touch—the more abstract it becomes. An aircraft carrier anchored outside a foreign harbor is concrete; the phrase "intervening in the name of democracy" is abstract.

You can see the problem of unsubstantiated assertions not only in papers but in everyday conversation. It occurs when people get in the habit of leaping to conclusions—forming impressions so quickly and automatically that what triggered these particular responses cannot even be recalled. Ask such people why they thought a party was boring or a new acquaintance pretentious, and they will rephrase the generalization rather than offer the evidence that led to it: the party was boring because nobody did anything; the person is pretentious because he puts on airs.

Rephrasing your generalizations rather than offering evidence tends to starve your thinking; it also has the effect of shutting out readers. If, for example, you defend your judgment that a person is pretentious by saying that he puts on airs, you have ruled on the matter and dismissed it. (You have also committed a logical flaw known as a circular argument; since "pretentious" and "putting on airs" mean virtually the same thing, using one in support of the other is arguing in a circle.)

If, by contrast, you include the *grounds* upon which your judgment is based—that he uses big words, say, or always wears a bow tie—you have given readers a glimpse of your criteria. Readers are far more likely to accept your views if you give them the chance to think *with* you about the evidence. The alternative—offering groundless assertions—is to expect them to take your word for it.

There is, of course, an element of risk in providing the details that have informed your judgment. You leave yourself open to attack if, for example, your readers wear bow ties or speak in polysyllables. But this is an essential risk to take, for, otherwise, you leave your readers wondering why you think as you do, or worse, unlikely to credit your point of view. Moreover, in laying out your evidence, you will be more likely to anticipate your readers' possible disagreement. This will make you more inclined to think openly and carefully about your judgments.

In order to check your drafts for unsubstantiated assertions, you first have to know how to recognize them. One of the most fundamental skills for a writer to possess is the ability to *distinguish* evidence from claims. It is sometimes difficult to separate facts from judgments, data from interpretations of the data. Writers who aren't practiced in this skill can believe that they are offering evidence when they are really offering only unsubstantiated claims. In your own reading and writing, pause once in a while to label the sentences of a paragraph as either evidence (E) or claims (C). What happens if we try to categorize the sentences of the following paragraph in this way?

> The owners are ruining baseball in America. Although they claim that they are losing money, they are really just being greedy. A few years ago, they even fired the commissioner, Fay Vincent, because he took the players' side. Baseball is a sport, not a business, and it is a sad fact that it is being threatened by greedy businessmen.

The first and last sentences of the paragraph are claims. They draw conclusions about as yet unstated evidence that the writer will need to provide. The middle two sentences are harder to classify. If particular owners have stated publicly that they are losing money, the existence of those statements is a fact. But the writer moves from evidence to claim when he suggests that the owners are lying about their financial situation and are doing so because of their greed. Both of these assertions are unsubstantiated claims. Unless the writer proceeds to ground them in evidence—relevant facts—they amount to little more than name-calling. Similarly, it is a fact that commissioner Fay Vincent was fired, but the assertion that he was fired "because he took the players' side" is another unsubstantiated claim. The writer needs to offer evidence in support of this claim, along with his reasons for believing that the evidence means what he says it does.

Without evidence and the reasoning you've done about it, your writing asks readers to accept your opinions as though they were facts. The central claim of the baseball paragraph—that greedy businessmen are ruining baseball—is an example of an opinion treated as though it were factual information. Although many readers might be inclined to accept some version of the claim as true, they should not be asked to accept the writer's opinion as a self-evident truth.

The word *evident* comes from a Latin verb meaning "to see." To say that the truth of a statement is "self-evident" means that it does not need proving because its truth should be plainly seen by all. The problem is that very few ideas—no matter how much you may believe in them—readily attest to their own truth. And precisely because what people have taken to be common knowledge ("women can't do math," for example, or "men don't talk about their feelings") so often turns out to be wrong, you should take care to avoid unsubstantiated claims.

You should be stingy, therefore, about treating your claims and evidence as factual. The more concrete information you gather, the less likely you will be to accept your opinions, partial information, or misinformation as fact. The writer of the baseball paragraph, for example, offers as fact that the owners claim they are losing money. If he were to search harder, however, he would find that his statement of the owners' claim is not entirely accurate. The owners have not unanimously claimed that they are losing money; they have acknowledged that the problem has to do with poorer "small-market" teams competing against richer "large-market" teams. This more complicated version of the facts might at first be discouraging to the writer, since it reveals his original thesis ("greed") to be oversimplified. But then, as we have been saying, the function of evidence is not just to corroborate your claims; it should also help you to *test* and *refine* your ideas and to *define* your key terms more precisely.

Most writers make at least some unsubstantiated claims as they draft. To remedy this problem:

1. Identify all claims, distinguishing them from evidence.
2. Locate evidence that could substantiate and test unsubstantiated claims.
3. Allow your analysis of this evidence to develop your claims, rather than simply confirming your original formulation.

Following these three steps will help you write more thoughtfully. You will also find yourself having much more to say.

POINTLESS EVIDENCE

problem: *Presenting a mass of evidence without explaining how it relates to the claims*

solution: *Make details speak. Explain how evidence confirms or qualifies the claim.*

Your thinking emerges in the way that you follow through on the implications of the evidence you have selected. You need to interpret it for your readers. It is not enough to insert evidence after your claim, expecting readers to draw the same conclusion about its meaning that you have. You cannot assume that the facts can speak for themselves. You must "make the details speak."

The following example illustrates what happens when a writer leaves the evidence to speak for itself:

Baseball is a sport, not a business, and it is a sad fact that it is being threatened by greedy businessmen. For example, Eli Jacobs, the previous owner of the Baltimore Orioles, recently sold the team to Peter Angelos for $100 million more than he had spent ten years earlier when he purchased it. Also, a new generation of baseball stadia have been built—for the Orioles in Baltimore, for the White Sox in Chicago, for the Rangers in Arlington, for the Indians in Cleveland. These parks are enormously expensive and include elaborate scoreboards and luxury boxes. The average baseball players, meanwhile, now earn over $1 million a year, and they all have agents to represent them. Barry Bonds, the left fielder for the San Francisco Giants, is paid $7 million a season. Sure, he has won the coveted Most Valuable Player award (MVP) in his league three times, but is any ballplayer worth that much money?

Unlike the previous example, which was all claims, this paragraph is all evidence, except for the opening claim and the closing question. The paragraph presents what we might call an "evidence sandwich": it encloses a series of facts between two quite different claims. (The opening statement blames "greedy businessmen," presumably owners, and the closing statement appears to indict greedy, or at least overpaid, players.) Readers are left with two problems. First, the mismatch between the opening and concluding claims leaves it not altogether clear what the writer is saying that the evidence suggests. And second, he has not told readers why they should believe that the evidence means what he says it does. Instead, he leaves it to speak for itself.

If you look again at the example, you'll see that each sentence after the opening claim offers facts but does not overtly interpret those facts by connecting them to the claims. The closest connection between claims and evidence is between the fact that Barry Bonds earns $7 million per year and the writer's implicit claim (phrased as a question) that no player is worth that much. Otherwise, the items of evidence do not bear directly on the claims made.

If readers are to accept the writer's implicit claims—that the spending is too much and that it is ruining baseball—he will have to show *how* and *why* the evidence supports these conclusions. The rule that applies here is that *evidence can almost always be interpreted in more than one way.*

You might, for instance, formulate at least three conclusions from the evidence offered in the baseball paragraph. You might decide that the writer believes baseball will be ruined by going broke or that he is saying its spirit will be ruined by becoming too commercial. Worst of all, you might disagree with his claim and conclude that baseball is not really being ruined, since the evidence could be read as signs of health rather than decay. The profitable resale of the Orioles, the expensive new ballparks (which, the writer neglects to mention, have drawn record crowds), and the skyrocketing salaries all could testify to the growing popularity rather than the decline of the sport.

How can you ensure that your readers will at least understand your interpretation of the data? Begin by constantly reminding yourself that the thought connections that have occurred to you will not automatically occur to others. This doesn't mean that you should assume your readers are stupid, but that you shouldn't expect them to read your mind and to do for themselves the thinking that you should be doing for them.

You can make the details speak if you take the time to stop and look at them, asking questions about what they imply. The two steps to follow are

1. Say explicitly what you take the details to mean.
2. State exactly how the evidence supports or qualifies your claims.

The writer of the baseball paragraph leaves both some of his claims and virtually all of his reasoning about the evidence implicit. What, for example, bothers him about the special luxury seating areas? What does this piece of information imply? Perhaps it demonstrates that economic interests are taking baseball away from its traditional fans because the new seating areas cost far more than the average person can afford to pay. This interpretation of the evidence could be used to support the writer's governing claim, but he would need to spell out the connection. He might say, for example, that baseball's time-honored role as the all-American sport—democratic and grass roots—is being displaced by the tendency of baseball as a business to orient its efforts around attracting higher box-office receipts and wealthier fans.

The writer could then make more explicit what his whole paragraph implies, that baseball's image as a popular pastime in which all Americans can participate is being tarnished by players and owners alike, whose primary concern appears to be making money. In making his evidence speak, the writer would also refine his claim by being much clearer about which aspect of baseball he thinks is being ruined. He could clarify in his revision, for instance, that the "greedy businessmen" to whom he refers include both owners and players.

The result of carefully pondering the implications of your evidence will almost always be a "smaller" idea than the one you may have set out to prove. This is what "qualifying" a generalization means: you shrink and restrict its scope. Sometimes it is hard to give up on the large, general assertions that were your first response to your subject. But your sacrifices in scope are exchanged for greater accuracy and validity. The sweeping claims you lose ("Greedy businessmen are ruining baseball") give way to less resounding but also more informed, more incisive, and less judgmental ideas ("Market pressures may not bring the end of baseball, but they are certainly changing the image and nature of the game").

Voices from Across the Curriculum

WHAT COUNTS AS EVIDENCE?

Thus far this chapter has concentrated on how to use evidence after you've assembled it. The professors quoted here, however, make clear that in many cases you need to consider a more basic and often hidden question before you begin collecting data: What counts as evidence?

This question raises two related concerns:

- Issues of *pertinence:* In what ways does the evidence bear on the claim or problem that you are addressing? Do the facts really apply in this particular case and, if so, how?

continued

- Issues of *framing:* In what ways is the evidence colored by the set of assumptions or point of view that designated it as evidence? At what point do these assumptions limit its authority or reliability?

To raise the issue of framing is not to imply that all evidence is *merely* subjective, somebody's impressionistic opinion. We are implying, however, that even the most apparently neutral evidence is the product of *some way of seeing* that qualifies the evidence as evidence in the first place. In some cases, this way of seeing is embedded in an established procedure. In the natural sciences, for example, the actual data that go into the "Results" section are the product of a highly controlled experimental procedure. As its name suggests, the section presents the *result* of seeing in a particular way.

The same kind of control is present in various quantitative operations in the social sciences, in which the evidence is usually framed in the language of statistics. And in somewhat less systematic but nonetheless similar ways, evidence in the humanities and some projects in the social sciences is always conditioned by methodological assumptions. As the following professors' comments make clear, even when it is not organized within any formalized, numbers-producing experimental procedure, evidence is never just some free-floating, absolutely reliable, objective entity for the casual observer to sample at random.

The advice I give on evidence always includes a warning on the tentative nature of what we think we know. New evidence can arrive at any time. Old evidence can be reworked. Conclusions held with certitude may have to be abandoned. This happens all the time in a social science like economics.

—*J. Marshall, Professor of Economics*

What counts as evidence? I try to impress upon students that they need to substantiate their claims with evidence. Most have little trouble with this. However, when I tell them that evidence itself is dependent upon *methodology*—that it's not just a question of gathering "information," but also a question of *how* it was accumulated—their eyes glaze over. Can we trust the source of information? What biases may exist in the way questions are posed in an opinion poll? Who counts as an authority on a subject? (No, Rush Limbaugh cannot be considered an authority on women's issues, or the environment, or, for that matter, anything else!) Is your evidence out of date? (In politics, books on electoral behavior have a shelf life only up to the next election. After two years, they may have severe limitations.)

Methodological concerns also determine the *relevance* of evidence. Some models of, say, democratic participation define as irrelevant certain kinds of evidence that other models might view as crucial. For instance, a pluralist view of democracy, which emphasizes the dominant role of competitive elites, views the evidence of low voter turnout and citizen apathy as a minor concern. More partic-

continued

ipatory models, in contrast, interpret the same evidence as an indication of the crisis afflicting contemporary democratic practices.

In addition to this question of relevance, methodology makes explicit the game plan of research: how did the student conduct his or her research? Why did he or she consider some information more relevant than others? Are there any gaps in the information? Does the writer distinguish cases in which evidence *strongly supports* a claim from evidence that is *suggestive* or *speculative?*

Finally, students need to be aware of the possible ideological nature of evidence. For instance, Americans typically seek to explain such problems as poverty in individualistic terms, a view consistent with our liberal heritage, rather than in terms of class structure as a Marxist would. Seeking the roots of poverty in individual behavior simply produces a particular kind of evidence different from that which would be produced if we began with the assumption that class structure plays a decisive influence in shaping individual behavior.

—G. Gambino, Professor of Political Science

As these comments suggest, it is always useful to try to figure out the methodological *how* behind the *what,* especially since methodology is always based in certain assumptions as opposed to others. And as both professors point out, evidence is always tentative and often short lived.

A useful example for thinking about evidence gathering in this context is Werner Heisenberg's famous formulation, the Uncertainty Principle. A theoretical physicist, Heisenberg hypothesized a subatomic particle orbiting the nucleus of an atom that could be observed only when it passed through a concentrated beam of light. At the instant of its illumination, however, the direction of the particle would necessarily be skewed by the beam. From this model, Heisenberg concluded that the act of observation invariably alters whatever is observed. This insight has made its way across the academic disciplines. In anthropology, for example, Clifford Geertz has written extensively on the ways that researchers into other cultures inevitably impose their own cultural assumptions onto their subjects (and then publish studies that influence subsequent researchers).

The challenge of determining what counts as evidence is also at issue when you start with a given problem or question and then must decide what you should look at. Say you are looking into the causes of child abuse. How do you decide what to look at? How do you even define what it is you are studying, since what conceivably constitutes child abuse now might have been considered normal child-rearing practices in the past? Or, staying within the field of sociology, suppose you are studying the causes of juvenile crime. What is the important evidence? In the past, the physical environment lay outside what sociologists usually considered, but what if the height of buildings in which juvenile crime occurs provides better data

continued

than the size of families? As this hypothetical example suggests, the relationship between cause and effect is always slippery, and the assumptions about what is and isn't evidence are potentially blinding.

The preferences of different disciplines for certain kinds of evidence notwithstanding, most professors share the conviction that the evidence you choose to present should not be one-sided. Our closing quotation is typical of professorial attitudes:

> Let's hear all the evidence: the good, the bad and the ugly. Students should not be made to feel that their papers are diminished by ambiguous, anomalous and contradictory evidence. They should learn to appreciate ambiguity, to accept that issues cannot always be nicely and neatly settled.

> —*J. Marshall, Professor of Economics*

ANALYZING EVIDENCE IN DEPTH

The more carefully you examine something, the more you will discover to say about it. But many writers (quite appropriately) believe that they don't have the space or the time to examine all of the pertinent data in depth, so they settle (perhaps inappropriately) for trying to cover everything a little. It is generally the case that such writers never develop their analysis past a superficial level. The remainder of the chapter offers a basic model for striking a compromise between coverage and depth that promotes writing analytically.

10 ON 1 VERSUS 1 ON 10

problem: *Insufficiently analyzed evidence about which the writer repeatedly makes the same general claim.*

solution: *It is generally better to make ten points on a single representative issue or example (10 on 1) than to make the same basic point about ten related issues or examples (1 on 10).*

The best way to enable yourself to say more about evidence is to narrow your focus. A paper built from detailed analysis of your most telling example is far more likely to take you to a good idea than a paper that keeps saying the same thing about a large number of examples.

Making ten points about your most telling example (10 on 1) is a fruitful alternative to repeatedly pointing to a similarity among ten related examples (1 on 10). (See Figure 7.1.) Certainly you need to examine more than one example in order to make a fair and accurate argument, but the problem with the method we are calling 1 on 10 is that it tries to cover too much ground and often ends by noticing little more than some general similarity that might be the starting point but should not be the final outcome of a paper. The number 10, we should add, is arbitrarily chosen. You could make 4 or 5 or 7 points. The important idea we intend 10 on 1 to communicate is that you should draw out as much meaning as possible from your best examples.

Say you were writing an essay on the role of faith in the biblical book of Exodus. You locate a number of examples that all point to the same conclusion: the Israelites falter because they cannot believe in an unseen God. Once most writers decide that all the evidence points to the same conclusion, they tend to stop really looking at the evidence. If you were to use all of your examples to repeatedly corroborate the same point, the repetition would deter you from exploring the evidence in more depth. Writing would then become not a matter of finding things

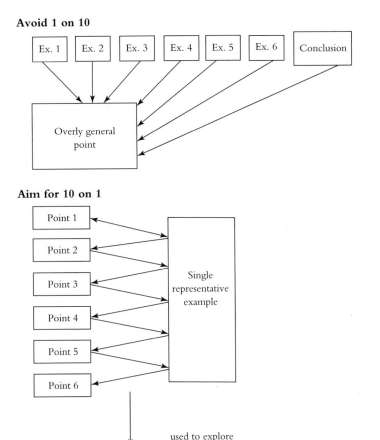

Figure 7.1   The horizontal pattern 1 on 10 (in which 10 stands arbitrarily for any number of examples) repeatedly makes the same point about every example; its analysis of evidence is superficial. The vertical pattern, 10 on 1 (in which 10 stands arbitrarily for any number of points), successively develops a series of points about a single, representative example; its analysis of evidence is in depth.

out or developing an idea but simply of dropping each example into place next to an unchanging conclusion. Rather than catalogue all of the instances of faltering faith, you would do better to scrutinize the most revealing instance. By drawing out its implications, you would more likely discover the questions and understand the issues that surround faith in Exodus—or any subject.

In a short paper (three to five pages), you might devote as much as 90 percent of your writing to illustrating what one example reveals about the larger subject. Even in a paper that uses several examples, however, as much as 50 percent might still be devoted to analysis of and generalization from a single case. The remaining half of the paper would make connections with other examples, testing and applying the ideas you arrived at from your single case. In-depth analysis of your best example thus creates a center from which you can move in two directions:

- Toward generalizations about the larger subject

- Toward other examples, using your primary example as a tool of exploration

Faced, for example, with writing a paper about the role slavery played in causing the Civil War, an inexperienced writer might offer a broad survey with a few paragraphs on abolitionism, a few paragraphs on various congressional attempts to legislate the slavery issue, and a few paragraphs on economic rivalries between the industrial North and the agrarian South. You could cover the same body of information in far more depth, however, by focusing almost entirely on the Missouri Compromise as a representative instance. Your analysis of this legislative battle would necessarily include discussion of the abolitionists' role and the economic interests of both parties, but it would do so within a tightly focused framework. Your assumption would be that if readers can see the collision of interests that led to this compromise and its failure, they will obtain a deeper understanding of the slavery issue than a survey could provide.

This same model, applicable across a wide variety of writing situations, can be reduced to a series of steps:

1. Narrow your focus.
2. Select a representative example.
3. Provide in-depth analysis (10 on 1).
4. Test your results in similar cases.

An analysis of the representation of blacks on television, for example, would fare better if you focused on one show—say, *Fresh Prince of Bel-Air*—narrowed the focus to comedies, and tested your results against other comedies, such as *The Cosby Show* and *Martin*. Similarly, a study of the national debt might focus on Social Security, working through specific evidence to arrive at generalizations to be tested and refined in the context, say, of health care or military spending. In sum, a close look at virtually anything will reveal its complexity, and you can bring that complex understanding to other examples for further testing and refining.

It is, of course, important to let your readers know that you are using the one primary example in this generalizable way. Note how the writer of the following discussion of the popular revolt in China in 1989 sets up his analysis. He first explains how his chosen example—a single photograph (Figure 7.2) from the media coverage of the event—illuminates his larger subject. The image is of a Chinese man in a white shirt who temporarily halted a line of tanks on their way to quell a demonstration in Tienanmen Square in Beijing.

> The tank image provided a miniature, simplified version of a larger, more complex revolution. The conflict between man and tank embodied the same tension found in the conflict between student demonstrators and the Peoples' Army. The man in the white shirt, like the students, displayed courage, defiance and rebellious individuality in the face of power. Initially, the peaceful revolution succeeded: the state allowed the students to protest; likewise, the tank spared the man's life. Empowered, the students' demands for democracy grew louder. Likewise, the man boldly jumped onto the tank and addressed the soldiers. The state's formerly unshakeable dominance appeared weak next to the strength of the individual. However, the state asserted its power: the Peoples' Army marched into the Square, and the tanks roared past the man into Beijing.
>
> The image appeals to American ideology. The man in the white shirt personifies the strength of the American individual. His rugged courage draws on contemporary heroes such as Rambo. His defiant gestures resemble the demonstrations of Martin Luther King Jr. and his followers. American history predisposes us to identify strongly with the Chinese demonstrators: we have rebelled against the establishment,

Figure 7.2   Tienanmen Square, Beijing, 1989

we have fought for freedom and democracy, and we have defended the rights of the individual. For example, the *New York Times* reported that President Bush watched the tank incident on television and said, "I'm convinced that the forces of democracy are going to overcome these unfortunate events in Tienanmen Square." Bush represents the popular American perspective of the Chinese rebellion; we support the student demonstrators.

This analysis is a striking example of 10 on 1. In the first paragraph, the writer constructs a detailed analogy between the particular image and the larger subject of which it was a part. The analogy allows the writer not just to describe but also to interpret the event. In the second paragraph, he develops his focus on the image as an image, a photographic representation tailor-made to appeal to American viewing audiences. Rather than generalizing about why Americans might find the image appealing, he establishes a number of explicit connections (10 on 1) between the details of the image and typical American heroes. By drawing out the implications of particular details, he manages to say more about the significance of the American response to the demonstrations in China than a broader survey of those events would have allowed. The rule of thumb here is to say more about less rather than less about more, allowing a carefully analyzed part of your subject to provide perspective on the whole.

DEMONSTRATE THE REPRESENTATIVENESS OF YOUR EXAMPLE

problem: *Generalizing on the basis of too little and unrepresentative evidence*

solution: *Survey the available evidence, and argue overtly for the representativeness of the examples on which you focus.*

One significant advantage of concentrating on your single, best example is its economy: you can cut quickly to the heart of a subject. But with this advantage comes a danger that the example you select will not in fact be representative. We have already mentioned the importance, when focusing on a single example (10 on 1), of selecting an example that is representative, but that's not the same thing as overtly demonstrating its representativeness. You need, in other words, to show that your example is part of a larger pattern of similar evidence and not an isolated instance.

In logical terms, the problem of generalizing from too little and unrepresentative evidence is known as an *unwarranted inductive leap.* That is, the writer leaps from one or two instances to a broad claim about an entire class or category. For example, because your economics professor and your biology professor wear corduroy jackets, you should not leap to the conclusion that all professors wear corduroy jackets.

The surest way you can guard against the problem of unwarranted inductive leaps is by reviewing the range of possible examples to make certain that the ones you choose to focus on are representative. If you were writing about faith in Exodus, for example, you might suggest the general trend by briefly mentioning instances in which the Israelites have difficulty believing in an unseen God. Then you could concentrate on the best example.

Not all illogical leaps are easy to spot. Here is a brief example from a writer who makes an unwarranted inductive leap:

> Some people feel that rock music videos are purely sexist propaganda, and they stereotype women as sex objects. I feel this is a generalization, and far from the truth. Many types of videos exist, a lot of which show no women in them at all. Others do contain women and could be considered sexist only if you choose to look at them from that point of view.

The writer of this paragraph next offers three examples in support of her generalization that rock videos do not stereotype women as sex objects. One video consists entirely of concert footage. In another the lead singer hugs and kisses his mother. Of the third, which shows a female passenger in a Jaguar who tries to get the attention of the male singer, who is driving, the writer asserts, "If anyone is being presented as the sex object, it is he."

Clearly, this writer is trying to correct an overgeneralization that all rock videos are sexist in their depiction of women, but her argument falls prey to the same kind of overgeneralization. Her sample is too small. Three examples of videos that do not depict women as sex objects constitute too small a sample to dismiss the charge of sexism. Her sample is also too selective. It does not confront examples that would challenge her point of view, examples that an opponent might use to prove that videos *do* stereotype women as sex objects. In other words, she avoids the difficult evidence, deliberately picking videos that may well be exceptions to the rule and then arguing that they are the rule.

Most of the time unwarranted leaps result from making too large a claim and avoiding examples that might contradict it. As a rule, you should *deliberately seek out the single piece of evidence that might most effectively oppose your point of view, and address it.* Doing so will prompt you to test the representativeness of your evidence and, in many cases, to qualify the claims you have made for it. The writer of the rock video example, for instance, can argue on the basis of three videos for a more limited version of her claim—that the representation of men and their relationship to women in rock videos is more varied and complex than the charge of sexism has allowed. In sum, if you select more complicated examples, or actively search out complication in evidence that at first seems simple and obvious, then you will be less likely to use unrepresentative examples to arrive at a claim that does not respond to the full range of relevant evidence.

In some cases, the conventions of a discipline would appear to discourage 10 on 1. The social sciences in particular tend to require a larger set of analogous examples to prove a hypothesis. Especially in certain kinds of research, the focus of inquiry rests on discerning broad statistical trends over a wide range of evidence. The inexperienced writer is likely to obey this disciplinary convention by providing a list of unanalyzed examples. But some trends deserve more attention than others, and some statistics similarly merit more interpretation than others. The best writers learn to choose examples carefully—each one for a reason—and to concentrate on developing the most revealing ones in depth; the interpretive and statistical models are not necessarily opposed to one another.

For instance, proving that tax laws are prejudiced in particularly subtle ways against unmarried people might require a number of analogous cases, along with a statistical summary of the evidence. But even with a subject such as this, you could still concentrate on some examples more than others. Rather than moving through each example as a separate case, you could use your analyses of these primary examples as *lenses* for investigating other evidence.

PAN, TRACK, AND ZOOM: THE FILM ANALOGY

The language of filmmaking offers a useful analogy for understanding the different ways that a writer can focus evidence. The writer, like the director of a film, controls the focus through three basic kinds of shots.

The Pan

The camera pivots around a stable axis, giving the viewer the "big picture." Using a pan, we see everything from a distance. Pans provide a context, the "forest" within which the writer can examine particular trees. Pans establish the representativeness of the example the writer examines in more detail, showing that it is not an isolated instance.

The Track

The camera no longer stays in one place but follows some sequence of action. For example, whereas a pan might survey a roomful of guests at a cocktail party, a track would follow a particular guest as she walks across the room, picks up a photograph, proceeds through the door, and throws the photo in a trash can. Analogously, a writer tracks by following selected pieces of the larger picture in order to make telling connections among them.

The Zoom

The camera moves in even closer on a selected piece of the scene, allowing us to notice more of its details. For example, a zoom might focus on the woman's hand as she crumples the photograph she's about to throw away, or on her face as she slams the lid on the trash can. A writer zooms by giving us more detail on a particular part of his or her evidence and by making the details say more. The zoom is the shot that enables you to do what we have been calling 10 on 1.

Extended Analysis

FLOOD STORIES: APPLYING THE FILM ANALOGY IN REVISION

The following student paper (about the recurrence of flood stories in religious texts and myth) shows what happens when a writer does not use the zoom. The paper is a workable first draft; it assembles some well-chosen evidence to support claims and generate conclusions. But, typical of the 1 on 10 pattern, the paper views everything from one relatively unrevealing distance. In our discussion of the paper, we will show how the writer could use zooms to test and refine his ideas rather than merely attaching the same basic point to each of his examples. (We use brackets and ellipses, [. . .], to indicate where we have abridged the essay.)

FLOOD STORIES

1   The role of man, as reflected in Genesis, Ovid's *Metamorphoses,* and the *Epic of Gilgamesh,* is solely to please the gods. Men, as the gods' subordinates, exist to do right in the gods' eyes and make them feel more like gods; for without men, whom could the gods be gods of? [. . .]

2   In Genesis, for example, God created man in his own image or likeness, and when men displeased Him, He destroyed them. If God could see wickedness in His creations, perhaps it was like seeing wickedness in himself. Further, the idea of having evidence of God being able to create an imperfect, "wicked" race of humans may have been a point God wasn't willing to deal with.

> The Lord saw that the wickedness of man was great in the earth, and that every imagination of the thoughts of his heart was only evil continually. And the Lord was sorry that he had made man on the earth and it grieved him to his heart.

It seems as though God had become unhappy with His creations so they were to be destroyed. Like a toy a child no longer has use for, man was to be wasted.

3   Similarly, in Ovid's *Metamorphoses,* God made man and "fashioned it into the image of the all-governing gods." Again here, man was made in the gods' image to serve as an everlasting monument of their glorification, to honor them and do good by them. In other words, men spent less time making the gods happy and therefore made them unhappy. Some men even questioned the reality of the gods' existence and the strength of their power. Lyacon, for example, had a driving tendency to try to belittle the gods and make them look like fools. The gods were very displeased with this trend, and now the entire race had to be destroyed. A flood would be sent to wipe out the race of men.

4   [The writer summarizes several examples in which the wicked are destroyed and a few upstanding citizens are preserved and arrives at the following conclusion:] Thus, the justification of yet another flood to appease the gods' egos.

5   Further evidence of man as being a mere whim of the gods to make them happy lies in the flood story in the *Epic of Gilgamesh.* It is obvious the gods weren't concerned with mankind, but rather with their own comfort. As the story goes, Enlil, the god of earth, wind, and air, couldn't bear the noise humans were making while he tried to sleep, so he gathered all the gods together, and thus they jointly decided to get rid of their grief of having all the humans around by destroying them. Ea [the god of wisdom], however, warned one man (Utnapishtim) of the flood to come. He told him to build a boat for himself and his wife and for the "seeds of all living creatures." [. . .]

6   Enlil later repented the harshness of his actions, deified Utnapishtim and his wife and then had the two live far away "on the distance of the mouths' rivers." It possibly could have been belittling to have Utnapishtim and his wife speaking to the new race of humans in terms of how rash and mindlessly the gods were capable of acting, so he immortalized them and had them live far out of the reach of man's ears—"the secret of the gods."

7   It seems that the main objective of the gods was to remain gods; for that is what made them happy. And man's role, then, was as the gods' stepping stone to their happiness. [. . .] Witnessing the fall of man, for the gods, was like witnessing imperfection in themselves, and thus their fall; anything causing these feelings didn't do the gods any good and therefore could be terminated without a second thought. It was man's job to make the gods happy, and upon failure at this task, man could be "fired" [death], only to be replaced later—it wasn't a position which the gods could hold vacant for long. Thus were the great flood stories.

In terms of the film analogy, the writer of this essay starts with a pan on the "big picture." Panning on all three stories allows him to discover similarities among his blocks of evidence and to demonstrate that the examples he has chosen are representative of his generalization—his *claim*—that in all three flood stories men exist "solely to please the gods." The writer then constructs a series of tracks, summaries of each of the three stories that isolate some interesting parallels for readers to ponder. The problem is that, rather than allowing his tracks to set up zooms, the writer returns again and again to versions of his original pan. The result is a 1 on 10 paper in which the writer sees, in effect, only what he wants to see—opportunities to repeatedly match the evidence to his one governing claim.

What's wrong, you might ask, with showing how the evidence fits the claim? Isn't this what writers are supposed to do? The answer is that you do want to use evidence to show that your claims have validity, but not in so general a way. The writer of the flood essay devotes much more space to repeating his central claim than he does to actually looking at his evidence. Because he never analyzes any one of his examples in detail (in the way a zoom would allow), he generalizes too quickly and too broadly, becoming blinded by similarity.

If evidence is used repeatedly to support the same overly general claim, there is no evolution of understanding. Look what happens, for example, in the writer's second paragraph. The evidence in that paragraph is a passage quoted from Genesis in which God sees "the wickedness of man" and "was sorry that he had made man . . . and it grieved him to his heart." The writer doesn't overtly say anything about the specific content of this quotation. Instead, he locates it after an opening claim, that

> God created man in his own image or likeness. . . . If God could see wickedness in His creations, perhaps it was like seeing wickedness in himself . . . [that He] wasn't willing to deal with.

This claim echoes the paper's thesis that humans exist solely to please the gods, but it also contains a potentially provocative speculation: that God wants to destroy man as a way of escaping the evidence of his own potential wickedness. This idea, which might have led him to an interpretation of God in Genesis as being complexly motivated (even repressed?), remains buried.

When evidence is forced to fit a static thesis, inconsistencies that would be at least interesting and possibly informative are lost. The writer follows the quotation from Genesis in the second paragraph with a brief paraphrase and then a comparison that contains a second claim:

> God had become unhappy with His creations so they were to be destroyed. Like a toy a child no longer has use for, man was to be wasted.

It is here that the writer allows the 1 on 10 pattern to rush his thinking and distract him from his evidence. Depicting man as God's toy may accurately describe Enlil, the god in *Gilgamesh* who, as we are later told, decides to get rid of humans because they make too much noise. But it does not fit the God of Genesis described in the evidence that the writer has quoted immediately prior to this claim. That "the wickedness of man . . . grieved him to his heart" would seem to reveal God's decision to flood the earth as wrenchingly ethical rather than child-ishly selfish and rash. And that "every imagination of the thoughts of [man's] heart was only evil continually" would seem to suggest that humans were not simply victims of divine prerogative, but rather that they deserved punishment. It is revealing that the writer's paraphrase of the evidence has left out these two key passages, since they are inconsistent with his thesis.

The writer doesn't consider these other possible interpretations because his reliance on pans—the general pattern—has predisposed him to see his evidence only as another sign of the gods' egotism, their desire to remain "happy" at any cost. Pressed by the desire to "match" examples to his one governing idea, the writer is not allowing himself to really examine his evidence. Thus, he is not pre-pared to deal with potentially significant differences among his examples.

Zooms give you the space and time to lay out and interpret more of the relevant facts in your evidence. They are one of your best means of avoiding overgeneralization and of locating implications that could help you to better develop your ideas. The writer of the flood essay might be reluctant to give up on his promising observa-tion that the flood stories, which recur in surprisingly parallel forms in different cultures, can be explained by the gods' desire to eliminate self-reflections that cause them to feel unhappy with themselves. Rather than having to throw out this thinking, the writer should consider (as is almost always the case in revision) that he hasn't refined it enough. As an interpretation of the evidence, his claim leaves too many things unaccounted for. To put it another way, the writer needs to see that what he took to be a reasonable "answer" is only a partial and inade-quately qualified theory about his evidence.

So how might the writer make better use of the evidence he has collected? In brief, he needs at least one carefully developed zoom. He should either examine one of the stories in more detail and refine his conclusions through comparison and contrast with the others, or he should pursue in more detail (zoom in on) what he takes to be the single most interesting aspect that the three stories share.

As the writer of the flood paper reexamines his draft and his evidence, he might look for the most promising zoom by having a conversation with himself that might sound something like this:

"What can I say with some certainty about my evidence?"

"Well, in all three of these stories, a first civilization created by a god is destroyed by the same means—a flood."

(Notice, by the way, that this is a factual reporting of the evidence rather than a speculation about it. You are always better off to state the facts in your evidence carefully and fully before moving to conclusions.)

"What else is certain about the evidence?"

"In each case the gods leave a surviving pair to rebuild the civilization rather than just wiping everybody out and inventing a new kind of being. Interestingly, the gods begin again by choosing from the same stock that failed the first time around."

Mulling over the evidence in this way, taking care to lay out the facts and distinguish them from speculation, will tell you what to zoom in on. One of the chief advantages of zooms is that they get you in close enough to your evidence to see the questions its details imply. So far, the writer of the flood paper has worked mostly from two quite general questions: Why did the gods decide to wipe out their creations? And why do the gods need human beings? But there are other questions his evidence requires him to ask. In each story, for example, the gods are disappointed by humankind, and yet they don't invent submissive robots who will dedicate their lives to making the deities feel good about themselves. Why not? This question might cause the writer to zoom in on a shared feature of his examples, the surviving pairs, especially since the existence of these pairs significantly complicates a part of his thesis.

Zooms can achieve the breadth of generalization at a new depth by focusing on a shared feature of several examples. Having selected the surviving pairs for more detailed examination, the writer might conclude what about them? One interesting fact that the surviving pairs reveal is that the flood stories are not only descriptions of the end of a world but also creation accounts, since they also tell us how a new civilization, the existing one, got started. What might this fact imply? For one thing, it suggests considerable skepticism about the possibility of progress through either individual or social change. Problematic people are simply eliminated, suggesting that the stories present violent intervention from a higher power as the only means of achieving pervasive reform. And although the stories do have a more optimistic side—the prospect of new beginnings—they also remind us that the world is still populated by the same fallible species who brought it to destruction once before. These implications about surviving pairs and creation accounts advance and complicate the writer's original thesis. The writer might proceed by investigating the differences in the fates of the survival pairs, thereby developing his interpretation still further.

LOOK FOR DIFFERENCE WITHIN SIMILARITY

Our revision suggestions for the flood paper were guided by a principle that we call "looking for difference within similarity." This is a two-step process:

1. Use similarity to locate a limited pool of evidence that will usually be rich in implication because it suggests larger trends or underlying patterns.
2. Analyze the significance of differences within the larger similarity. Figuring out the significance of the difference is an effective way to avoid plugging in the same "answer" (a general similarity) again and again.

As a rule, if you find yourself repeatedly making the same general point about a series of examples, develop that idea by looking for examples that are similar but not virtually identical. By analyzing significant differences, you will be building on and revising your idea—rather than just repeating it—as you move through evidence.

The writer of the flood essay has accomplished the first of these two steps effectively. He has discerned a pattern common to several flood stories, composed a set of shared characteristics (such as the use of the floods to destroy human beings), and drafted a general explanation (the destructions were motivated by the gods' self-serving reactions). Stopping at this point, however, left him blinded by similarity and proving an overly general point.

A potentially significant difference implicit in the flood paper's pool of evidence involves the survival pair (and seed carriers) in the story of *Gilgamesh,* who are segregated from the new world and granted immortality. So what? Perhaps this separation suggests that the new civilization will not be haunted by the painful memory of a higher power's intervention, leaving humans less fearful of what might happen in the future. This distinction could focus the argument in the essay; it does not distract from the writer's overall generalization but rather develops it.

The principle of looking for difference within similarity is a common strategic move in analytical writing. To take one more quick example: in Irish studies, scholars characteristically acknowledge the extent to which contemporary Irish culture is the product of colonization. To this extent, Irish culture shares certain traits with other former colonies in Africa, Asia, Latin America, and elsewhere. But instead of simply demonstrating how Irish culture fits the general pattern of colonialism, these scholars isolate and analyze the particular ways that Ireland fits and does not fit the model—how, for example, its proximity and racial similarity to England, its colonizer, have distinguished the kinds of problems it encounters today.

FACING THE FEAR

As this chapter began by suggesting, your ability to discover ideas and improve on them in revision depends largely on your attitude toward evidence. And so we've spoken throughout the chapter about thinking of evidence as a means of testing and developing your ideas rather than just confirming and reasserting them. What we have not yet fully acknowledged is a fear that writers sometimes express about acknowledging significant differences and potential contradictions in their evidence. This fear commonly takes two forms:

1. The fear of losing readers by including evidence that might encourage them to reject or lose track of the writer's point of view
2. The fear that recognizing contradictions and complications in the evidence might cancel out all of a writer's potential ideas, leaving him or her with nothing to say

The "Guidelines" section that follows provides advice for negotiating these quite reasonable fears, but there are no easy antidotes.

In regard to quelling the first fear, you need to realize that avoiding evidence that doesn't easily fit with your thesis will not make that evidence go away. If your readers know of evidence that might challenge your ideas, but you fail to address it, the credibility of your argument will be damaged far more than if you had brought up that awkward evidence yourself and tried to account for it. In regard to quelling the second fear, if you are worried that acknowledging complications in your evidence will cancel out your ideas, you need to understand that qualifying or limiting your claim is an advantage, not a liability. The resulting claim, though smaller in scope, will be more accurate and therefore stronger.

More generally, it might help to realize that evidence is often (and perhaps usually) *suggestive* rather than *conclusive*. In the realm of analysis, there are precious few smoking guns and absolutely reliable eyewitnesses. When there are, you have an open-and-shut case that probably does not need proving. Most analysis is a matter of assembling evidence circumstantially.

Our premise, then, is that there are a variety of ways of assembling evidence to arrive at different conclusions. Think of evidence as stars and of analysis as the means by which those stars may be connected into constellations. Writers are invariably constelling evidence, and the challenge, given that a star can be a part of more than one constellation, comes in drawing the lines that connect the stars.

In any case, if you make a point of substantiating your claims, of showing the logic by which you moved from the evidence to the claim, and of acknowledging the possibility of other explanations, you will almost surely arrive at a plausible interpretation. Your readers may not agree with you, but they will be able neither to dismiss your point nor to attack your method.

GUIDELINES FOR ANALYZING EVIDENCE

1. Support your assertions with evidence. Locate the details that have led you to your conclusions.
2. Interpret the evidence for your readers, rather than leaving examples to speak for themselves. Make details speak.
3. Make explicit what is implicit in both your evidence and your claims.
4. State the connection between the evidence and the claims, rather than just putting the evidence next to the claims. Explain how each example supports, refines, or extends the point you are making.
5. Allow your evidence to shape your claim, rather than trying to force the evidence to fit a preconceived and overly broad generalization.
6. Give yourself the chance to discover a workable idea by narrowing your focus. Say more about less rather than less about more, allowing a carefully analyzed part of your subject to provide perspective on the whole.
7. It is generally better to make ten points on a representative issue or example than to make the same basic point about ten related issues or examples.
8. When writing about a number of examples, explore the significant differences among them, rather than just pointing to a general similarity.
9. Use your best example as a lens through which to examine other evidence. Your analysis of subsequent examples should test and develop the conclusions derived from your best example, rather than just confirming that you are right.
10. Argue overtly that the examples on which you focus are representative. Be careful not to generalize on the basis of too little or unrepresentative evidence.
11. To test the representativeness of your evidence and qualify your claims, seek out and address the single piece of evidence that most effectively opposes your point of view.

USING SOURCES

SECONDARY SOURCES ARE A FORM OF EVIDENCE

SINCE THE USE OF secondary sources is a special case of the use of evidence, the strategies for analyzing sources resemble those we offered in the preceding chapter on analyzing evidence. As with factual examples, where you need to make the details speak, in using sources you need to make the secondary materials speak. Clarify the meaning of the material you have quoted or paraphrased, and explain its significance in light of your evolving thesis. In other words, be overt about why you have bothered to quote (or paraphrase or summarize) in the first place.

Many inexperienced writers have difficulty using secondary materials because they believe that once they have introduced what the experts have said, they need no longer speak themselves. Such writers characteristically make a generalization in their own words and then juxtapose it to an illustrative quotation and assume the meaning of the quotation will be self-evident. This practice not only leaves the connection between the writer's thinking and his or her source material unstated, but it also substitutes mere repetition of someone else's viewpoint for a more active interpretation. The source offers the final word, stopping the discussion and the writer's thinking.

The risk of using sources uncritically does not mean that you should ignore them altogether. *A writer needs to find the middle ground between developing an idea independent of what experts have written on a subject and producing a paper that does nothing but repeat other people's ideas.* The writer who does not consult what others have said may omit viewpoints that are crucial to understanding his or her subject. By remaining unaware of existing thinking, he or she in effect chooses to stand outside of the conversation that others interested in the subject are having. Standing in this sort of intellectual vacuum sometimes appeals to inexperienced writers who fear that consulting sources will leave them with nothing to say. But it is possible, as this chapter shows, to learn what others have had to say without allowing your sources to do all of your thinking for you.

THE CONVERSATION ANALOGY

The first step in using sources effectively—neither discounting nor overrelying on them—is to reject the assumption that sources provide final and complete answers. If they did, there would be no reason for others to continue writing on the subject. As in conversation, we raise ideas for others to respond to. Accepting that no source has the final word does not mean, however, that you should shift from unquestioning approval to the opposite pole and necessarily assume an antagonistic position toward all sources. Indeed, a habitually antagonistic response to others' ideas is just as likely to bring your conversation with your sources to a halt as the habit of always assuming that the source must have the final word.

Most people would probably agree on the attributes of a really good conversation. There is room for agreement and disagreement, for give and take, among a variety of viewpoints. Generally, people don't deliberately misunderstand each other, but a significant amount of the discussion may go into clarifying one's own as well as others' positions. Such conversations construct a genuinely collaborative *chain* of thinking: Karl builds on what David has said, which induces Jill to respond to Karl's comment and so forth.

There are, of course, obvious differences between conversing aloud with friends and conversing on paper with sources. As a writer, you must construct the chain of thinking, orchestrate the exchange of views with and among your sources, and give the conversation direction and point. A good place to begin in using sources is to recognize that you need not respond to everything another writer says, nor do you need to come up with an entirely original point of view— one that completely revises or refutes the source. You are performing analysis, for example, when you note that two experiments (or historical accounts or whatever) are similar but have different priorities, or that they ask similar questions in different ways. Building from this kind of observation, you could then analyze what these differences imply.

There are, in any case, a variety of ways of approaching sources, but they generally share a common goal: *to use the source as a point of departure.* Here is a brief list of how to use sources in this way:

- Make as many points as you can about a single representative passage, and then branch out from this center to analyze other passages that "speak" to it in some way. (See Chapter 7, the section "10 on 1 versus 1 on 10.")

- Build upon the source's point of view, extending its implications.

- Apply the idea in the source to another subject.

- Agree with most of what the source says, but take issue with one small part that you want to modify.

- Identify a contradiction in the source and explore its implications, without necessarily arriving at a solution.

If you quote with the aim of conversing with your sources rather than allowing them to do your thinking for you, you will discover that sources can promote rather than stifle your analysis. In short, think of sources not as answers but as voices inviting you into a community of interpretation, discussion, and debate.

Before continuing our treatment of how to converse with sources, let us first address a few underlying questions. Why should you use sources at all? When should you consult them? What kinds of sources should you consult? Then we will focus on integrating sources (especially quotations) into your own prose and acknowledging that you've used them. The final section of this chapter returns to strategies, with examples, for conversing analytically with your sources.

WHY USE SOURCES AT ALL?

Why use sources at all? The simple answer is to increase your pool of information. It's obviously a good idea to get some notion of what people are saying about a subject before you join in. After all, the conversation has already been going on out there for a long time. The danger in using sources, of course, is that you can lose track of your own ideas. Confronted with the seasoned views of experts in a discipline, you may well feel that there is nothing left for you to say because it has all been said before. (This anxiety explains why so many writers surrender to the role of conduit for the voices of the experts, providing conjunctions between quotations.)

A good rule of thumb is to formulate a tentative position before you consult sources. In other words, give yourself time to do some preliminary thinking. A particularly useful strategy is to prewrite about the topic, analyzing some piece of pertinent information already at your disposal. That way you will have in writing your initial responses to weigh against what others have said. Prewriting of this sort also helps you to select what to look at in the sources you eventually consult.

On balance, the argument for consulting sources far outweighs the one for avoiding them. The risks in not doing any research, in other words, are more severe than being overwhelmed by others' ideas. However daunting it may be to have to find something to say about the sources, you generally cannot take the risk of pretending they don't exist. The risk is twofold: (1) You will waste your time reinventing the wheel, or (2) you will undermine your analysis (or at least leave it incomplete) by not considering information or acknowledging positions that are commonly discussed in the field. A little research—even if it's only an hour's browse in the reference collection of the library—will virtually always raise the level of what you have to say above what it would have been if you had consulted only the information and opinions that you carry around in your head.

Voices from Across the Curriculum

FINDING SOURCES

A useful research technique is to begin in the reference and periodical section of your library rather than beginning with books. Most scholarly journals have an index in the last issue for each year. Listed alphabetically by author, subject, or title are articles for a given year. Also, you may want to use any number of indexes. Here you look up a key word or phrase (of your choosing) and the index tells you when, what, where, etc. for the word/phrase. Some of the key indexes are: *Social Science Index*, *Wall Street Journal Index* (for *WSJ* stories), *New York Times Index* (for *NYT* stories), and *The Public Affairs Information Service*.

—*F. Norling, Professor of Business*

The advice that this professor offers can help you to be efficient. If you start with specialized dictionaries, abstracts, and bibliographies, you can rapidly gain both a broad perspective on your subject and a summary of what particular sources contain. This is the purpose of the reference room: to review and summarize material for you in shorthand forms. Inexperienced writers generally waste time and effort by starting with the card catalogue.

Ask your reference librarian to direct you to the printed and on-line *indexes, bibliographies, specialized dictionaries,* and compilations of *abstracts* that are pertinent to your subject or discipline. These tools vary in their scope and in the information they contain. An index offers a list of titles directing you to scholarly journals; often this list is sufficient to give you a clearer idea of the kinds of topics about which writers in the field are conversing. More information is provided by compilations of abstracts and annotated bibliographies—usually a few sentences that summarize each source. Specialized dictionaries are sometimes extraordinarily useful in sketching the general terrain for a subject, and they often include bibliographical leads as well. Finally, book review indices can direct you to how others in a particular field have evaluated a given book. If, for example, a given book seems to have said everything there is to say, a few book reviews can be invaluable in helping you to develop a different point of view toward the book in question.

Once you leave the reference room, an effective next step in finding sources is to consult periodicals and journals, which are generally more up to date and concise than books. In any case, you should take care not to get bogged down in one author's book-length argument until you've achieved a wider view of how other sources treat your subject.

Whether you are working in the reference room or at the library's book catalogue, don't be surprised if the subject headings you type in initially yield nothing.

A critical part of the bibliographic effort is to find a topic on which there are materials. Most topics can be researched. The key is to choose a flexible key-

continued

word/phrase and then try out different versions of it. For example, a bibliography on Women in Management might lead you to look up Women, Females, Business (women in), Business (females in), Gender in the workplace, Sexism and the workplace, Careers (of men, of women, in business), Women and CEOs, Women in management, Affirmative Action and women, Women in corporations, Female accountants, and so on. Be imaginative and flexible. A little bit of time with some of the indexes listed above will provide you with a wealth of sources.

—F. Norling, Professor of Business

If you are using the subject headings section of a computerized library catalogue, you should first check to see what the Library of Congress heading would be for your subject. An index of these headings is usually available at the reference desk. It will tell you, for example, that fraternities and sororities are listed not under "fraternities and sororities," but under "Greek letter organizations."

Once you've begun to find source materials, your next task is to find a way of choosing among them. It's important to avoid sources that for one reason or another are viewed by members of your discipline as insufficiently rigorous.

Use quality psychological references. That is, use references professional psychologists use and regard highly. *Psychology Today* is not a good reference; *Newsweek* and *Reader's Digest* are worse. And don't even think about *The National Enquirer.* APA journals, such as the *Journal of Abnormal Psychology,* on the other hand, are excellent.

In looking for reference material, be sure to search under several headings. For example, look under "depression," "affective disorders," and "mood disorders."

Books (e.g., *The Handbook of Affective Disorders*) are often very helpful, especially for giving a general overview of a topic. Books addressing a professional audience are generally preferable to those addressing a general, popular audience.

Finally, references should be reasonably current. In general, the newer the better. For example, with rare exceptions (classic articles), articles from before 1970 are outdated and so should not be used.

—A. Tjeltveit, Professor of Psychology

We might generalize a rule from this professor's final comment: *start in the present and work backward.* Usually the most current materials will include bibliographical citations that can help you identify the most important sources in the past. We would also note that *Newsweek* can be a useful source if you want evidence about popular understanding of a subject or issue; in this case, the fact that the material comes from *Newsweek* provides the central reason for citing it. As we discussed in Chapter 7, the evidence is always qualified by the frame.

Voices from Across the Curriculum

CITING SOURCES

There are three ways of incorporating material from sources into your own text—summary, paraphrase, and quotation—and all three require citation. *Summarizing* condenses the information (often radically); *paraphrasing* restates the material in your own words; and *quotation* preserves it exactly as you found it in the source. In all three cases, since the information or ideas did not originate with you, it is *plagiarism* if you do not openly acknowledge the source. To do otherwise is misleading and dishonest.

From the early years of their schooling, most students have been lectured on the unethical nature of plagiarism, so we won't belabor the issue. You need to include a source citation unless the information or ideas are common knowledge (for example, the American Revolution was fought to free the colonies from England's economic and political domination; the technique of electrophoresis can separate various proteins from a given bacterium). If you're unsure whether a given fact or viewpoint is common knowledge, you're better off including a citation.

Another important reason for giving credit where it's due is that these references provide a courtesy to your readers. Citations enable them to find out more about a given position and to pursue other conversations on the subject. Along these lines, it is important to identify your source (make an attribution) *within* the text of your paper as well as in the parenthetical citation that follows your quotation or summary.

Provide sources (reference citations) for the factual claims you make, especially for specific information you obtain from a particular source and include in your paper. Make it clear which idea or information comes from which source. Where possible, integrate references into the structure of the paragraph (rather than listing sources at the end of the paragraph).

Also, as a general rule, you should not use as a reference any sources (a) for which you have read only the abstract, or (b) which you have not read but which are cited in a source you have read.

—*A. Tjeltveit, Professor of Psychology*

In other words, when you introduce a source, word that introduction so that readers can easily distinguish between what the source is saying and what you are saying. When you are including information from several sources, it is especially important that you attribute this information when you introduce it; otherwise, readers will encounter a series of citations at the end of a paragraph and will be bewildered about which information comes from which source.

SIX TECHNIQUES FOR
INTEGRATING QUOTATIONS INTO YOUR PAPER

Integrating quotations into a paper is a technical matter that obeys a few basic rules, each of which is discussed briefly and exemplified next.

TECHNIQUE 1: ACKNOWLEDGE SOURCES IN YOUR TEXT,
NOT JUST IN CITATIONS

When you incorporate material from a source, attribute it to the source explicitly in your text—not just in a citation. In other words, when you introduce the material, frame it with a phrase such as "according to Marsh" or "as Cartelli argues." Such attributions are not required if you have cited the source within parentheses or with a footnote at the end of the last sentence you have quoted, paraphrased, or summarized. You are, however, usually much better off making the attribution overtly as well. If a passage does not contain an attribution, your readers will not know that it comes from a source until they reach the citation at the end. Attributing up front clearly distinguishes what one source says from what another says and, perhaps more important, what your sources say from what you say. Useful verbs for introducing attributions include the following: *notes, observes, argues, comments, writes, says, reports, suggests,* and *claims.* Note: Generally speaking, you should cite the author by last name only—as Cartelli, not Thomas Cartelli and not Mr. Cartelli.

TECHNIQUE 2: SPLICE QUOTATIONS ONTO YOUR OWN WORDS

Always attach quotations to some of your own language; don't let them sit in your text as independent sentences with quotation marks around them. You can normally satisfy this rule with an attributive phrase introducing the quotation—"As Bloom suggests, . . ." Alternatively, you can splice quotations into your text with a colon. For example:

> Patrick Henry's famous phrase is one of the first that American schoolchildren memorize: "Give me liberty, or give me death."

(Note that in this usage, the material that precedes the colon is normally an independent clause.) The rationale for this rule is essentially the same as for the previous one. If you are going to move to a quotation, you first need to identify its author so that your readers will be able to put it in context quickly.

TECHNIQUE 3: SPLICE QUOTATIONS IN A WAY THAT IS
GRAMMATICALLY CORRECT

Make sure that the quotation obeys the grammar of the sentence to which it is spliced. You obviously don't want to commit a grammatical error, and, in many cases, such an error will render the sentence incoherent. Suppose, for example, you want to use at least a part of the following quotation:

> Where contemporaries like Wordsworth and Coleridge found their subject matter in a direct contemplation of the natural world, Keats was never more interested in nature than when it was mediated through art, through the words or pictures or statuary of other artists (Scott xi).

You would not want to preface this quotation with an opening such as "In Keats's 'Ode on a Grecian Urn,' the urn illustrates." Try to read such a sentence:

> In Keats's "Ode on a Grecian Urn," the urn illustrates, says Scott, "where contemporaries like Wordsworth and Coleridge found their subject matter in a direct contemplation of the natural world, Keats was never more interested in nature than when it was mediated through art, through the words or pictures or statuary of other artists (xi).

The splicing here is awkward and misleading. Scott is not referring explicitly to the ode, but the sentence suggests that the urn is an example of where the other poets find their subject matter.

There are various ways to insert quoted material smoothly and correctly into your sentences. We illustrate a few of these below, using revised versions of the prefatory statement about the urn.

Example 1

> As is evident in his treatment of the urn in "Ode on a Grecian Urn," Keats was, as Scott observes, "never more interested. . . ."

Here the lead-in moves effortlessly into the second half of the original quotation.

Example 2

> Keats's "Ode on a Grecian Urn" illustrates the poet's tendency, as Scott notes, "never [to be] more interested. . . ."

To maintain the grammatical fluency in the splicing above, it is necessary to add words inside square brackets. The brackets indicate that you are doing this editing. Brackets are also used when you insert explanatory information, such as a definition or example, within a quotation.

Example 3

> As Scott has suggested, poems by Wordsworth and Coleridge find "their subject matter in a direct contemplation of the natural world," unlike Keats, who, in poems such as "Ode on a Grecian Urn," "was never more interested. . . ."

This version inserts pieces of the original quotation in two places in the sentence. Note that only the second insertion ("was never more interested") is preceded by a comma, because grammar requires it. It is a common misconception that a comma always precedes a quotation.

TECHNIQUE 4: USE ELLIPSES TO SHORTEN QUOTATIONS

Use ellipsis points to shorten quotations. These marks—typed as three dots with spaces around them—indicate that you have omitted words from within the quotation. Four dots indicate that the deletion continues to the end of the sentence (the fourth dot being a period). The example below illustrates both uses of ellipsis marks, adding a sentence from later in Scott's paragraph.

> Keats's "Ode on a Grecian Urn" illustrates Scott's argument that "Keats was . . . more interested in nature . . . when it was mediated . . . through the words or pictures or statuary of other artists. . . . His best poetry is composed largely of representations of representations" (xi).

In most cases, the gap between quoted passages should be short, and in any case, you should be careful to preserve the sense of the original. The standard joke about ellipses is apposite here: a reviewer writes that a film "will delight no one and appeal to the intelligence of invertebrates only, but not average viewers." An unethical advertiser cobbles together pieces of the review to say that the film "will delight . . . and appeal to the intelligence of . . . average viewers."

TECHNIQUE 5: CITE SOURCES AFTER QUOTATIONS

Locate citations in parentheses after the quotation and before the final period. As shown in the citation of Scott above, the information about the source appears at the end of the sentence, with the final period following the closing parenthesis. There is normally no punctuation at the end of the quotation itself, either before or after the closing quotation mark. Quotations that end in question marks and exclamation points are exceptions to this rule, since these signs are an integral part of the quotation's meaning. For example: "As Hamlet says to Rosencrantz and Guildenstern, 'And yet to me what is this quintessence of dust?'" (2.2.304-05).

TECHNIQUE 6: USE A CITATION FORM APPROPRIATE TO THE DISCIPLINE

Use the form of citation appropriate to the discipline in which you are writing. In most academic writing, the division (humanities, social sciences, natural sciences) or the discipline (psychology) usually stipulates a particular citational form. Your best source on this matter is your professor and the specialized reference manual of the discipline in question. We have included in Appendix A extensive descriptions of the most commonly used citation formats: APA (American Psychological Association) and MLA (Modern Language Association). As the appendix demonstrates, the differences among the various formats are not limited to bibliographical citations. In APA form, for example, quotations of more than forty words should be indented to set them off from the text; in MLA form, quotations of more than three lines receive this treatment.

SIX STRATEGIES FOR
CRITICAL ANALYSIS OF SOURCES

Having addressed some of the basic issues in using sources—why and when to use them, where to find them, how to acknowledge them—we now return to our primary focus on how to use sources analytically. This section of the chapter is divided into strategies, each one followed by discussion and examples.

STRATEGY 1: MAKE YOUR SOURCES SPEAK

Quote, paraphrase, or summarize *in order to* analyze. Don't assume that either the meaning of the source material or your reason for including it is self-evident. Don't just string together citations for which you provide little more than conjunctions. You also need to explain to your readers what the quotation or paraphrase or summary of the source means. What elements of it do you want to emphasize? How does it relate to your evolving thesis?

In making sources speak, focus on articulating how the source has led to the conclusion you draw from it. Beware of simply putting a generalization and a quotation next to each other (juxtaposing them) without explaining the connection. Consider the following paragraph from a student's paper on political conservatism:

> Edmund Burke's philosophy evolved into contemporary American conservative ideology. There is an important distinction between philosophy and political ideology: philosophy is "the knowledge of general principles that explain facts and existences." Political ideology, on the other hand, is "an overarching conception of society, a stance that is reflected in numerous sectors of social life" (Edwards 22). Therefore, conservatism should be regarded as an ideology rather than a philosophy.

The final sentence offers the writer's conclusion—what the source information has led him to—but how did it get him there? The word "therefore" indicates to the reader that the conclusion is the result of a process of logical reasoning, but this reasoning has been omitted. Instead, the writer assumes that the reader will be able to connect the quotations with his conclusion. The writer needs to make the quotation speak. What is "an overarching conception of society," and how does it differ from "knowledge of general principles"? More important, why is it necessary or useful to categorize conservatism as either an ideology or a philosophy?

Here, by contrast, is a writer who makes her sources speak. Note how she integrates analysis with quotation:

> Stephen Greenblatt uses the phrase "self-fashioning" to refer to an idea he believes developed during the Renaissance—the idea that one's identity is not created or born but shaped, both by one's self and by others. The idea of self-fashioning is incorporated into an attitude toward literature which has as its ideal what Greenblatt calls "poetics of culture." A text is examined with three elements in mind: the author's own self, the cultural self-fashioning process which created that self, and the author's reaction to that process. Since our selves, like texts, are "fashioned," an author's life is just as open to interpretation as that of a literary character.
>
> If this is so, then biography does not provide a repository of unshakeable facts from which to interpret an author's work. Greenblatt criticizes the fact that the methods of literary interpretation are applied just to art and not to life. As he observes, "We wall off literary symbolism from the symbolic structures operative

elsewhere, as if art alone were a human creation." If the line between art and life is indeed blurred, then we need a more complex model for understanding the relationship between the life and work of an author.

In this example, we can see how the writer's thinking has been stimulated by the source. At the end of the first paragraph and the beginning of the second, for example, she not only specifies what she takes to be the meaning of the quotation but also draws a conclusion about its implications (that the facts of an author's life, like his or her art, require interpretation). And this manner of proceeding is habitual: the writer repeats the pattern in the second paragraph, moving beyond what the quotation says to explore what its logic suggests.

STRATEGY 2: USE YOUR SOURCES TO ASK QUESTIONS, NOT JUST TO PROVIDE ANSWERS

Avoid the temptation to plug in quotations as "answers" that require no further commentary or elaboration. Instead, use your selections from sources as a means of raising issues and questions. Ironically, it is perfectly reasonable to search sources for answers, provided that you don't use them as answers. In other words, in your source reading you will no doubt find viewpoints you believe to be valid, but it is not enough to drop these "answers" from the source into your own writing at the appropriate spots. You need to *do* something with the secondary material, even with those sources that seem to have said what you want to say.

As long as you only consider the source in isolation, you may not discover much to say about it. Once you begin considering it in other contexts and with other sources, you may begin to see aspects of your subject that your source does not adequately address. Having recognized that the source does not answer all questions, you should not conclude that the source is "wrong"—only that it is limited in some ways. More important, it is advantageous to find such limitations. Discovering areas of your subject that your source does not adequately address can lead you to identify a place from which to launch your own analysis.

It does not necessarily follow that you will then provide your own answer in place of one offered by a source. Often—in fact, far more often than most inexperienced writers suspect—it is enough to discover an issue or problem and raise it clearly. Phrasing *explicitly* the issues and questions that remain *implicit* in a source is an important part of what analytical writers do, especially with cases in which there is no solution, or at least none that can be presented in a relatively short paper. Here, for example, is how the writer on Stephen Greenblatt's concept of "self-fashioning" concludes her essay:

> It is not only the author whose role is complicated by New Historicism; the critic is subject to some of the same qualifications and restrictions. According to Adam Begley, "it is the essence of the new-historicist project to uncover the moments at which works of art absorb and refashion social energy, an endless process of circulation and exchange." In other words, the work is both affected by and has an effect on the culture. But if this is so, how then can we decide which elements of

culture (and text) are causes and which are effects? If we add the critic to this picture, the process does indeed appear endless. The New Historicists' relationship with their culture infuses itself into their assessment of the Renaissance, and this assessment may in turn become part of their own self-fashioning process, which will affect their interpretations, and so forth. . . .

Notice that this writer incorporates the quotation into her own chain of thinking. By paraphrasing the quotation ("In other words"), she arrives at a question ("how then") that follows as a logical consequence of accepting its position ("but if this is so"). Note, however, that she does not then label the quotation right or wrong. Instead, she tries to figure out *to what position it might lead* and to what possible problems.

By contrast, the writer of the following excerpt, from a paper comparing two films aimed at teenagers, settles for plugging in sources as answers and consequently does not pursue the questions implicit in her quotations.

> In both films, the adults are one-dimensional caricatures, evil beings whose only goal in life is to make the kids' lives a living hell. In *Risky Business,* director Paul Brickman's solution to all of Joel's problems is to have him hire a prostitute and then turn his house into a whorehouse. Of course, as one critic observes, "the prostitutes who make themselves available to his pimply faced buddies are all centerfold beauties: elegant, svelte, benign and unquestionably healthy (after all, what does V.D. have to do with prostitutes?)" (Gould 41)—not exactly a realistic or legal solution. Allan Moyle, the director of *Pump Up the Volume,* provides an equally unrealistic solution to Mark's problem. According to David Denby, Moyle "offers self-expression as the cure to adolescent funk. Everyone should start his own radio station and talk about his feelings" (59). Like Brickman, Moyle offers solutions that are neither realistic nor legal.

This writer is having a hard time figuring out what to do with sources that offer well-phrased and seemingly accurate answers ("self-expression as the cure to adolescent funk"). Her analysis of both quotations leads her to settle for the bland and undeveloped conclusion that films aimed at teenagers are "not . . . realistic"— an observation that most readers would already recognize as true. But unlike the writer of the previous example, she does not ask herself, *"if this is true, then what follows?"* Had she done so, she might, for example, have inquired how the illegality of the solutions is related to their unrealistic quality. (So what, for example, that the main characters in both films are not marginalized as criminals and made to suffer for their illegal actions, but celebrated as heroes? What different kinds of illegality do the two films apparently condone, and how might these be related to the different decades in which each film was produced?) Rather than use her sources to think with, the writer has simply used them to confirm an obvious generalization.

STRATEGY 3: CONVERSE WITH YOUR SOURCES

Rather than limiting yourself to agreeing or disagreeing with your sources, aim for conversation with and among them. Although it is not "wrong" to agree or disagree with your sources, it is wrong to see these as your only possible moves. You should also understand that although it is sometimes useful and perhaps even necessary to agree and disagree, these judgments should (1) always be *qualified* and (2) occur only *in certain contexts*.

Especially near the beginning of a paper, for example, a source can be extraordinarily helpful in orienting your readers for the discussion to follow. This practice of "framing the discussion" typically locates the writer either for or against some well-known point of view or frame of reference. That is, a source can succinctly summarize a position that you plan to develop, or it can present a series of statements that you can challenge. This latter strategy—sometimes known as a *straw man*, because you construct a "dummy" position specifically in order to knock it down—can stimulate you to formulate a point of view, especially if you are not accustomed to responding critically to sources.

As this boxing analogy suggests, however, setting up a straw man can be a dangerous game. If you do not fairly represent and put into context the straw man's argument, you risk encouraging readers to dismiss your counterargument as a cheap shot and to dismiss you for being *reductive*. On the other hand, if you spend a great deal of time detailing the straw man's position, you risk losing momentum in developing your own point of view. In any case, if you are citing a source in order to establish some context, the safer and more reasonable move is both to agree *and* disagree with it. First, identify shared premises; give the source some credit. Then distinguish the part of what you have cited that you intend to develop or complicate or dispute. This method of proceeding is obviously less combative than the typically blunt straw man approach; it verges on conversation.

In the following passage from a student's paper on Darwin's theory of evolution, the student clearly recognizes that he needs to do more than summarize what Darwin says, but he seems not to know any way of conversing with his source other than indicating his agreement and disagreement with it.

> The struggle for existence also includes the dependence of one being on another being to survive. Darwin also believes that all organic beings tend to increase. I do not fully agree with Darwin's belief here. I can not conceive of the fact of all beings increasing in number. Darwin goes on to explain that food, competition, climate, and the location of a certain species contribute to its survival and existence in nature. I believe this statement is very valid and that it could be very easily understood through experimentation in nature.

This writer's use of the word "here" in his third sentence is revealing. He is tagging summaries of Darwin with what he seems to feel is an obligatory response—a polite shake or nod of the head: I can't fully agree with you there, Darwin, but here I think you might have a point. The writer's tentative language lets us see how uncomfortable, even embarrassed, he feels about venturing these judgments on a subject that is too complex for this kind of response. It's as though the writer moves along, talking about Darwin's theory for a while, and then says to himself, "Time for a response," and lets a particular summary sentence trigger a yes/no switch. Having pressed that switch, which he does periodically, the writer resumes his summary, having registered but not analyzed his own interjections. There is no reasoning in a chain from his own observations, just random insertions of unanalyzed agree/disagree responses.

Here, by contrast, is the introduction of an essay that frames the conversation that the writer is preparing to have with her source:

> In *Renaissance Thought: The Classic, Scholastic and Humanist Strains,* Paul Kristeller responds to two problems that he perceives in Renaissance scholarship. The first is the haze of cultural meaning surrounding the word "humanism": he seeks to clarify the term and its origins, as well as to explain the apparent lack of religious concern in humanism. Kristeller also reacts to the notion of humanism as an improvement upon medieval Aristotelian scholasticism.

Rather than leading with her own beliefs about the source, the writer emphasizes the issues and problems she believes are central in it. Although the writer's position on her source is apparently neutral, she is not summarizing passively. In addition to making choices about what is especially significant in the source, she has also located it within the conversation that Kristeller was having with his own sources—other practitioners of Renaissance scholarship who have developed a widely accepted view of humanism he wants to revise ("Kristeller responds to two problems"). Further on in the paper, the writer achieves a clearer picture of Kristeller's point of view by putting it into conversation with another source:

> Unlike Kristeller, Tillyard also tries to place the seeds of individualism in the minds of the medievals. "Those who know most about the Middle Ages," he claims, "now assure us that humanism and a belief in the present life were powerful by the 12th century." Kristeller would undoubtedly reply that it was scholasticism, lacking the humanist emphasis on individualism, which was powerful in the Middle Ages. True humanism was not evident in the Middle Ages.
>
> In Kristeller's view, Tillyard's attempts to assign humanism to medievals are not only unwarranted, but also counterproductive. Kristeller ends his chapter on "Humanism and Scholasticism" with an exhortation to "develop a kind of historical pluralism. It is easy to praise everything in the past which appears to resemble certain favorable ideas of our own time, or to ridicule and minimize everything that disagrees with them. This method is neither fair nor helpful." Tillyard, in trying to locate humanism within the medieval world, allows the value of humanism to supersede the worth of medieval scholarship. Kristeller argues that there is inherent worth in every intellectual movement, not simply in the ones that we find most agreeable.
>
> Kristeller's work is valuable to us primarily for its forthright definition of humanism. Tillyard has cleverly avoided this undertaking: he provides many textual references, usually with the companion comment that "this is an example of Renaissance humanism," but he never overtly and fully formulates the definition in the way that Kristeller does.

As this excerpt makes evident, the writer has found something to say about her source by putting it into conversation with another source ("Kristeller would undoubtedly reply") with which she believes Kristeller would disagree. Although it seems obvious that the writer prefers Kristeller to Tillyard, her agreement with him is not the main point of her analysis. She focuses instead on foregrounding the problem that Kristeller is trying to solve and on relating that problem to different attitudes toward history. In so doing, she is deftly orchestrating the conversation between her sources. Her next step would be to distinguish her position from Kristeller's. Having used Kristeller to get a perspective on Tillyard, she now needs somehow to get a perspective on Kristeller. The next guideline will address this issue.

STRATEGY 4: FIND YOUR OWN VOICE IN THE CONVERSATION

Even in cases in which you find a source's position entirely congenial, it is not enough simply to agree with it. In order to converse with a source, you need to find some way of being a distinct voice in that conversation. This does not mean that you should feel compelled to attack the source, but that you need to find something of your own to say about it.

In general, you have two options when you find yourself strongly in agreement with a source.

1. You can *work with* the source by expanding its implications, by applying it to new situations, and by pointing out areas in it that deserve more attention. In other words, you can maintain your general agreement with the source, but try to go somewhere else with it.
2. You can seek out other perspectives on the source in order to break the spell it has cast upon you. Breaking the spell means that you will necessarily become somewhat disillusioned, but not that you will then need to dismiss everything you previously believed.

How, in the first option, do you take a source somewhere else? Rather than focusing solely on what the writer believes Kristeller finds most important, she might locate a point she finds especially interesting that Kristeller did not choose to emphasize and that she wished he had developed further. Then she could follow through on his lead and uncover new implications that depend upon Kristeller but that lie outside his own governing preoccupations. Or she might apply his principles to new geographic (rather than theoretical) areas, such as Germany instead of Italy.

The second option, researching new perspectives on the source, can also lead to uncovering new implications. Your aim need not be simply to find a source that disagrees with the one that has convinced you and then switch your allegiance, since this move would perpetuate the problem from which you are trying to escape. Instead, you would use additional perspectives to gain some critical distance on your source. As noted earlier in this chapter, consulting book reviews in scholarly journals is an ideal way of sampling possible critical approaches to a source. Once the original source is taken down from the pedestal through additional reading, there is a greater likelihood that you will see how to distinguish your views from those it offers.

You may think, for example, that another source's critique of your original source is partly valid and that both sources miss things that you could point out, in effect refereeing the conversation between them. The writer on Kristeller might play this role by asking herself, So what that subsequent historians have viewed his objective—a disinterested historical pluralism—as not necessarily desirable and in any case impossible? How might Kristeller respond to this charge, and how has he responded already in ways that his critics have failed to notice? Using additional research in this way can lead you to *situate* your source more fully and fairly, acknowledging its limits as well as its strengths.

In other words, this writer, in using Kristeller to critique Tillyard, has arrived less at a conclusion than at her next point of departure. A good rule to follow, especially when you find a source entirely persuasive, is that *if you can't find a perspective on your source, you haven't done enough research.* Having established Kristeller's achievement in relation to his predecessor, Tillyard, what does the writer want to do with it? Good analytical writing always moves in such a chain, and if you are analyzing your sources as you perform your research, your thinking will tell you what direction your research needs to go in.

STRATEGY 5: SUPPLY ONGOING ANALYSIS OF SOURCES (DON'T WAIT UNTIL THE END)

Unless disciplinary conventions dictate otherwise, analyze *as* you quote or paraphrase sources, rather than summarizing everything first and leaving your analysis for the end. A good conversation does not consist of long monologues alternating among the speakers. Participants exchange views, query, and modify what other speakers have said. Similarly, when you orchestrate conversations with and among your sources, you need to *integrate your analysis into your presentation* of them.

Voices from Across the Curriculum

INTEGRATING SOURCES

Avoid serial citation summaries; that is, rather than discussing what author A found, then what author B found, then what author C found, and so forth, *integrate* material from all your sources. For instance, if writing about the cause and treatment of a disorder, discuss what all authors say about cause, then what all authors have to say about treatment, and so forth, addressing any contradictions or tensions between authors.

—*A. Tjeltveit, Professor of Psychology*

If you integrate your analysis as you go along, you will be more likely to explain how the information in the source fits into your unfolding presentation, and your readers will be more likely to follow your train of thought and grasp the logic of your organization.

THE FLIGHT FROM TEACHING

The following example of a research paper typifies the problems that result from leaving the analysis for the end. We have summarized parts of the essay in the interest of brevity.

THE FLIGHT FROM TEACHING

1   The "flight from teaching" (Smith 6) in higher education is a controversial issue of the academic world. The amount of importance placed on research and publishing is the major cause of this flight. I will show different views and aspects concerning the problem plaguing our colleges and universities, through the authors that I have consulted.

2   Page Smith takes an in-depth look at the "flight from teaching" in *Killing the Spirit*. Smith's views on this subject are interesting, for he is a professor with tenure at UCLA. Throughout the book, Smith stresses the sentiment of the student being the enemy, as expressed by many of his colleagues. Some professors resent the fact that the students take up their precious time—time which could be better used for research. Smith goes on about how much some of his colleagues go out of their way to avoid their students. They go as far as making strange office hours to avoid contact. Smith disagrees with the hands-off approach being taken by the professors: "There is no decent, adequate, respectable education, in the proper sense of that much-abused word, without personal involvement by a teacher with the needs and concerns, academic and personal, of his/her students. All the rest is 'instruction' or 'information transferral,' 'communication technique,' or some other impersonal and antiseptic phrase, but *it is not teaching* and the student is not truly learning" (7).

3   Page Smith devotes a chapter to the ideal of "publish or perish," "since teaching is shunned in the name of research." Smith refutes the idea that "research enhances teaching" and that there is a "direct relationship between research and teaching" (178). In actuality, research inhibits teaching. The research that is being done, in most cases, is too specialized for the student. Like teaching and research, Smith believes there is not necessarily a relationship between research and publication. Unfortunately those professors who are devoted to teaching find themselves without a job and/or tenure unless they conform to the requirements of publishing. Smith asks, "Is not the atmosphere hopelessly polluted when professors are forced to do research in order to validate themselves, in order to make a living, in order to avoid being humiliated (and terminated)?" (197) Not only are the students and the professors suffering, but as a whole, "Under the publish-or-perish standard, the university is perishing" (180).

4   Charles J. Sykes looks at the "flight from teaching" in *Profscam: Professors and the Demise of Higher Education*. Sykes cites statistics to show the results of the reduction of professors' teaching loads enabling them time for more research. The call to research is the cause of many problems. The reduced number of professors actually teaching increases both the size of classes and the likelihood that students will find at registration that their courses are closed. Students will also find they do not have to write papers and often exams are multiple choice, because of the large classes. Consequently, the effects of the "flight from teaching" have "had dramatic ramifications for the way undergraduates are taught" (40).

[Here the writer includes two more paragraphs, each containing a summary of a different source.]

5   E. Peter Volpe, in his chapter "Teaching, Research, and Service: Union or Coexistence?" in the book *Whose Goals for American Higher Education?* disagrees strongly that there is an overemphasis on research. Volpe believes that only the research scholar can provide the best form of teaching because "Teaching and research are as inseparable as the two faces of the same coin" (80). The whole idea of education is to increase the student's curiosity. When the enthusiasm of the professor, because of his research, is brought into the classroom, it intensifies that curiosity and therefore provides "the deepest kind of intellectual enjoyment" (80). Volpe provides suggestions for solving the rift between students and professors, such as "replacing formal discourse by informal seminars and independent study programs" (81). He feels that this will get students to think for themselves and professors to learn to communicate with students again. Another suggestion is that the government provide funding for "research programs that are related to the education function" (82). This would allow students the opportunity to share in the research. In conclusion, Volpe states his thesis to be, "A professor in any discipline stays alive when he carries his enthusiasm for discovery into the classroom. The professor is academically dead when the spark of inquiry is extinguished within him. It is then that he betrays his student. The student becomes merely an acquirer of knowledge rather than an inquirer into knowledge" (80).

6   The "flight from teaching" is certainly a problem in colleges and universities. When beginning to research this topic, I had some very definite opinions. I believed that research and publication should not play any role in teaching. Through the authors utilized in this paper and other sources, I have determined that there is a need for some "research" but not to the extent that teaching is pushed aside. College and universities exist to provide an education; therefore, their first responsibility is to the student.

7   I agree with Smith that research, such as reading in the professor's field, is beneficial to his or her teaching. But requiring research to the extent of publication so as to secure a tenured position is actually denying education to both the professors and their students. I understand that some of the pressure stems from the fact that it is easier to decide tenure by the "tangible" evidence of research and publication. The emphasis on "publish or perish" should revert to "teach or perish" (Smith 6). If more of an effort is required to base tenure upon teaching, then that effort should be made. After all, it is the education of the people of our nation that is at risk.

8   In conclusion, I believe that the problem of the "flight from teaching" can and must be addressed. The continuation of the problem will lead to greater damage in the academic community. The leaders of our colleges and universities will need to take the first steps towards a solution. [Here the writer concludes with an example of one university that has attempted to restore more emphasis to teaching.]

After studying this research paper, we can see that the first five paragraphs mechanically string together unanalyzed summaries of sources, followed by three paragraphs in which the writer offers her opinion of all this material. The gap between presentation and discussion leaves the analysis too loose: especially at first reading, we are left unsure where the writer stands in relation to her sources and how to interpret the various points of view that she is summarizing for us. Although the writer declares in the third sentence of the paper that she intends to "show different views and aspects concerning the problem," some of her remarks seem to be not just those of her sources but interjections of her own opinions as well.

For example, when she refers to the professors' concern for their "precious time" in paragraph 2, or when she writes that "In actuality, research inhibits teaching" in paragraph 3, is she simply summarizing Smith or endorsing his position? The problem is not that she—or any writer—should stay out of the summary, but that she has not carefully differentiated her own remarks from those of her sources. As a general rule, when you are providing ongoing analysis of your sources it is imperative that you clarify for your readers when you are speaking for your source and when you are speaking for yourself. You can, as noted earlier, easily achieve this clarity by inserting attributive tag phrases that distinguish who's saying what: "in Smith's view" or "In response to Smith, one might argue that."

When, in the final three paragraphs, the writer finally does get around to responding to her sources, she just comes down on one side of the issue she has raised, but she has never closely analyzed the position she has chosen. In effect, she has first told us what her sources have said and then rendered her final judgment, but she has omitted the necessary middle step of analyzing their claims. For example, is it only professors' desire to be off doing their own research that explains closed courses, large class size, and multiple-choice tests, as Sykes argues in paragraph 4? What about other causes for these problems, such as the cost of hiring additional professors or the pressure a university puts on professors to publish in order to increase the status of the institution?

We do not intend to suggest that the writer should have recognized these particular problems with her sources, but that she needs, somewhere in the paper, to raise questions about the reasoning implicit in them. The large gap between the writer's presentation of her sources and her own conclusions about them allows her to avoid analyzing the arguments that her sources make. And as we have been suggesting, her chosen mode of organization exacerbates this problem. By constructing a mechanical list of summaries, she does not establish a conversation among sources that might have led her to develop her ideas more carefully.

In other words, the writer needs both to get her sources to speak to one another and more actively to referee the conflicts among them. Instead, she seems to think that once she has presented what her sources have said, she can leave the sources behind and render her judgment: "I have determined that there is a need for some 'research' but not to the extent that teaching is pushed aside. Colleges and universities exist to provide an education; therefore, their first responsibility is to the student" (paragraph 6). This conclusion glosses over the key question. At exactly what point *does* research push teaching aside?

Her sources have repeatedly addressed this very question, offering opposing answers that she should have put into debate. For example, Smith asserts that "research inhibits teaching" (paragraph 3), whereas Volpe contends that "only the research scholar can provide the best form of teaching because 'Teaching and research are as inseparable as the two faces of the same coin'" (paragraph 5). Both sides *agree* that educating students is the "first responsibility" of colleges and universities, but they disagree radically on how this responsibility is best fulfilled. Smith believes that professors' research gets in the way of excellent teaching, while Volpe believes that research is essential to it. If the writer had brought these sources into dialogue, she could have discovered that the assertion she offers as her conclusion is, in fact, an evasion.

To generalize from this paper: it is no coincidence that a research paper that summarizes its sources and delays discussing them should have difficulty constructing a logically coherent and analytically revealing point of view. The organization of "The Flight from Teaching" obstructs the writer's ability to have ideas about her material. The alternative, where disciplinary conventions allow, is to analyze your sources as you go along—a project that will be made easier if you put them into conversation with one another. In this light, "The Flight from Teaching" represents a useful first draft—for it is beneficial to summarize sources insofar as that enables you to locate the issues and break them down into their components. But now the writer is ready to *reorganize her essay around issues or topics, letting her sources debate them.*

Here, by contrast, is the opening paragraph of an essay that offers continual analysis of its sources:

> Alan Friedman's Spider's Web argues in elaborate detail that the United States illegally armed Iraq prior to the Gulf War. Although the book relies on exhaustive description to focus on individual strands of the "web" in order to better understand the whole, it by no means offers the complete story. If anything, Friedman's accusations call for a comprehensive investigation. He has no pretensions about the book—that is, Friedman recognizes that his argument is only the first step. He writes in the closing paragraphs, "The issue far transcends Iraqgate or even the particular circumstances described in these pages. It is therefore up to Congress, the Clinton Administration, the Scott inquiry and the British Parliament to pursue allegations wherever they lead" (AF 287). It would almost be ridiculous to argue that Friedman's thesis is not based on some truth. There are far too many documents, testimonies, and coincidences for this entire situation to be a hoax. What is at issue is the extent of culpability.

At the very outset of his paper, the writer has synthesized his summary of the central source with a first stab at analyzing it. He tells us that Friedman's book does not offer "the complete story," quotes the author's closing admission to this effect, and suggests that at the least the book's argument contains (only) "some truth." Although the paragraph still remains too close to summary, the writer could take the next step—getting more analytical about his source—by using the questions supplied by the political science professor in our last chapter, on using evidence:

Are there any gaps in the information? Does the writer distinguish cases in which evidence *strongly supports* a claim from evidence that is *suggestive* or *speculative?*

A revised version of this paragraph would more clearly indicate the writer's point of view toward the limitations of Friedman's analysis.

STRATEGY 6: WHEN THE LANGUAGE IS IMPORTANT, QUOTE (DON'T PARAPHRASE)

Quote sources—as opposed to paraphrasing them—when the actual language that they use is important to your point. Consciously asking yourself why it is important to quote rather than paraphrase a passage can benefit your analysis not only by helping you to break the habit of using quotations as "answers" but, more importantly, by also getting you to pay more careful attention to *the language itself.* If you quote, you should spell out what you think is significant about key words in the quotation. This practice will help you to represent the view of your source fairly and accurately; you will be less likely to overgeneralize and thereby distort your source's position.

In most cases, paying close attention to the language will lead you to uncover attitudes implicit in the source. That is, your focus will rest at least as much on the *way* the source represents its position as on the information it contains. If you are quoting *Newsweek* on Bosnia, for example, what matters most is not some truth about American involvement in this eastern European nation but how this involvement is being represented in a magazine that is a mouthpiece for popular culture. Similarly, if you quote President Bill Clinton on Bosnia, what probably matters most is that the president is choosing particular words to represent—and promote—the government's position. It is not neutral information. In short, the person speaking and the kind of source in which his or her words appear will acquire added significance when you quote rather than paraphrase.

Take, for example, a single sentence from the research paper, "The Flight from Teaching":

> Smith disagrees with the hands-off approach being taken by the professors: "There is no decent, adequate, respectable education, in the proper sense of that much-abused word, without personal involvement by a teacher with the needs and concerns, academic and personal, of his/her students" (7).

The writer uses this passage as part of an apparently neutral summary of Smith's position, and she does not comment upon it further. But notice how the source's word choices provide additional information about the central idea being articulated. The repetition of "personal" and the quarrelsome tone of "much-abused" suggest that the writer's characterization of Smith as one who "disagrees with the hands-off approach" is extremely understated. Smith is writing a polemic, and he is preoccupied with the personal to the extent that he wishes to restrict the definition of education to it. The writer may agree or disagree with Smith's outlook, but the point is that if she attends to his actual language, she will be able to characterize that outlook much more accurately.

By contrast, the writer analyzing the *Spider's Web* quotes in order to analyze the implications of the source's language:

> If allegations that top levels of United States and British governments acted covertly to shape foreign policy are truthful, then this scandal, according to Friedman, poses serious questions concerning American democracy. Friedman explains, "The government's lack of accountability, either to Congress or to the public, was so egregious as to pose a silent threat to the principles of American democracy" (AF 286). The word "principles" is especially important. In Friedman's view, without fundamental ideals such as a democracy based on rule by elected representatives

and the people, where does the average citizen stand? What will happen to faith in the government, Friedman seems to be questioning, if elected representatives such as the president sully that respected office?

This writer's use of quotation serves not only to convey information but also to frame it. By emphasizing Friedman's diction ("principles"), he makes a point about that author's point of view.

As with all uses of evidence, in analyzing sources you will usually do better to say more about less, rather than less about more. If you rely too heavily on quotation as a means of explaining your source, you will not be able to address any of your quotations adequately, and you will be tempted to try to let them speak for themselves.

GUIDELINES FOR USING SOURCES

1. Avoid the temptation to plug in sources as "answers." Aim for a *conversation* with them. Think of sources as voices inviting you into a community of interpretation, discussion, and debate.
2. Quote, paraphrase, or summarize in order to analyze. Explain what you take the source to mean, showing the reasoning that has led to the conclusion you draw from it.
3. Quote, rather than summarize or paraphrase, when the actual language is important to your point. Then analyze the important terms directly, bringing out their implications.
4. Quote sparingly. You are usually better off centering your analysis on a few quotations and branching out to aspects of your subject that the quotations illuminate.
5. Put your source in a context that will give your readers perspective on its concerns. Which of its points does the source find most important? What positions does it want to modify or refute, and why?
6. Attribute sources ("According to Einstein, . . .") in the text of your paper, not just in parenthetical citations. Such attributions (a) help your readers evaluate the source material as they read it and (b) distinguish source material from your remarks about it.
7. Look for ways to develop, modify, or apply what a source has said, rather than simply agreeing or disagreeing with it. Ask yourself, "If we accept this position as true, then what follows?"
8. If you challenge a position found in a source, be sure to represent it fairly. First give the source some credit by identifying assumptions you share with it. Then isolate the part that you intend to complicate or dispute.
9. Look for sources that address your subject from different perspectives. Avoid relying too heavily on any one source.
10. When your sources disagree, consider playing mediator. Instead of immediately agreeing with one or the other, clarify areas of agreement and disagreement among them.

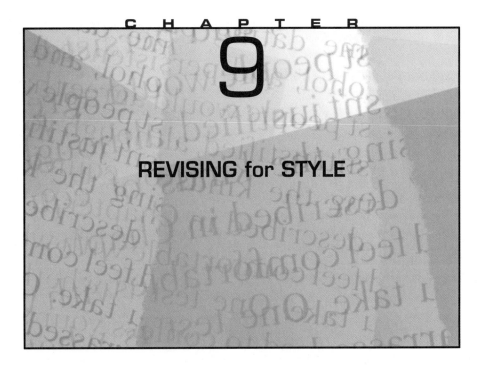

CHAPTER 9

REVISING for STYLE

R EVISING IS THE VERY heart of writing. The best ideas develop over time, through your repeated attempts to find the language that best articulates your thinking. *Revision* is a very broad term, however, and so it is useful to distinguish two kinds of revision.

CONCEPTUAL VERSUS TECHNICAL REVISION

As we have been using it thus far, the term *revision* refers to the process by which writers continually evaluate and rethink what they have written to improve the clarity and accuracy of their ideas. Revision, in this sense of "re-vision," to see again, might involve choosing the best point you've made in an early draft and building the next draft around it, cutting the majority of what you had written. Or it might mean discovering an entirely different way of analyzing your topic and working to reconcile this viewpoint with your formulation from a previous draft. Such revisions are *conceptual:* they involve wide-scale changes in content and organization. In the first eight chapters, we have demonstrated how to do this kind of revision.

We now turn to the more *technical* kinds of revision associated with editing and correcting a draft. Chapter 9 concentrates on the stylistic choices that are available to you as you write and revise your draft for greater clarity and effect.

Chapter 10 addresses the issue of grammatical correctness and offers ways of recognizing and fixing (or avoiding) the most serious errors.

WAIT TO FOCUS ON TECHNICAL REVISION

Perhaps the first guideline in technical revision is to *wait* to do it until you have arrived at a reasonably complete conceptual draft. We have delayed until the end of the book our consideration of technical revisions precisely because most writers avoid worrying about them in the early stages of the writing process. As we have suggested, writers need a stage in which they are allowed to make mistakes and use writing to help them discover what they want to say. If you get too focused on producing polished copy right up front, you may never explore the subject enough to learn how to have ideas about it. In other words, it doesn't make sense for you to let your worries about proper form or persuasive phrasing prematurely distract you from the more important matter of having something substantial to polish in the first place. But in the appropriate place—the later stages of the writing process—technical revision becomes very important.

USE TECHNICAL REVISION AS A FORM OF CONCEPTUAL REVISION

A second guideline in doing technical revision is to avoid thinking of it solely as a matter of communicating more effectively with your audience. Rethinking the way you have said something will often lead you to rethink the substance of what you have said. Put another way: in practice, technical revision often spills over into conceptual revision. When you reorder the words in your sentences, you will frequently be able to recognize your ideas more clearly and, for that matter, discover new ideas that were shrouded in foggy constructions.

Suppose, for example, that in revising your sentence structure you decide to give more prominence to one of the two ideas that your original draft treated as equal. Your draft reads,

> The history of Indochina is marked by colonial exploitation as well as international cooperation.

Here, the claim that Indochina has experienced colonial exploitation is equal in weight to the claim that it has also experienced international cooperation. But consider what happens when your revision, by using an *although* clause, makes the claim of exploitation secondary to the claim of cooperation:

> The history of Indochina, *although* marked by colonial exploitation, testifies to the possibility of international cooperation.

The first version of the sentence would probably lead you to a broad survey of foreign intervention in Indochina. The result would likely be a static list in which you judged some interventions to be "beneficial" and others "not beneficial." The revised sentence redirects your thinking, tightens your paper's focus to prioritize evidence of cooperation, and presses you to make decisions, such as whether the positive consequences of cooperation outweigh the negative consequences of colonialism. In short, the revision leads you to examine the dynamic relations between your two initial claims.

Just as commonly, the spill-over from technical to conceptual revision can occur when you are revising at the level of word choice. Let's say that you've drafted an analysis of the president's approach to military spending, and, having encountered some apparently contradictory evidence, you've chosen to call his stance "ambiguous" (open to many interpretations). As you focus on the transitions among your examples, though, you realize that his approach actually tends to fall into one of two responses. You then understand that his approach should more accurately be termed "ambivalent" (possessing two opposite or conflicting views). This recognition, in turn, would lead you not only to reorganize your final version but also to refocus your argument, building to the significance of this ambivalence (that the president is trying to adopt two stances simultaneously) rather than to your previous conclusion (that presidential policy is simply incoherent).

As you read this chapter and apply its advice, keep in mind that revision is the essence of writing. Assume that your first draft—indeed, your first several drafts— will not be polished. When you allow time to rewrite, to dwell with your writing, you will begin to notice how to make it cleaner, clearer, and more persuasive. On the other hand, you should also recognize that the process of revision is, in theory, endless. Near the end of his career, Sigmund Freud considered the question of when a person should stop undergoing psychoanalysis, given that one is never totally "cured." His answer was that at a certain point one has simply had enough and so stops arbitrarily. At some arbitrary point you will have to decide to stop revising. The more of it you can find the time to do, however, the more successful your final product is likely to become.

WHAT IS STYLE?

Broadly defined, *style* refers to all of a writer's decisions in selecting, arranging, and expressing what he or she has to say. Many factors affect your style: your aim and sense of audience, the ways you approach and develop a topic, the kinds of evidence you choose, and, particularly, the kinds of syntax and diction you characteristically select. In this sense, style is personal.

The foundations of your style emerge in the dialogue you have with yourself about your topic. When you revise for style, you consciously reorient yourself toward communicating the results of that dialogue to your audience. Stylistic decisions, then, are a mix of the unconscious and conscious, of chance and choice. You don't simply impose style onto your prose; it's not a mask you don or your way of icing the cake. Revising for style is more like sculpting. As a sculptor uses a chisel to "bring out" a shape from a block of walnut or marble, a writer uses style to "bring out" the shape of the conceptual connections in a draft of an essay.

As the rest of this chapter will suggest in various ways, this "bringing out" demands a certain detachment from your own language. It requires that you *become aware* of your words as words and of your sentences as sentences.

LEVELS OF STYLE: WHO'S WRITING TO WHOM, AND WHY DOES IT MATTER?

How you say something is always a significant part of *what* you are saying. To look at words as words is to focus on the *how* as well as the *what*. Imagine that you call your friend on the phone, and a voice you don't recognize answers. You ask to speak with your friend, and the voice responds, "With whom have I the pleasure of speaking?" By contrast, what if the voice had instead responded, "Who's this?" What information do these two versions of the question convey, beyond the obvious request for your name?

The first response—"With whom have I the pleasure of speaking?"—tells you that the speaker is formal and polite. He is also probably fastidiously well-educated: he not only knows the difference between *who* and *whom,* but he also obeys the etiquette that outlaws ending a sentence with a preposition ("Whom have I the pleasure of speaking *with*?"). The very formality of the utterance, however, might lead you to label the speaker pretentious. His assumption that conversing with you is a "pleasure" suggests empty flattery. On the other hand, the second version—"Who's this?"—although also grammatically correct, is less formal. It is more direct but also terse to a fault: the speaker does not seem particularly interested in treating you politely.

Is one response better than the other? The answer would seem to depend on your point of view and your understanding of the situation. Let's consider one more hypothetical example. You answer the phone, and a voice asks to speak with a member of your household but mispronounces the name. You might reasonably surmise that the caller is working from a list and trying to sell something. If you dislike telephone solicitation, you probably would be more likely to ask "Who's this?" than "With whom have I the pleasure of speaking?"

What generalizations about style do these examples suggest?

- There are many ways of conveying a message.

- The way you phrase a message constitutes a significant part of its meaning.

- Your phrasing gives your reader cues that suggest your attitude and your ways of thinking.

- All stylistic decisions depend on your sensitivity to context—who's talking to whom about what subject and with what aims.

The last of these generalizations concerns what is called the *rhetorical situation*. *Rhetoric* is the subject that deals with the use of language to inform or persuade or move an audience in some way. Obviously, as you make stylistic choices, you need to be aware of the possible consequences of making certain statements to a certain audience in a certain fashion. In reference to our telephone examples, for instance, you should recognize that in daily speech a proper *whom* can lead others, however unfortunately, to view you with suspicion.

In an academic context, though, most of the analytical writing that you do occurs in a rhetorical situation that is quite formal. As Chapter 3 ("Questions of Format") discussed, academic discourse tends to be full of conventions—rules and protocols—and these are not simply a matter of etiquette. They also provide guidelines designed to help writers organize and develop their thinking. Along similar lines, the diction you choose to use in academic situations will not only reflect your ability to "talk the talk" but will also, if you respect the terms, help you to think.

Formal and Informal Styles

Formal English obeys the basic conventions of standard written prose, and most academic writing is fairly formal. An informal style—one that is conversational and full of slang—can have severe limitations in an academic setting. The syntax and vocabulary of written prose aren't the same as those of speech, and attempts to import the language of speech into academic writing can result in your communicating less meaning with less precision.

Let's take one brief example:

> Internecine quarrels within the corporation destroyed morale and sent the value of the stock plummeting.

The phrase *internecine quarrels* may strike some readers as a pretentious display of formal language, but consider how difficult it is to communicate this concept economically. "Fights that go on between people related to each other" is awkward; "brother against brother" is sexist and a cliché; and "mutually destructive disputes" is acceptable but long-winded.

It is arguably a part of our national culture to value the simple and the direct as more genuine and democratic than the sophisticated, which is supposedly more aristocratic and pretentious. This "plain-speaking" style, however, can hinder your ability to develop and communicate your ideas. In the case of *internecine,* the more formal diction choice actually communicates more, and more effectively, than the less formal equivalents.

When in doubt about how your readers will respond to the formality or informality of your style, you are usually better off opting for some version of "With whom have I the pleasure of speaking?" rather than "Who's this?" The best solution will usually lie somewhere in between: "May I ask who's calling?" would protect you against the imputation of either priggishness or piggishness.

REVISING WORD CHOICE (DICTION)

The rest of this chapter examines the kinds of choices that you need to consider as you revise your drafts. The choices that arise in contemplating and reconsidering your words involve not only *precision* but also *appropriateness.* That is, you want the words with the most accurate meanings but also those that are most acceptable in the given rhetorical situation within which you are writing.

GETTING THE RIGHT WORD

The "right" word contributes accuracy and precision to your meaning. The "wrong" word, it follows, is inaccurate and vague. The most reliable guide to choosing the right word and avoiding the wrong words is the dictionary. A good one will give you not only concise definitions but also the origin of the word (known as its *etymology)* and, in some cases, synonyms and advice on the differences among related words. As an alternative to a dictionary, a thesaurus (a dictionary of synonyms) can provide a list of similar words from which to choose, but unless you are certain of the fine distinctions among related words (which a dictionary will generally provide), you run a fairly high risk of choosing an inappropriate word. In any case, you should not overlook one of the best ways to learn more about word choice (also known as *diction):* pay attention in your reading to how unfamiliar words are used.

If you confuse *then* and *than* or *infer* and *imply,* you will not convey the meaning that you intend, and you will probably bewilder your readers. Getting the wrong word is, of course, not limited to pairs of words that are spelled similarly. A *notorious* figure is widely but unfavorably known, whereas a *famous* person is usually recognized for accomplishments that are praiseworthy. (For further discussion, see "Diction Errors That Interfere with Meaning" in Chapter 10.)

Shades of Meaning

A slightly less severe version of getting the wrong word occurs when a writer uses a word with a shade of meaning that is inappropriate or inaccurate in a particular context. Take, for example, the words *assertive* and *aggressive.* Often used interchangeably, they don't really mean the same thing—and the difference matters. Loosely defined, both terms mean "forceful." But assertive suggests being "bold and self-confident," while aggressive carries the sense of being "eager to attack." In most cases, you compliment the person you call assertive but raise doubts about the one you label aggressive (depending on the situation: aggressive is a term of praise on the football field but less so if used to describe an acquaintance's behavior during conversation at the dinner table).

One particularly charged context in which shades of meaning matter to many readers involves the potentially sexist implications of using one term for women and another for men. If, for example, in describing a woman and a man up for the same job, we referred to the woman as aggressive but the man as assertive, our diction would deservedly be considered sexist, since it would imply that her behavior was inappropriately belligerent and therefore "unwomanly," whereas his behavior was poised and therefore full of "manly" leadership potential. The sexism comes in when word choice suggests that what is assertive in a man is aggressive in a woman.

In choosing the right shade of meaning, you can often get a sharper sense for the word by knowing its etymological history—the word or words from which it evolved. In the previous example, aggressive derives from the Latin *aggressus,* meaning "to go to or approach"; and *aggressus* is itself a combination of *ad,* a prefix expressing motion, and *gradus,* "a step." An aggressive person, then, is "coming at you." Assertive, on the other hand, comes from the Latin *asserere,* combining *ad* and *serere,* meaning "to join or bind together." An assertive person is "coming to build or put things together"—certainly not to threaten.

The point is, words embody rich and complex histories that distinguish them from other words and that allow you to discriminate fine shades of meaning. The nineteenth-century English statesman Benjamin Disraeli once differentiated between *misfortune* and *calamity* by commenting on his political rival William Gladstone: "If Mr. Gladstone fell into the Thames, it would be a misfortune; but if someone dragged him out, it would be a calamity."

What's Bad about *Good* and *Bad* (and Other Broad Terms)

Vague terms such as *good* and *bad* can seduce you into stopping your thinking while it is still too general and ill-defined. If you train yourself to select a more precise word whenever you encounter these words in your drafts, not only will your prose become clearer, but also the search for a new word will probably start you thinking again, sharpening your ideas. If, for example, you find a sentence such as "The subcommittee made a *bad* decision," ask yourself *why* you called it a bad decision. A revision to "The subcommittee made a shortsighted decision" indicates what in fact is "bad" about the decision and sets you up to discuss why the decision was myopic, further developing the idea. Nor are evaluative terms the only ones whose broadness can create problems. In a sentence such as "Society disapproves of interracial marriage," the broad term *society* can blind you to a host of important distinctions about social class, about a particular culture, and so on.

Concrete and Abstract Diction

At its best, effective analytical prose uses both concrete and abstract words. Simply defined, *concrete diction* evokes: it brings things to life by offering your readers words that they can use their senses upon. *Telephone, eggshell, crystalline, azure, striped, kneel, flare,* and *burp* are examples of concrete diction. In academic writing, there is no substitute for concrete language whenever you are describing what happens or what something looks like—in a laboratory experiment, in a military action, or in a painting or film sequence. In short, the language of evidence usually consists of concrete diction.

By contrast, *abstract diction* refers to words that lie beyond the senses, to concepts. *Virility, ideology, love, definitive, conscientious, classify,* and *ameliorate* are examples of abstract diction. In academic writing, by and large, this is the language of ideas.

Just as evidence needs to be organized by a thesis and a thesis needs to be developed by evidence, so concrete and abstract diction need each other. Use concrete diction to illustrate and anchor the generalizations that abstract diction

---

Hint Box: Latinate Diction

   Much abstract diction comes from Latin roots, words with such endings as *-tion, -ive, -ity, -ate,* and *-ent.* (Such words will be designated by an *L* in the etymological section of dictionary definitions.) Taken to an extreme, Latinate diction can leave your meaning vague and your readers confused. Note how impenetrable the Latinate terms make the following example:

> The examination of different perspectives on the representations of sociopolitical anarchy in media coverage of revolutions can be revelatory of the invisible biases that afflict television news.

   This sentence actually makes sense, but the demands it makes upon readers will surely drive off most of them before they have gotten through it. Reducing the amount of Latinate diction can make it more readable:

> Because we tend to believe what we see, the political biases that afflict television news coverage of revolutions are largely invisible. We can begin to see these biases when we focus on how the medium reports events, studying the kinds of footage used, for example, or finding facts from other sources that the news has left out.

   Although the revision above retains a lot of Latinate words, it provides a ballast of concrete, sensory details that allow readers to follow the idea. Although many textbooks on writing argue against using Latinate terms where shorter, concrete terms (usually of Anglo-Saxon origin) might be used instead, such an argument seems needlessly limiting in comparison with the advantages offered by a thorough mixture of the two levels of diction. It's fine to use Latinate diction; just don't make it the sole staple of your verbal diet.

---

expresses. Note the concrete language used to define the abstraction *provinciality* in this example:

> There is no cure for *provinciality* like traveling abroad. In America the waiter who fails to bring the check promptly at the end of the meal we rightly convict for not being watchful. But in England, after waiting interminably for the check and becoming increasingly irate, we learn that only an ill-mannered waiter would bring it without being asked. We have been rude, not he.

   In the example below, the abstract terms *causality, fiction,* and *conjunction* are integrated with concrete diction in the second sentence.

> According to the philosopher David Hume, *causality* is a kind of *fiction* that we ascribe to what he called "the constant *conjunction* of observed events." If a person gets hit in the eye and a black semicircle develops underneath it, that does not necessarily mean the blow caused the black eye.

   The best academic writing integrates concrete and abstract diction. A style that omits concrete language can leave readers lost in a fog of abstraction that only tangible details can illuminate. The concrete language helps readers see what you mean, much in the way that examples help them understand your ideas. Without the shaping power of abstract diction, however, concrete evocation can leave you with a list of lively but finally pointless facts.

USING AND AVOIDING JARGON

Jargon—the specialized vocabulary of a particular group—is one of those terms with unstable shades of meaning. Many people assume that all jargon is "bad": pretentious language designed to make most readers feel inferior. Many guidebooks on writing style attack jargon in similar terms, calling it either polysyllabic balderdash or a specialized, "gatekeeping" language designed by an in-group to keep others out.

Yet in many academic contexts, jargon is downright essential. It is a conceptual shorthand, a technical vocabulary that allows the members of a group (or a discipline) to converse with one another more clearly and efficiently. Certain words that may seem odd to outsiders actually function as connective tissue for a way of thought shared by insiders. The following sentence, for example, although full of botanical jargon, is also admirably cogent:

> In angiosperm reproduction, if the number of pollen grains deposited on the stigma exceeds the number of ovules in the ovary, then pollen tubes may compete for access to ovules, which results in fertilization by the fastest growing pollen tubes.

We might label this use of jargon acceptable, for it is written, clearly, by insiders *for* fellow insiders. It might not be acceptable language for an article intended for readers who are not botanists, or at least not scientists.

The problem with jargon comes when this insiders' language is ostensibly directed at outsiders as well. The language of contracts offers a prime example of such jargon at work:

> The Author hereby indemnifies and agrees to hold the Publisher, its licensees, and any seller of the Work harmless from any liability, damage, cost, and expense, including reasonable attorney's fees and costs of settlement, for or in connection with any claim, action, or proceeding inconsistent with the Author's warranties or representations herein, or based upon or arising out of any contribution of the Author to the Work.

Run for the lawyer! What does it mean to "hold the Publisher . . . harmless"? To what do "the Author's warranties or representations" refer? What exactly is the author being asked to do here—release the publisher from all possible lawsuits that the author might bring? We might label this use of jargon obfuscating; while it may aim at precision, it leaves most readers bewildered. While average readers are asked to sign such documents, they are really written by lawyers for other lawyers.

As the botanical and legal examples suggest, the line between acceptable and obfuscating jargon has far more to do with the audience to whom it is addressed than with the actual content of the language. Because most academic writing is addressed to insiders, you need to know the acceptable jargon in a given field. Your ability to use the technical language of the discipline is a necessary skill for conversing with others. Moreover, by demonstrating that you can "talk the talk," you will validate your authority to pronounce an opinion on matters in the discipline.

The following two guidelines can help you in your use of jargon:

1. When addressing *insiders,* use jargon accurately ("talk the talk").
2. When addressing *outsiders*—the general public or members of another discipline—either define the jargon carefully or avoid it altogether.

USING PRONOUNS: THE PERSON QUESTION

The person of a pronoun takes one of three forms:

"I read Nietzsche" is in the first person. The pronoun *(I)* identifies the speaker.

"You read Nietzsche" is in the second person. The pronoun *(you)* identifies the person spoken to.

"He reads Nietzsche" is in the third person. The pronoun *(he)* identifies the person or thing spoken about.

Table 9.1 distinguishes among first-, second- and third-person pronouns, indicating the various forms for each of the three persons.

"The Person Question" concerns which of these forms you should use when you write. As a general rule, in academic writing you should discuss your subject matter in the third person and avoid the first and second person.

third person: Heraclitus is an underrated philosopher.

first person: I believe Heraclitus is an underrated philosopher.

second person: You should recognize that Heraclitus is an underrated philosopher.

Table 9.1   First-, Second-, and Third-Person Pronouns

	Singular	Plural
First Person	I, me, mine	we, us, ours
Second Person	you, yours	you, yours
Third Person	he, him, his she, her, hers it, its	they, them, theirs

There is logic to this rule: most academic analysis focuses on the subject matter rather than on you as you respond to it. If you use the third person, you will keep the attention where it belongs. (This does not mean that you should write about yourself in the third person—"This writer believes"—as we discuss in the following section.)

The First-Person *I*: Pro and Con

Using the first-person *I* throws the emphasis on the wrong place. Repeated assertions of "in my opinion" actually distract your readers from what you have to say. Omit them except in the most informal cases. You might, however, consider using the first person as a strategy for loosening up and saying what you really think about a subject rather than adopting conventional and faceless positions. This is not a bad idea in the drafting stage, especially if you are having trouble bringing your own point of view to the forefront. In the final analysis, though, most analytical prose will be more precise and direct in the third person.

Let's take an example. Say that you are considering the extent to which models of local, state, and national government effectively provide social services for the homeless in an economy in which dwindling funds are available. After considering the strengths and weaknesses of each model, you might conclude, "I am convinced that local governments are most effective at providing services for the homeless, because they avoid the bureaucratic red tape that afflicts efforts on the state and national levels." The first four words of this sentence, although they may serve a rhetorical purpose—announcing to your audience your willingness to take a stand—are arguably an unnecessary and distracting addition. In fact, they grammatically subordinate the stand you have taken. If you cut "I am convinced that," what you lose in personal conviction you gain in concision and directness by keeping the focus on the main idea in the main clause.

Voices from Across the Curriculum

THE FIRST-PERSON *I*

Are there cases when you should use *I*? Some professors do prefer the first-person pronoun in particular cases, as noted in the three observations that follow.

I prefer that personal opinion or voice (for example, "I this," or "I that") appear throughout. I like the first person. No "the author feels" or "this author found that," please! Who is the author? Hey, it's you!

—*F. Norling, Professor of Business*

Avoid phrases like "*The author* believes (or will discuss). . . ." Except in the paper's abstract, "*I* believe (or will discuss)" is okay, and often best.

—*A. Tjeltveit, Professor of Psychology*

continued

The biggest stylistic problem is that students tend to be too personal or colloquial in their writing, using phrases such as the following: *"Scientists all agree . . .": "I find it amazing that . . ."; "the thing that I find most interesting . . ."* Students are urged to present data and existing information in their own words, but in an objective way. My preference in writing is to use the active voice in the past tense. I feel this is the most direct and least wordy approach: *I asked this . . . ; I found out that . . . ; These data show. . . .*

—*R. Niesenbaum, Professor of Biology*

Most professors prefer the first-person "I think" to the more awkward "the writer (or "one") thinks." We would only point out that, in the service of reducing wordiness, you can often avoid both options. One case in which the first person is particularly appropriate occurs when you are citing an example from your own experience (taking into account the danger of merely anecdotal evidence).

In certain contexts and disciplines, moreover, the first-person plural *we* is acceptable usage. When, for example, you are doing rhetorical analysis, studying the relation of a piece of writing to its audience, you might well write that "The president's speech assumes that we are all dutiful but disgruntled taxpayers" or "When we examine the president's actual program for cutting taxes, we discover a version of his opponents' proposals." Ultimately, if you are in doubt about using *I* or *we,* either check with your professor or avoid these first-person pronouns.

The Second-Person *You* and the Imperative Mood

As for the second person, proceed with caution. Using *you* is a fairly assertive gesture. Many readers will be annoyed, for example, by a paper about advertising that states, "When you read about a sale at the mall, you know it's hard to resist." Most readers resent having a writer airily making assumptions about them or telling them what to do. Some rhetorical situations, however, call for the use of *you.* Textbooks, for example, use *you* frequently because it creates a more direct relationship between authors and readers. Yet even in appropriate situations, directly addressing readers as *you* may alienate them by ascribing to them attitudes and needs they may not have.

The readiest alternative to *you,* the imperative mood, requires careful handling for similar reasons. The *imperative mood* of a verb expresses a direct request or command, leaving *you* understood, as in the following example: "Don't [you] scorn Aaron Burr too quickly." Such a sentence, though, runs the same kind of risk as the sentences discussed above that use the *you* explicitly: readers might resent your assumption that they would scorn Aaron Burr or, at any rate, dislike being told so forcefully how to think about him.

On the other hand, in certain writing situations—when, for instance, you are giving a set of step-by-step instructions or politely soliciting your reader's attention—the imperative address is both appropriate and useful. Here are two examples:

Imperatives

Unscrew the distributor cap, and then *take* a spark plug wrench and *loosen* the plugs.

Consider how England responded to the new treaty between its historical enemies.

In the first sentence, the insertion of *you should* or *one should* before each verb would be wordy and distracting. In the second example, the imperative invites the reader into the discussion fairly unobtrusively.

The conventional argument for using the first and second person is that *I* and *you* are personal and engage readers. It is not necessarily the case, however, that the third person is therefore impersonal. Just as film directors put their stamp on a film by the way they organize the images, move among camera viewpoints, and orchestrate the soundtrack, so writers have a wide variety of resources at their disposal for making the writing more personal and accessible for their audiences, even when writing in the third person. Some of these stylistic resources can be found in the next section: syntax.

REVISING SENTENCE STRUCTURE (SYNTAX)

The term *syntax* refers to a sentence's structure, the way it arranges words, phrases, and clauses. As such, it is an essential aspect of *grammar,* the systematic explanation of the structure of a language. Syntax is, first and foremost, a tool of logic. It clarifies the relationships within a sentence and gives some parts of the sentence more emphasis than others. The key to revising the syntax of your sentences is to make sure that the relationships are clear and the emphasis falls where you intend.

ACTIVE AND PASSIVE VOICES: DOING AND BEING DONE TO

In the *active voice,* the grammatical subject acts; in the *passive voice,* the subject is acted upon. Here are two examples:

Active Voice

Adam Smith wrote *The Wealth of Nations* in 1776.

Passive Voice

The Wealth of Nations was written by Adam Smith in 1776.

The two sentences convey identical information, but the emphasis differs—the first focuses on the author, the second on the book. As the examples illustrate, using the passive normally results in a longer sentence than using the active. If we consider how to convert the passive into the active, you can see why. In the passive, the verb requires a form of *to be* plus a past participle (for more on participles, see the "Glossary of Grammatical Terms" in Chapter 10). In this case, the active *wrote* becomes the passive *was written,* the subject (Smith) becomes the object of the preposition *by,* and the direct object *(The Wealth of Nations)* becomes the grammatical subject.

Passive Voice: Pro and Con

Consider the activity being described in the two versions of the sentence about Adam Smith: a man wrote a book. That was what happened in life. The grammar of the active version captures that action most clearly: the grammatical subject (Smith) performs the action, and the direct object *(The Wealth of Nations)* receives it, just as in life. By contrast, the passive version alters the close link between the syntax and the event: the object of the action in life *(The Wealth of Nations)* has become the grammatical subject, while the doer in life (Smith) becomes the grammatical object of a prepositional phrase.

Note, too, that the passive would allow us to omit Smith altogether: *"The Wealth of Nations* was written in 1776." A reader who desired to know more and was not aware of the author would not appreciate this sentence. More troubling, the passive can also be used to avoid naming the doer of an action—not "I made a mistake" (active) but "A mistake has been made" (passive).

In sum, there are three reasons for avoiding the passive voice when you can: (1) it's longer, (2) its grammatical relationships often reverse what happened in life, and (3) it can omit the performer responsible for the action.

On the other hand, there are also good reasons for using the passive. If you want to emphasize the object or recipient of the action rather than the performer, the passive will do that for you: *"The Wealth of Nations* was written in 1776 by Adam Smith" places the stress on the book. The passive is also preferable when the doer remains unknown: "The president has been shot!" is probably a better sentence than "Some unknown assailant has shot the president!"

Passive Voice and Scientific Writing (Avoiding *I*)

Especially in the natural sciences, the use of the passive voice is a standard practice. There are sound reasons for this disciplinary convention: science tends to focus on what happens *to* something in a given experiment rather than on the actions of that something. Consider the following passive sentence:

Separation of the protein was achieved by using an electrophoretic gel.

Although you could convert this sentence into the active voice ("The researcher used an electrophoretic gel to separate the protein"), the emphasis would then rest, *illogically,* on the agent of the action (the researcher) rather than on what happened and how (electrophoretic separation of the protein).

More generally, the passive voice can provide a way to avoid using the pronoun *I,* whether for reasons of convention, as above, or for other reasons. For example, the following passive sentence begins a business memo from a supervisor to the staff in her office.

Passive

The Inventory and Reprint departments have recently been restructured and merged.

Like many passive sentences, this one names no actor; we do not know for sure who did the restructuring and merging, though we might imagine that the author of the memo is the responsible party. The supervisor might, then, have written the sentence as an active one:

Active

I have recently restructured and merged the Inventory and Reprint departments.

But the active version is less satisfactory than the passive one for two reasons: one of practical emphasis and one of sensitivity to the audience (tone). First, the fact of the changes is more important for the memo's readers than is announcing who made the changes. The passive sentence appropriately emphasizes the changes; the active sentence inappropriately emphasizes the person who made the changes. Second, the emphasis of the active sentence on *I* (the supervisor) risks alienating the readers by its autocratic tone and by seeming to exclude all others from possible credit for the presumably worthwhile reorganization.

On balance, *consider* is the operative term when you choose between passive and active as you revise the syntax of your draft. What matters is that you recognize there is a choice—in emphasis, in relative directness, and in economy. All things being equal, and disciplinary conventions permitting, the active is usually the better choice.

STATIC VERSUS ACTIVE VERBS: *TO BE* OR NOT *TO BE*

Verbs energize sentences. They do the work, connecting the parts of the sentence with each other. In a sentence of the subject-verb–direct object pattern, the verb functions as a kind of engine, driving the subject into the predicate, as in the following examples.

Active Verbs

John F. Kennedy effectively *manipulated* his image in the media.

Thomas Jefferson *embraced* the idea of America as a country of yeoman farmers.

By contrast, *is* and other forms of the verb *to be* provide an equals sign between the subject and the predicate but otherwise tell us nothing about the relationship between them. Compare the two sentences above, which use active verbs, with the following versions of the same sentences using forms of the verb *to be*.

To Be Verbs

John F. Kennedy *was* effective at the manipulation of his image in the media.

Thomas Jefferson's idea *was* an America of yeoman farmers.

Rather than making things happen through an active verb, these sentences let everything just hang around in a state of being. In the first version, Kennedy did something—*manipulated* his image—but in the second he just *is* (or *was),* and the energy of the original verb has been siphoned into an abstract noun, *manipulation.* The Jefferson example suffers from a similar lack of momentum compared with the original active version: the syntax doesn't help the sentence get anywhere. Yet because the forms of *to be* are so easy to use, writers tend to place them every-where habitually, thus producing relatively static and wordy sentences.

Certain situations, however, dictate the use of forms of *to be.* For definitions in particular, in which a term does in fact equal some meaning, *is* works well. For in-stance, "Organic gardening *is* a method of growing crops without using synthetic fertilizers or pesticides." As with choosing between active and passive voices, the decision to use *to be* or not should be just that—a conscious decision on your part.

If you can train yourself to eliminate every unnecessary use of *to be* in a draft, you will make your prose more vital and direct. In most cases, you will find a verb that you can substitute for *is* lurking somewhere in the sentence in some other grammatical form. In the sentence about Kennedy, *manipulate* is implicit in *manipu-lation.* In Table 9.2, each of the examples in the left-hand column uses a form of *to be* for its verb (italicized) and contains a potentially strong active verb lurking in the sentence in some other form (underlined). These "lurkers" have been converted into active verbs (italicized) in the revisions in the right-hand column.

Clearly, the examples in the left-hand column have problems other than their reliance on *to be* verbs—notably wordiness. *To be* syntax tends to encourage this

Table 9.2   Static and Active Verbs

Action Hidden in Nouns and *To Be* Verbs	Action Emphasized in Verbs
The <u>cost</u> of the book *is* ten dollars.	The book *costs* ten dollars.
The <u>acknowledgment</u> of the fact *is* increasingly widespread that television *is* a <u>replacement</u> for reading in American culture.	People increasingly *acknowledge* that television *has replaced* reading in American culture.
A computer *is* ostensibly a labor-<u>saving</u> device—until the hard disk *is* the victim of a <u>crash</u>.	A computer ostensibly *saves* labor—until the hard disk *crashes.*
In the <u>laying</u> of a flagstsone patio, the important preliminary steps to remem-ber *are* the <u>excavating</u> and the <u>leveling</u> of the area and then the <u>filling</u> of it with a fine grade of gravel.	To *lay* a flagstone patio, first *excavate* and *level* the area, and then *fill* it with a fine grade of gravel.

circumlocution and verbosity. In revising a draft, try the following experiment. First, circle the sentences that rely on forms of *to be*. Then examine the other words in these sentences, looking for "lurkers." Rewrite the sentences, converting the lurkers into vigorous verbs. You will usually discover many lurkers, and your revision will acquire more energy and directness.

COORDINATION, SUBORDINATION, AND THE ORDER OF CLAUSES

Nowhere is the interrelationship between conceptual and technical revision more evident than in the choices you make about coordination, subordination, and the order of clauses (a *clause* is a group of words containing a subject and a predicate). As the first example in this chapter, about Indochina, demonstrated, the syntax of a sentence can give your readers cues about whether the idea in one clause is equal to (coordinate) or subordinate to the idea in another clause. In this context, grammar operates as a form of implicit logic, defining relationships among the clauses in a sentence. In revising your sentences, it is useful to think of coordination and subordination as tools of logic and emphasis, helping to rank your meanings.

Coordination

Coordination uses grammatically equivalent constructions to link ideas. These ideas should carry roughly equal weight as well. Sentences that use coordination connect clauses with coordinating conjunctions (such as *and, but, or*). Here are two examples:

Coordinate Sentences with *And*

Historians organize the past, *and* they can never do so with absolute neutrality.

Homegrown corn is incredibly sweet, *and* it is very difficult to grow.

If you ponder these sentences, you may begin to detect the danger of the word *and*. It does not specify a precise logical relationship between the things it connects but instead simply adds them.

Notice that the sentences get more precise if we substitute *but* for *and:*

Coordinate Sentences with *But*

Historians organize the past, *but* they can never do so with absolute neutrality.

Homegrown corn is incredibly sweet, *but* it is very difficult to grow.

These sentences are still coordinate, but they achieve more emphasis than the *and* versions. In both cases, the *but* clause carries more weight, since *but* always introduces information that qualifies or contradicts what precedes it.

Reversing the Order of Coordinate Clauses

In both the *and* and *but* examples, the second clause tends to be stressed. The reason is simple: the end is usually a position of emphasis.

You can see the effect of *clause order* more starkly if we reverse the clauses in our examples:

> Historians are never absolutely neutral, but they organize the past.

> Homegrown corn is very difficult to grow, but it is incredibly sweet.

Note how the meanings have changed in these versions by emphasizing what now comes last. Rather than having their objectivity undermined *(Historians are never absolutely neutral),* historians are now credited with at least providing organization *(they organize the past).* Similarly, whereas the previous version of the *corn* sentence was likely to dissuade a gardener from trying to grow it *(it is very difficult to grow),* the one above is more likely to lure him or her to nurture it *(it is incredibly sweet).*

Nonetheless, all of these sentences are examples of coordination because the clauses are grammatically equal. As you revise, notice when you use coordinate syntax, and think about whether you really intend to give the ideas equal weight. Consider as well whether reversing the order of clauses will more accurately convey your desired emphasis to your readers.

Subordination

A *main* or *independent clause* can stand alone, but a *subordinate* or *dependent clause* relies on some other statement to complete it. In sentences that contain *subordination,* there are two "levels" of grammar—the main clause and the subordinate clause— which create two levels of meaning. When you put something in a main clause, you emphasize its significance. When you put something in a subordinate clause, you make it less important than the main clause. (For more information, see the "Glossary of Grammatical Terms" and discussion of sentence fragments in Chapter 10.)

A subordinate clause is linked to a main clause by words known as *subordinating conjunctions.* Here is a list of the most common ones: *after, although, as, as if, as long as, because, before, if, rather than, since, than, that, though, unless, until, when, where, whether,* and *while.* All of these words define something *in relation to* something else:

> *If* you study hard, you will continue to do well.

> You will continue to do well, *if* you study hard.

In both of these examples, *if* subordinates "you study hard" to "you will continue to do well," regardless of whether the *if* clause comes first or last in the sentence.

Reversing Main and Subordinate Clauses

Unlike the situation with coordinate clauses, the emphasis in subordination rests on the relation of the subordinate to the main clause, regardless of the clause order. Nevertheless, the principle of end emphasis still applies, though to a lesser extent than among coordinate clauses. Let's consider two versions of the same sentence:

Hint Box: Expletive Constructions

The syntactic pattern for *"It is true that* more government services mean higher taxes" is known as an *expletive* construction. The term *expletive* comes from a Latin word that means "serving to fill out." The most common expletives are *it* and *there*. Consider how the expletives function in the following examples:

Expletives

There are several prototypes for the artificial heart.

It is obvious that the American West exerted a profound influence on the photography of Ansel Adams.

Expletives Eliminated

The artificial heart has several prototypes.

The American West obviously exerted a profound influence on the photography of Ansel Adams.

As the revisions demonstrate, most of the time you can streamline your prose by getting rid of expletive constructions. The "It is obvious" opening above, for example, causes the sentence to subordinate its real emphasis. In some cases, however, an expletive can provide a useful way of emphasizing, as in the following example: "There are three primary reasons that you should avoid litigation." Although this sentence subordinates its real content (avoiding litigation), the expletive provides a useful frame for what is to follow.

Subordinate Clause First

Although the art of the people was crude, it was original.

Subordinate Clause Last

The art of the people was original, although it was crude.

Both sentences emphasize the idea in the main clause ("original"). Because the second version locates the *although* clause at the end, however, the subordinated idea ("crude") has more emphasis than it does in the first version.

CUTTING THE FAT

If you can reduce verbiage, your prose will communicate more directly and effectively. In cutting the fat, you need to consider both the diction and the syntax. As regards diction, the way to eliminate superfluous words is deceptively simple: ask yourself if you need all the words you've included in order to say what you want to say. Such revision requires an aggressive attitude. *Expect* to find unnecessary restatements or intensifiers such as *quite* and *very* that add words but not significance.

As regards syntax, there are a few technical operations that you can perform on your sentences to reduce the number of words. Most of these have been mentioned in other contexts. Here, with a slightly different focus, is a recap:

- Convert sentences from the passive into the active voice. "He read the book" reduces by a third "The book was read by him," and eliminating the prepositional phrase clarifies the relationships within the sentence.

- Replace anemic forms of *to be* with vigorous verbs and direct subject-verb-object syntax. Often you will find such verbs lurking in the original sentence, and once you've recognized them, conversion is easy: "The Watergate *scandal* was an event the effects of which were felt across the nation" becomes "Watergate *scandalized* people across the nation."

- Avoid unnecessary subordination. It is illogical to write "*It is true that* more government services mean higher taxes." If "it is true that," then just write "More government services mean higher taxes"—don't muffle your meaning in a subordinate *(that)* clause.

Beyond these technical operations, perhaps the most useful way to cut the fat is to have confidence in your position on a subject and state it clearly in your paper. A lot of fat in essays consists of throat clearings, attempts to avoid stating your position. Move quickly to an example that raises the question or issue you wish to analyze.

THE SHAPES OF SENTENCES

When you write, you build. Writing, after all, is also known as composition—from the Latin *compositio,* made up of parts. We speak of *constructing* sentences and paragraphs and essays. The fundamental unit of composition is the sentence. Every sentence has a shape, and learning to see that shape is essential to revising for style. Once you see the shape of a sentence, you can recast it to make it more graceful or logical or emphatic.

When you revise your sentences for style, your goal is not to prettify your language but to reveal the organization of your thought, clarifying your meaning and delivering it more accessibly to your readers. Since meanings are rarely simple themselves, clarifying often does not involve simplifying. Meanings usually involve complex relationships, placing two or more items in balance or elevating one over the others. These relationships can be built into the structure of your sentences. A series of short sentences that breaks up items that belong together will make your prose less readable than a long sentence that makes the connections for your readers. Note the choppiness of the following passage.

Interactive computer games teach children skills. The games introduce kids to computers. The games enact power fantasies of destroying enemies. These power fantasies are potentially disturbing.

Compare that to the revision below:

Although interactive computer games teach children certain skills, they also encourage certain potentially disturbing power fantasies.

Because this version connects the items with tighter logic, it generates more forward momentum and is easier to comprehend than the first version, even though the sentence structure is more complex.

It is useful to think about style in this technical, syntactic way because revising your sentences ceases to become vague and undirected. If something sounds awkward but you don't know why, or if you want to make a passage more forceful but you don't know how, there are fairly standard ways of assessing and altering the shapes of your sentences to make them communicate more effectively.

How to Recognize the Four Basic Sentence Types

Style, as defined earlier, has to do with choice—the decisions a writer makes about how to express something. But these choices can be realized only if you can recognize and use the basic building blocks of composition.

Every sentence is built upon the skeleton of its *independent clause*(s), the subject and verb combination that can stand alone. Consider the following four sentences:

Consumers shop.

Consumers shop; producers manufacture.

Consumers shop in predictable ways, so producers manufacture with different target groups in mind.

Consumers shop in ways that can be predicted by such determinants as income level, gender, and age; consequently, producers use market research to identify different target groups for their products.

Certainly these four sentences become progressively longer, and the information that they contain becomes increasingly detailed, but they also differ in their structure—specifically, in the number of independent and dependent clauses they contain. Given that the sentence is the fundamental unit of composition, you will benefit immensely, both in composing and revising your sentences, if you can identify and construct the four basic sentence types.

The Simple Sentence

The *simple sentence* consists of a single independent clause. At its simplest, it contains a single subject and verb.

Consumers shop.

Other words and phrases can be added to this sentence, but it will remain simple so long as "Consumers shop" is the only clause.

Most consumers shop unwisely.

Even if the sentence contains more than one grammatical subject or more than one verb, it still remains simple in structure.

Most consumers *shop* unwisely and *spend* more than they can afford. [two verbs]

Both female *consumers* and their *husbands* shop unwisely. [two subjects]

The sentence structure in the first example above is known as a *compound predicate (shop* and *spend),* the second as a *compound subject (consumers* and *husbands).* The first adds another verb, the second another subject. If, however, you were to add both another subject and another verb to your simple sentence, then you would have the next sentence type, a compound sentence.

The Compound Sentence

The *compound sentence* consists of at least two independent clauses and no subordinate clauses. The information conveyed in these clauses should be of roughly equal importance:

Producers manufacture, and consumers shop.

Producers manufacture, marketers sell, and consumers shop.

As with the simple sentence, you can also add qualifying phrases to the compound sentence, and it will remain compound, as long as no dependent clauses are added:

Consumers shop in predictable ways, so producers manufacture with different target groups in mind.

Consumers shop recklessly during holidays; marketers are keenly aware of this fact.

Note that a compound sentence can connect its independent clauses with either a coordinate conjunction or a semicolon. If you were to substitute a subordinating conjunction for either of these connectors, however, you would then have a sentence with one independent clause and one dependent clause. For example,

Because consumers shop in predictable ways, producers manufacture with different target groups in mind.

This revision changes the compound sentence into the next sentence type, the complex sentence.

The Complex Sentence

The *complex sentence* consists of a single independent clause and one or more dependent clauses. As discussed under "Subordination, Coordination, and the Order of Clauses," the information conveyed in the dependent clause is subordinated to the more important independent clause. In the following example, the subject and verb of the main clause are underlined, and the subordinating conjunctions are italicized.

Although mail-order merchandising—*which* generally saves shoppers money—has increased, most <u>consumers</u> still <u>shop</u> unwisely, buying on impulse rather than deliberation.

This sentence contains one independent clause *(consumers shop)*. Hanging upon it are two introductory dependent clauses *(Although . . . merchandising . . . has increased* and *which . . . saves)* and a participial phrase *(buying on impulse)*. If you converted either of these dependent clauses into an independent clause, you would have a sentence with two independent clauses (a compound sentence) and a dependent clause. In the example below, the subjects and verbs of the two main clauses are underlined, and the conjunctions are italicized.

> Mail-order <u>merchandising</u>—*which* generally saves shoppers money—<u>has increased</u>, *but* <u>consumers</u> still <u>shop</u> unwisely, buying on impulse rather than deliberation.

This revision changes the complex sentence into the next sentence type, the compound-complex sentence.

The Compound-Complex Sentence

The *compound-complex sentence* consists of two or more independent clauses and one or more dependent clauses.

> Consumers shop in ways that can be predicted by such determinants as income level, gender, and age; consequently, producers use market research that aims to identify different target groups for their products.

This sentence contains two independent clauses *(Consumers shop* and *producers use)* and two dependent ones *(that can be predicted* and *that aims)*.

Parallel Structure

Besides sentence type, probably the most important and useful device for shaping sentences is *parallel structure* or, as it is also known, *parallelism*. Parallelism is a form of symmetry: it involves placing sentence elements that correspond in some way into the same (that is, parallel) grammatical form. Consider the following examples, in which the parallel items are underlined or italicized:

> The three kinds of partners in a law firm who receive money from a case are popularly known as <u>finders</u>, <u>binders</u>, and <u>grinders</u>.

> The Beatles acknowledged their musical debts <u>to</u> American rhythm and blues, <u>to</u> English music hall ballads and ditties, and later <u>to</u> classical Indian ragas.

> There was <u>no way that</u> the president <u>could gain</u> the support of party regulars *without alienating* the Congress and <u>no way that</u> he <u>could appeal</u> to the electorate at large *without alienating* both of these groups.

> In the entertainment industry, the money that <u>goes out</u> to hire *film stars* or *sports stars* <u>comes back</u> in increased ticket sales and video or television rights.

> Where *bravura* <u>failed</u> to settle the negotiations, *tact and patience* <u>succeeded</u>.

As all of these examples illustrate, at the core of parallelism lies *repetition*—of a word, a phrase, or a grammatical structure. Parallelism uses repetition to organize and emphasize certain elements in a sentence, so that readers can perceive more clearly the shape of your thought. In the Beatles example, each of the prepositional phrases beginning with *to* contains a musical debt; in the president example, the repetition of the phrase *no way that* emphasizes the president's entrapment.

Parallelism has the added advantage of *economy*: each of the musical debts or presidential problems might have had its own sentence, but in that case, the prose would have been wordier and the relationships among the parallel items more obscure. Along with this economy comes *balance* and *emphasis.* The trio of rhyming words *(finders, binders,* and *grinders)* that concludes the law firm example gives each item equal weight; in the entertainment industry example, *comes back* "answers" *goes out* in a way that accentuates their symmetry.

Antithesis

One particularly useful form of balance that parallel structure accommodates is known as *antithesis* (from the Greek word for opposition), a conjoining of contrasting ideas. Here the pattern sets this against that, as in the last of the parallelism examples:

Where <u>bravura</u> *failed* to settle the negotiations, <u>tact</u> <u>and</u> <u>patience</u> *succeeded.*

Failed is balanced antithetically against *succeeded,* as *bravura* is against *tact and patience.* Antithesis commonly takes the form of "if not *x,* at least *y*" or "not *x* but *y.*"

Faulty Parallelism

When you employ parallelism in revising for style, there is one grammatical rule you should obey. It is important to avoid what is known as *faulty parallelism,* which occurs when the items that are parallel in content are not placed in the same grammatical form.

    faulty: *To study* hard for four years and then *getting* ignored once they enter the job market is a hard thing for many recent college graduates to accept.

    revised: *To study* hard for four years and then *to get* ignored once they enter the job market is a hard thing for many recent college graduates to accept.

As you revise your draft for style, search for opportunities to place sentence elements in parallel structure. Often the parallels will be hidden in your sentences, but they can be brought out with a minimum of labor. In emphasizing the parallels, you will make your prose more graceful, clear, and logically connected.

The Periodic Sentence: Snapping Shut

The shape of a sentence governs the way it delivers information. The order of clauses, especially the placement of the main clause, affects what and how the sentence means. The two most common sentence shapes are known as periodic and cumulative. The main clause in a *periodic sentence* builds to a climax that is not completed until the end. Often, a piece of the main clause (such as the subject) is located earlier in the sentence, as in the following example.

The *way* that beverage companies market health—"No Preservatives," "No Artificial Color," "All Natural," "Real Brewed"—*is* often, because the product also contains a high percentage of sugar or fructose, *misleading*.

We have italicized the main clause to clarify how various modifiers interrupt it. The effect is suspenseful: not until the final word does the sentence consummate its fundamental idea. The main clause is spread out across the sentence. (The term *periodic* originates in classical rhetoric to refer to the length of such sentences.)

Another version of the periodic sentence locates the entire main clause at the end, after introductory modifiers:

Using labels that market health—such as "No Preservatives," "No Artificial Color," "All Natural," and "Real Brewed"—while producing drinks that contain a high percentage of sugar or fructose, *beverage companies are misleading*.

As we discussed in "Coordination, Subordination, and the Order of Clauses," the end of a sentence normally receives emphasis. When you use a periodic construction, the pressure on the end intensifies because the sentence needs the end to complete its grammatical sense. In both of the examples above, the sentences snap shut. They string the reader along, delaying *closure*—the point at which the sentence can stand alone independently—until they arrive at a climactic end. (Periodic sentences are also known as climactic sentences.)

You should be aware of one risk that attends using periodic constructions. If the delay lasts too long because there are too many "interrupters" before the main clause gets completed, your readers may forget the subject that is being predicated. To illustrate, let's add more subordinated material to one of the examples above:

The way that beverage companies market health—"No Preservatives," "No Artificial Color," "All Natural," "Real Brewed"—is often, because the product also contains a high percentage of sugar or fructose, not just what New Agers would probably term immoral and misleading but what a government agency such as the Food and Drug Administration should find illegal.

Arguably, the additions (the *not just/but* clauses after *fructose*) push the sentence into incoherence. The main clause has been stretched past the breaking point. If readers don't get lost in such a sentence, they are at least likely to get irritated, wishing the writer would finally get to the point.

Nonetheless, with a little care, periodic sentences can be extraordinarily useful in giving emphasis. If you are revising and want to underscore some point, try letting the sentence snap shut upon it. Often the periodic *potential* will already be present in draft, and revising for style can bring it out more forcefully. Note how minor the revisions are in the following example:

draft: The novelist Virginia Woolf suffered from acute anxieties for most of her life. She had several breakdowns and finally committed suicide on the eve of World War II.

revision: Suffering from acute anxieties for most of her life, the novelist Virginia Woolf not only *had* several *breakdowns but also,* finally, on the eve of World War II, *committed suicide.*

This revision has made two primary changes. It has combined two short sentences into a longer sentence, and it has made the sentence periodic by stringing out the main clause (italicized). What is the effect of this revision? Stylistically speaking, the revision radiates a greater sense of the writer's authority. The information has been arranged for us. Following the opening dependent clause *(Suffering . . .),* the subject of the main clause *(Woolf)* is introduced, and the predicate is protracted in a *not only/but also* parallelism. The interrupters that follow *had . . . breakdowns (finally, on the eve of World War II)* increase the suspense, before the sentence snaps shut with *committed suicide.* In general, when you construct a periodic sentence with care, you can give readers the sense that you are in control of your material. You do not seem to be writing off the top of your ahead but rather, from a position of greater detachment, rationally composing your meaning.

The Cumulative Sentence: Starting Fast

A cumulative sentence is in many respects the opposite of the periodic. Rather than delaying the main clause or its final piece, the cumulative sentence begins by presenting the independent clause as a foundation and then *accumulates* a number of modifications and qualifications. As the following examples illustrate, the independent clause (italicized) provides quick grammatical closure, freeing the rest of the sentence to amplify and develop the main idea.

Robert F. Kennedy was assassinated by Sirhan B. Sirhan, a 24-year-old Palestinian immigrant prone to occultism and unsophisticated left-wing politics and sociopathically devoted to leaving his mark in history, even if as a notorious figure.

There are two piano concerti composed solely for the left hand, one by Serge Prokofiev and one by Maurice Ravel and both commissioned by Paul Wittgenstein, a concert pianist (and the brother of the famous philosopher Ludwig Wittgenstein) who had lost his right hand in combat during World War I.

Anchored by the main clause, a cumulative sentence moves serially through this and that and the next thing, close to the associative manner in which people think. To an extent, then, cumulative sentences can convey more immediacy and a more conversational tone than other sentence shapes. Look at the following example:

The film version of *Lady Chatterley's Lover* changed D. H. Lawrence's famous novel a lot, omitting the heroine's adolescent experience in Germany, making her husband much older than she, leaving out her father and sister, including a lot more lovemaking, and virtually eliminating all of the philosophizing about sex and marriage.

Here we get the impression of a mind in the act of thinking. Using the generalization of changes in the film as a base, the sentence then appends a series of parallel participial phrases *(omitting, making, leaving, including, eliminating)* that move forward associatively, gathering a range of information and laying out possibilities. Cumulative sentences perform this outlining and prospecting function effectively. On the other hand, if we were to add four or five more changes to the sentence, readers would likely find it tedious or, worse, directionless. As with periodic sentences, overloading the shape can short-circuit its desired effect.

CONSISTENCY OF TONE

The *tone* of a piece of writing is its implied attitude toward its subject and audience. Whenever you revise for style, your choices in syntax and diction will affect the tone. There are no hard and fast rules to govern matters of tone, and your control of it will depend upon your sensitivity to the particular context—your understanding of your own intentions and your readers' expectations.

Let's consider, for example, the tonal implications of the warning signs in the subways of London and New York.

London: Leaning out of the window may cause harm.

New York: Do not lean out of the window.

Initially, you may find the English injunction laughably indirect and verbose in comparison with the shoot-from-the-hip clarity of the American sign. But that is to ignore the very thing we are calling style. The American version appeals to authority, commanding readers what not to do without telling them why. The English version, by contrast, appeals to logic; it is more collegial toward its readers and assumes they are rational beings.

In revising for tone, you need to ask yourself if the attitude suggested by your language is appropriate to the aim of your message and to your audience. Your goal is to keep the tone *consistent* with your rhetorical intentions. The following paragraph, from a college catalogue, offers a classic mismatch between the overtly stated aim and the tonal implications:

The student affairs staff believes that the college years provide a growth and development process for students. Students need to learn about themselves and others and to learn how to relate to individuals and groups of individuals with vastly different backgrounds, interests, attitudes and values. Not only is the tolerance of differences expected, but an appreciation and a celebration of these differences must be an outcome of the student's experience. In addition, the student must progress toward self-reliance and independence tempered by a concern for the social order.

The explicit content of this passage—*what* it says—concerns tolerance. The professed point of view is student-friendly, asserting that the college exists to allow students *to learn about themselves and others* and to support the individual in accord with the *appreciation . . . of differences.*

But note that the implicit tone—*how* the passage goes about saying *what* it says—is condescending and intolerant. Look at the verbs. An imperious authority lectures students about what they *need* to learn; tolerance is *expected;* celebration *must* be an outcome; and the student *must* progress along these lines. Presumably, the paragraph does not intend to adopt this high-handed manner, but its deafness to tone subverts its desired meaning.

Voices from Across the Curriculum

DICTION AND SYNTAX

By way of a final word on how to improve your diction and syntax, consider the following two comments from professors. The first articulates the crucial interrelationship between writing well and reading attentively:

Aside from the usual basic writing errors, the stylistic problems I most frequently encounter in students' papers are odd word selection and awkward sentence structure. I think both problems find their genesis in the same broader problem. You learn how to make telling use of the vocabulary you've been forced to memorize only by reading. You fashion an appealing sentence based on what you've read others doing.

—*J. Marshall, Professor of Economics*

The following anecdote, by contrast, argues for resisting the "officious" jargon of the workplace, in order to say what you mean.

I worked for the Feds for many years before seeking the doctorate. My job required immense amounts of writing: reports, directives, correspondence, etc. But, on a day-to-day basis for almost seven years I had to write short "write-ups" assessing the qualifications of young people for the Peace Corps and VISTA programs. I'd generate "list-like," "bullet-like" assessments: "Looks good with farm machinery, has wonderful volunteer experience, would be best in a rural setting, speaks French." But I had to conclude each of these assessments with a one-page narrative. Here I tended to reject officious government-ese for a more personal style. I'd write as I spoke. Rather than "Has an inclination for a direction in the facilitation of regulation," I'd write "Would be very good directing people on projects." I'd drop the "-tion" stuff and write in "speak form," not incomplete sentences, but in what I call "candid, personal" style. I carry this with me today.

—*F. Norling, Professor of Business*

GUIDELINES FOR STYLISTIC REVISION

1. Strive for distance as you edit: place yourself in the position of the reader, not the writer.
2. Check the diction. Is it precise? Have you pondered your definitions of terms? Is there sufficient balance between abstractions and concrete details?
3. Cut the fat. Don't use five words *(due to the fact that)* when one will do *(because)*. Root out expletives that needlessly subordinate *(It is true that . . .)*. Avoid redundancy.
4. Tighten the syntax of your sentences by energizing the verbs. The active voice generally achieves directness and economy; it will promote clarity and cut fat.
5. Look for potentially strong active verbs "lurking" in sentences that use a form of *to be*. Beware of habitual use of *to be* and passives, since these forms tend to blur or submerge the action, omit its performers, and generally lack momentum.
6. Look at the order and arrangement of clauses. Are ideas of equal importance in coordinate constructions? Have you used subordination to rank ideas? Have your sentences exploited the end as a position of emphasis?
7. Look at the shapes of your sentences. Do they use parallelism to keep your ideas clear? Where do you find opportunities for composing periodic and cumulative sentences that revision can bring out?

C H A P T E R

10

REVISING for CORRECTNESS

W HEN A PAPER OBEYS the rules of grammar, punctuation, and spelling, it has achieved *correctness*. Unlike revising for style (see Chapter 9), which involves you in making choices between more and less effective ways of phrasing, revising for correctness locates you in the domain of right or wrong. As with revising for style, though, most writers delay revising for correctness until late in the process of composition. By postponing this kind of revision until you have revised the paper conceptually and stylistically, you can prevent a premature concern with technical errors from interfering with your thinking.

In its place, though, revising for correctness matters deeply, because your prose may be unreadable without it. If your prose is ungrammatical, you will not only risk incoherence (in which case your readers will not be able to follow what you are saying), but you will also inadvertently invite them to dismiss you as illiterate. Is it fair of readers to reject your ideas because of the way you've phrased them? Perhaps not, but the fact is they often will. A great many readers regard technical errors as an inattention to detail that also signals sloppiness at more important levels of thinking. In producing writing that contains such errors, you risk not only distracting readers from your message but also undermining your authority to deliver the message in the first place.

BASIC WRITING ERRORS (BWEs)

You get a paper back, and it's a sea of red ink. But if you look more closely, you'll often find that you haven't made a million mistakes—you've made only a few, but over and over in various forms. This phenomenon is what the rhetorician Mina Shaughnessy addressed in creating the category of Basic Writing Errors, or BWEs. Shaughnessy argues that in order to improve your writing for correctness, you need to do two things:

- Look for a pattern of error, which will require you to understand your own logic in the mistakes you typically make.

- Recognize that not all errors are created equal, which means that you need to address errors in some order of importance—beginning with those most likely to interfere with your readers' understanding.

The following BWE guide that we have composed reflects Shaughnessy's view. First, it aims to teach you how to recognize and correct the basic kinds of errors that are potentially the most damaging to the clarity of your writing and to your credibility with readers. Second, the discussions in the guide seek to help you become aware of the patterns of error in your writing and discover the logic that has misled you into making them. If you can learn to see the pattern and then look for it in your editing and proofreading—expecting to find it—you will quickly get in the habit of avoiding the error. In short, you will learn that your problem is not that you can't write correctly but simply that you have to remember, for example, to check for possessive apostrophes.

Our BWE guide does not cover all of the rules of grammar, punctuation, diction, and usage, such as where to place the comma or period when you close a quotation or whether or not to write out numerals. For comprehensive coverage of the conventions of standard written English, you can consult one of the many handbooks available for this purpose. Our purpose is to provide a short guide to grammar—identifying the most common errors, providing remedies, and offering the logic that underlies them. This chapter's coverage of nine basic writing errors and how to fix them will help you eliminate most of the problems that routinely turn up in student essays. We have arranged the error types in a hierarchy, moving in descending order of severity (from most to least problematic).

Most of the relevant terminology for talking about grammar appears within the discussion of the Basic Writing Errors. For definitions of terms that for reasons of space are not included there, we have compiled a "Glossary of Grammatical Terms," which appears at the end of the chapter. The key explanatory terms used in the BWE list have been boldfaced to indicate that they can also be found, alphabetically organized, in this glossary. Some of the nine BWEs also recur briefly in the glossary, but we have tried to avoid unnecessary repetition.

NINE BASIC WRITING ERRORS
AND HOW TO FIX THEM

BWE 1: Sentence Fragments

The most basic of writing errors, a **sentence fragment,** is a group of words punctuated like a complete sentence but lacking the necessary structure: it is only part of a sentence. Typically, a sentence fragment occurs when the group of words in question (a) lacks a subject, (b) lacks a predicate, or (c) is a subordinate (or dependent) clause.

To fix a sentence fragment, either turn it into an independent clause by providing whatever is missing—a **subject** or a **predicate**—or attach it to an independent **clause** upon which it can depend.

Noun Clause (No Predicate) as a Fragment

A world where imagination takes over and sorrow is left behind.

The fragment is not a sentence but a noun clause—a sentence subject with no predicate. The fragment lacks a verb that would assert something about the subject. (The verbs *takes over* and *is left* are in a dependent clause created by the **subordinating conjunction** *where*.)

Corrections

A world *arose* where imagination takes over and sorrow is left behind.
[new verb matched to *A world*]

She entered a world where imagination takes over and sorrow is left behind.
[new subject and verb added]

The first correction adds a new verb *(arose)*. The second introduces a new subject and verb, converting the fragment into the direct object of *She entered*.

Verbal as a Fragment

Falling into debt for the fourth consecutive year.

Falling in the fragment above is not a verb. Depending on the correction, *Falling* is either a **verbal** or part of a verb phrase.

Corrections

The company was falling into debt for the fourth consecutive year.
[subject and helping verb added]

Falling into debt for the fourth consecutive year *led the company to consider relocating.*
[new predicate added]

Falling into debt for the fourth consecutive year, *the company considered relocating.*
[new subject and verb added]

In the first correction, the addition of a subject and the helping verb *was* converts the fragment into a sentence. The second correction turns the fragment into a **gerund** phrase functioning as the subject of a new sentence. The third correction converts the fragment into a **participial phrase** attached to a new independent clause. (See glossary under **verbals** for definitions of *gerund* and *participle*.)

Subordinate Clause as a Fragment

I had an appointment for 11:00 and was still waiting at 11:30. Although I did get to see the dean before lunch.

Although is a **subordinating conjunction** that calls for some kind of completion. Like *if, when, because, whereas,* and other subordinating conjunctions (see glossary), *although* always makes the clause that it introduces dependent.

Hint Box: Dashes and Colons

One way to correct a fragment is to replace the period with a dash: "The campaign required commitment. Not just money." becomes "The campaign required commitment—not just money." The dash offers you one way of attaching a phrase or clause to a sentence without having to construct another independent clause. In short, it's succinct. (Compare the correction that uses the dash with another possible correction: "The campaign required commitment. It also needed money.") Moreover, with the air of sudden interruption that the dash conveys, it can capture the informality and immediacy that the intentional fragment offers a writer.

You should be wary of overusing the dash in this way, as the slightly more presentable cousin of the intentional fragment. The energy it carries can clash with the decorum of formal writing contexts; its staccato effect quickly becomes too much of a good thing.

One alternative to this usage of the dash, in some cases, is the colon. It can substitute because it also can be followed by a phrase, a list, or a clause. As with the dash, it must be preceded by an independent clause. And it, too, carries dramatic force because it abruptly halts the flow of the sentence. The colon, however, does not convey informality. In place of a slapdash effect, it offers a spotlight on what is to follow it. Hence, as in this sentence, it is especially appropriate for setting up certain kinds of information: explanations, lists, or results. In the case of results, the cause or action precedes the colon; the effect or reaction follows it.

Before leaving this hint box, let us quickly offer the other legitimate use of the dash: to enclose information within a sentence. In this use, dashes precede and follow the information, taking the role usually assigned to commas. Consider the following example:

Shortly before the election—timing its disclosures for maximal destructive effect— the candidate's campaign staff levied a series of charges against the incumbent.

Note that if the information within the dashes is omitted, the sentence must still read grammatically. That is the rule for using dashes in this way.

Correction

I had an appointment for 11:00 and was still waiting at *11:30, although* I did get to see the dean before lunch.

[fragment attached to preceding sentence]

As the correction demonstrates, the remedy lies in attaching the fragment to an independent clause on which it can depend (or alternatively, making the fragment into a sentence by dropping the conjunction).

Sometimes writers use sentence fragments deliberately, usually for rhythm and emphasis or to create a conversational tone. In less formal contexts, they are generally permissible, but you run the risk that the fragment will not be perceived as intentional. In formal writing assignments, it is safer to avoid intentional fragments.

There are fragments in each of the three examples below, probably the result of their proximity to legitimate sentences. What's the problem in each case, and how would you fix it?

> Margaret Mead studied non-Western cultures in such works as *Coming of Age in Samoa*. And influenced theories of childhood development in America.

> The catastrophe resulted from an engineering flaw. Because the bridge lacked sufficient support.

> In the 1840s the potato famine decimated Ireland. It being a country with poor soil and antiquated methods of agriculture.

BWE 2: COMMA SPLICES AND FUSED (OR RUN-ON) SENTENCES

A **comma splice** consists of two independent clauses connected ("spliced") with a comma; a **fused** or **run-on sentence** combines two such clauses with no conjunction or punctuation. The remedies for both comma splices and fused sentences are the same:

1. Place a conjunction (such as *and* or *because*) between the clauses.
2. Place a semicolon between the clauses.
3. Make the clauses into separate sentences.

All of these solutions solve the same logical problem: they clarify the boundaries of the independent clauses for your readers.

Comma Splice

> He disliked discipline, he avoided anything demanding.

Correction

> *Because* he disliked discipline, he avoided anything demanding.
> [subordinating conjunction added]

Comma Splice

> Today most TV programs are violent, almost every program is about cops and detectives.

Correction

> Today most TV programs are violent; almost every program is about cops and detectives.
> [semicolon replaces comma]

Since the two independent clauses in the first example contain ideas that are closely connected logically, the most effective of the three comma-splice remedies is to add a subordinating conjunction *(Because)* to the first of the two clauses, making it depend on the second. For the same reason—close conceptual connection—the best remedy for the next comma splice is to substitute a semicolon for the comma. The semicolon signals that the two independent clauses are closely linked in meaning. In general, you can use a semicolon where you could also use a period.

The best cures for the perpetual comma splicer are to learn to recognize the difference between independent and dependent clauses and to get rid of the "pause theory" of punctuation. All of the clauses in our two examples are independent. As written, each of these should be punctuated not with a comma but a period or a semicolon. Instead, the perpetual comma splicer usually acts on the pause theory: because the ideas in the independent clauses are closely connected, the writer hesitates to separate them with a period. And so the writer inserts what he or she takes to be a shorter pause—the comma. But a comma is not a breath mark; it provides readers with specific grammatical information, in this case (erroneously) that there is only one independent clause separated by the comma from modifying information. In the corrections, by contrast, the semicolon sends the appropriate signal to the reader: the message that it is joining two associated but independent statements. (A coordinating conjunction such as *and* would also be grammatically correct, though possibly awkward.)

Fused Sentence

The Indo-European language family includes many groups most languages in Europe belong to it.

Correction

The Indo-European language family includes many groups. Most languages in Europe belong to it.
[period inserted after first independent clause]

You could also fix this fused sentence with the coordinating conjunction *and*. Alternatively, you might condense the whole into a single independent clause:

Most languages in Europe belong to the Indo-European language family.

Comma Splices with Conjunctive Adverbs

Quantitative methods of data collection show broad trends, however, they ignore specific cases.

Sociobiology poses a threat to traditional ethics, for example, it asserts that human behavior is genetically motivated by the "selfish gene" to perpetuate itself.

Corrections

Quantitative methods of data collection show broad trends; however, they ignore specific cases.
[semicolon replaces comma before *however*]

Sociobiology poses a threat to traditional ethics; for example, it asserts that human behavior is genetically motivated by the "selfish gene" to perpetuate itself.
[semicolon replaces comma before *for example*]

Both of these examples contain one of the most common forms of comma splices. Both of them are *compound sentences*—that is, they contain two independent clauses. (See Chapter 9, the section "The Compound Sentence.") Normally, connecting the clauses with a comma and a conjunction would be correct: for example, "Most hawks hunt alone, but osprey hunt in pairs." In the two comma splices given, however, the independent clauses are joined by transitional expressions known as **conjunctive adverbs.** (See glossary.) When conjunctive adverbs are used to link two independent clauses, they always require a semicolon. By contrast, when a coordinating conjunction links the two clauses of a compound sentence, it is always preceded by a comma.

In most cases, depending on the sense of the sentence, the semicolon precedes the conjunctive adverb and has the effect of clarifying the division between the two clauses. There are exceptions to this general rule, though, as in the following sentence.

The lazy boy did finally read a *book, however;* it was the least he could do.

Here *however* is a part of the first independent clause, qualifying its claim. The sentence thus suggests that the boy was not totally lazy, since he did get around to reading a book. Note how the meaning changes when *however* becomes the introductory word for the second independent clause:

The lazy boy did finally read a *book; however,* it was the least he could do.

Here the restricting force of *however* suggests that reading the book was not much of an accomplishment.

TEST YOURSELF: COMMA SPLICES

What makes each of the sentences below a comma splice? What would be the best way to fix each one and why?

"Virtual reality" is a new buzzword, so is "hyperspace."

Many popular cures for cancer have been discredited, nevertheless, many people continue to buy them.

Elvis Presley's home, Graceland, attracts many musicians as a kind of shrine, even Paul Simon has been there.

She didn't play well with others, she sat on the bench and watched.

BWE 3: ERRORS IN SUBJECT-VERB AGREEMENT

The subject and the verb must agree in number, singular subjects taking singular verbs and plural subjects taking plural verbs. Errors in subject-verb agreement usually occur when a writer misidentifies the subject or verb of a clause.

Agreement Problem
Various kinds of vandalism has been rapidly increasing.

Correction
Various kinds of vandalism *have* been rapidly increasing.
[verb made plural to match *kinds*]

> ### Hint Box: Nonstandard English
>
> The term *standard written English* refers to language that conforms to the rules and conventions adhered to by the majority of English-speaking writers. The fact is, however, that not all speakers of English grow up hearing, reading, and writing standard written English. Some linguistic cultures in America, for example, follow a different set of conventions for subject/verb agreement. Their speakers do not differentiate singular from plural verb forms with a terminal *-s,* as in standard English:
>
> She walks home after work.
>
> They walk home after work.
>
> Some speakers of English do not observe this distinction, so that the first sentence above becomes:
>
> She walk home after work.
>
> These two ways of handling subject/verb agreement are recognized by linguists not in terms of right versus wrong, but in terms of dialect difference. A dialect is a variety of a language that is characteristic of a region or culture and is sometimes unintelligible to outsiders. The problem for speakers of a dialect that differs from the norm is that they can't always rely on their ear—on what sounds right—when they are editing according to the rules of standard written English. If you consistently fail to detect a particular kind of error because it looks and sounds right to you, the best solution is to add a proofreading stage to your final draft in which you check every sentence only for that error.

When you isolate the grammatical subject *(kinds)* and the verb *(has)* of the original sentence, you can tell that they do not agree. While *vandalism* might seem to be the subject because it is closest to the verb, it is actually the **object of the preposition** *of.* The majority of agreement problems arise from mistaking the object of a preposition for the actual subject of a sentence. If you habitually make this mistake, you can begin to remedy it by familiarizing yourself with the most common **prepositions.** (See glossary.)

Agreement Problem
Another aspect of territoriality that differentiates humans from animals are their possession of ideas and objects.

Correction
Another aspect of territoriality that differentiates humans from animals *is* their possession of ideas and objects.
[verb made singular to match subject *aspect*]

The subject of the sentence is *aspect.* The two plural nouns *(humans* and *animals)* probably encourage the mistake of using a plural verb *(are),* but *humans* is part of the *that* clause modifying *aspect,* and *animals* is the object of the preposition *from.*

Agreement Problem

The Republican and the Democrat both believe in doing what's best for America, but each believe that the other doesn't understand what's best.

Correction

The Republican and the Democrat both believe in doing what's best for America, but each *believes* that the other doesn't understand what's best.

[verb made singular to agree with subject *each*]

The word *each* is always singular, so the verb must be singular as well *(believes)*. The presence of a plural subject and verb in the sentence's first independent clause *(The Republican and the Democrat both believe)* has probably encouraged the error.

TEST YOURSELF: **SUBJECT-VERB AGREEMENT**

Test yourself by diagnosing and correcting the error in the example below:

The controversies surrounding the placement of Arthur Ashe's statue in Richmond was difficult for the various factions to resolve.

BWE 4: SHIFTS IN SENTENCE STRUCTURE (FAULTY PREDICATION)

This error involves an illogical mismatch between subject and predicate. If you continually run afoul of faulty predication, you might use the exercises in a handbook to drill you on isolating the grammatical subjects and verbs of sentences, since that is the first move you need to make in fixing the problem.

Shift

In 1987, the release of more information became available.

Correction

In 1987, more *information* became available *for release.*

[new subject]

It was the *information,* not the *release,* that *became more available.* The correction relocates *information* from its position as object of the preposition *of* to the subject position in the sentence; it also moves *release* into a prepositional phrase.

Shift

The busing controversy was intended to rectify the inequality of educational opportunities.

Correction

Busing was intended to rectify the inequality of educational opportunities.

[new subject formulated to match verb]

The *controversy* wasn't *intended to rectify,* but *busing* was.

TEST YOURSELF: **FAULTY PREDICATION**

Identify and correct the faulty predication in the example below:

The subject of learning disabilities is difficult to identify accurately.

BWE 5: Errors in Pronoun Reference

There are at least three forms of this problem. All of them involve a lack of clarity about who or what a **pronoun** (a word that substitutes for a noun) refers to. The surest way to avoid difficulties is to make certain that the pronoun relates back unambiguously to a specific word, known as the *antecedent*. In the sentence "Nowadays appliances don't last as long as they once did," the noun *appliances* is the antecedent of the pronoun *they*.

Pronoun-Antecedent Agreement

A pronoun must agree in number (and gender) with the noun or noun phrase that it refers to.

Pronoun Error

It can be dangerous if a child, after watching television, decides to practice what they saw.

Corrections

It can be dangerous if *children,* after watching television, *decide* to practice what *they* saw.
[antecedent (and verb) made plural to agree with pronoun]

It can be dangerous if a child, after watching television, decides to practice what *he or she* saw.
[singular pronouns substituted to match singular antecedent *child*]

The error occurs because *child* is singular but its matching pronoun, *they*, is plural. The first correction makes both plural; the second makes both singular. You might also observe in the first word of the example—the impersonal *it*—an exception to the rule that pronouns must have antecedents.

TEST YOURSELF: PRONOUN-ANTECEDENT AGREEMENT

What is wrong with the following sentence, and how would you fix it?

Every dog has its day, but all too often when that day happens, they can be found barking up the wrong tree.

Ambiguous Reference

A pronoun should have only one possible antecedent.

Pronoun Error

Children like comedians because they have a sense of humor.

Corrections

Because children have a sense of humor, *they* like comedians.
[subordinate *because* clause placed first, and relationship between noun *children* and pronoun *they* tightened]

Children like comedians because *comedians* have a sense of humor.
[pronoun eliminated and replaced by repetition of noun]

Hint Box: Sexism and Pronoun Usage

Errors in pronoun reference sometimes occur because of a writer's praiseworthy desire to avoid sexism. In most circles, the following correction of the preceding example would be considered sexist:

It can be dangerous if a child, after watching TV, decides to practice what *he* saw.

Though the writer of such a sentence may intend *he* to function as a gender-neutral, impersonal pronoun, it in fact excludes girls on the basis of gender. Implicitly, it also conveys sexual stereotypes (for example, that only boys are violent, or perhaps stupid enough to confuse TV with reality).

The easiest way to avoid the problem of sexism in pronoun usage usually lies in putting things into the plural, since plural pronouns *(we, you, they)* have no gender. (See the use of *children* in the first correction of the "Pronoun-Antecedent Agreement" example.) Alternatively, you can use the phrase *he or she,* as in the second correction above. Many readers, however, find *he or she* and its variant, *s/he,* to be awkward constructions. Another remedy lies in rewriting the sentence to avoid pronouns altogether, as in the following revision:

It can be dangerous if a child, after watching television, decides to practice *some violent activity portrayed on the screen.*

Does *they* in the original example refer to *children* or *comedians?* The rule in such cases of ambiguity is that the pronoun refers to the nearest possible antecedent, so here *comedians* possess the sense of humor, regardless of what the writer may intend. As the corrections demonstrate, either reordering the sentence or repeating the noun can remove the ambiguity.

***TEST YOURSELF:* AMBIGUOUS REFERENCE**

As you proofread, it's a good idea to target your pronouns to make sure that they cannot conceivably refer to more than one noun. What's wrong with the following sentences, and how would you fix them?

Alexander the Great's father, Philip of Macedon, died when he was twenty-six.

The committee could not look into the problem because it was too involved.

Broad Reference

Broad reference occurs when a pronoun refers loosely to a number of ideas expressed in preceding clauses or sentences. It causes confusion because the reader cannot be sure which of the ideas the pronoun refers to.

Pronoun Error

As a number of scholars have noted, Sigmund Freud and Karl Marx offered competing but also at times complementary critiques of the dehumanizing tendencies of Western capitalist society. We see this in Christopher Lasch's analysis of conspicuous consumption in *The Culture of Narcissism*.

Correction

As a number of scholars have noted, Sigmund Freud and Karl Marx offered competing but also at times complementary critiques of the dehumanizing tendencies of Western capitalist society. We see *this complementary view* in Christopher Lasch's analysis of conspicuous consumption in *The Culture of Narcissism*.
[broad *this* clarified by addition of noun phrase]

The word *this* in the second sentence of the uncorrected example could refer to the fact that *a number of scholars have noted* the relationship between Marx and Freud, to the competition between Freud's and Marx's critiques of capitalism, or to the complementary nature of their critiques.

Broad reference most commonly occurs when *this* is used as a pronoun; the remedy is generally to avoid using the word as a pronoun. Instead, convert *this* into an adjective, and let it modify some noun that more clearly specifies the referent: *this complementary view,* as in the correction or, alternatively, *this competition* or *this scholarly perspective.*

TEST YOURSELF: BROAD REFERENCE

Locate the errors in the following examples and provide a remedy:

Regardless of whether the film is foreign or domestic, they can be found in your neighborhood video store.

Many experts now claim that dogs and other higher mammals dream; for those who don't own such pets, this is often difficult to believe.

BWE 6: Misplaced Modifiers and Dangling Participles

Before you can detect misplaced modifiers, you first need to understand what modifiers are. *Modifiers* are words or groups of words used to qualify, limit, intensify, or explain some other element in a sentence. A *misplaced modifier* is a word or phrase that appears to modify the wrong word or words.

Misplaced Modifier

At the age of three he caught a fish with a broken arm.

Correction

At the age of three *the boy with a broken arm* caught a fish.
[noun replaces pronoun; prepositional phrase revised and relocated]

The original sentence mistakenly implies that the fish has a broken arm.

Misplaced Modifier

According to legend, General George Washington crossed the Delaware and celebrated Christmas in a small boat.

Correction

According to legend, General George Washington crossed the Delaware *in a small boat* and *then* celebrated Christmas *on shore.*

[prepositional phrase relocated; modifiers added to second verb]

As a general rule, you can avoid misplacing a modifier by keeping it as close as possible to what it modifies. Thus, the second correction removes the implication that Washington celebrated Christmas in a small boat. When you cannot relocate the modifier, separate it from the rest of the sentence with a comma to prevent readers from connecting it to the nearest noun.

A *dangling participle* creates a particular kind of problem in modification: the noun or pronoun that the writer intends the participial phrase to modify is not actually present in the sentence.

Dangling Participle

After debating the issue of tax credits for the elderly, the bill passed in a close vote.

Correction

After debating the issue of tax credits for the elderly, *the Senate passed the bill* in a close vote.
[appropriate noun added for participle to modify]

The bill did not debate the issue, as the original example implies. As the correction demonstrates, fixing a dangling participle involves tightening the link between the activity implied by the participle *(debating)* and the entity performing that action *(the Senate)*.

TEST YOURSELF: **MODIFICATION ERRORS**

Find the modification errors in the examples below. How would you correct each of them?

After eating their sandwiches, the steamboat left the dock.

The social workers saw an elderly woman on a bus with a cane standing up.

Crossing the street, a car hit the pedestrian.

BWE 7: ERRORS IN USING POSSESSIVE APOSTROPHES

Adding *'s* to most singular nouns will make them show possession: the plant*'s* roots, the accountant*'s* ledger. You can add the apostrophe alone, without the *s,* to make plural nouns that already end with *s* show possession: the flower*s'* fragrances, the ship*s'* berths.

Apostrophe Error

The loyal opposition scorned the committees decisions.

Corrections

The loyal opposition scorned the *committee's* decisions.

The loyal opposition scorned the *committees'* decisions.
[possessive apostrophe added]

The first correction assumes there was one committee; the second assumes there were two or more.

Apostrophe Error

The advisory board swiftly transacted it's business.

Correction

The advisory board swiftly transacted *its* business.
[apostrophe dropped]

Unlike possessive nouns, possessive pronouns *(my, your, yours, her, hers, his, its, our, ours, their, theirs)* do not take an apostrophe. (See BWE 9.)

TEST YOURSELF: **POSSESSIVE APOSTROPHES**

Find the error in the following sentence.

The womens movement has been misunderstood by many of its detractors.

BWE 8: COMMA ERRORS

As with other rules of punctuation and grammar, the many that pertain to comma usage share an underlying aim: to clarify the relationships among the parts of a sentence. Commas separate the parts of a sentence. They are particularly useful in separating the main clause from dependent elements, such as subordinate clauses and long prepositional phrases. One of their primary uses, then, is to help your readers distinguish the main clause from the rest of the sentence.

Comma Error

After eating the couple went home.

Correction

After *eating,* the couple went home.
[comma added before independent clause]

The comma after *eating* is needed to keep the main clause *visible* or separate; it marks the point at which the prepositional phrase ends and the independent clause begins. Without this separation, readers would be invited to contemplate cannibalism as they move across the sentence.

Comma Error

In the absence of rhetoric study teachers and students lack a vocabulary for talking about their prose.

Correction

In the absence of rhetoric *study,* teachers and students lack a vocabulary for talking about their prose.
[comma added to separate prepositional phrase from main clause]

Readers have to read the sentence twice to find out where the prepositional phrase ends—with *study*—in order to figure out where the main clause begins.

Comma Error

Dog owners, despite their many objections will have to obey the new law.

Correction

Dog owners, despite their many *objections,* will have to obey the new law.
[single comma converted to a pair of commas]

A comma is needed after *objections* in order to isolate the phrase in the middle of the sentence *(despite their many objections)* from the main clause. This phrase is *nonrestrictive;* that is, the information it contains provides additional information that is not essential to the meaning of what it modifies. The test of nonrestrictive phrases and clauses is to see if they can be omitted without substantially changing the message that a sentence conveys ("Dog owners will have to obey the new law"). Nonrestrictive elements always take two commas—a comma "sandwich"—to set them off. Using only one comma separates the sentence's subject *(dog owners)* from its predicate *(will have to obey)* illogically. This problem is easier to see in a shorter sentence. You wouldn't, for example, write "I, fell down."

Comma Error

Most people regardless of age like to spend money.

Correction

Most *people,* regardless of age, like to spend money.
[comma sandwich added]

Commas enclose the nonrestrictive elements in the corrected example above. You could omit this information without significantly affecting the sense. Such is not the case in the two examples below.

Comma Error

People, who live in glass houses, should not throw stones.

Correction

People *who live in glass houses* should not throw stones.
[commas omitted]

Comma Error

Please return the library book, that I left on the table.

Correction

Please return the library *book that* I left on the table.
[comma omitted]

It is incorrect to place commas around *who live in glass houses* or a comma before *that I left on the table.* Each of these is a *restrictive clause*—that is, it contains information that is an essential part of what it modifies. In the first sentence, for example, if *who live in glass houses* is left out, the meaning of the sentence is lost: *People should not throw stones. Who* is defined by restricting it to *people* in the category of glass-house dwellers. Similarly, in the second example the *that* clause contributes an essential meaning to *book*—the sentence is referring to not just any book but a particular one, the one *on the table.*

As a general rule, if the information in a phrase or clause can be omitted—if it is nonessential and therefore nonrestrictive—it needs to be separated by commas from the rest of the sentence. Also be aware that restrictive clauses use *that* and nonrestrictive clauses use *which*.

***TEST YOURSELF:* COMMA ERRORS**

How would you fix the following example?

The book which I had read a few years ago contained a lot of outdated data.

BWE 9: Spelling/Diction Errors That Interfere with Meaning

Misspellings are always a problem in a final draft, insofar as they undermine your authority by inviting readers to perceive you as careless (at best). If you make a habit of using the spell-checking function of a word processor, you will take care of most misspellings. But the problems that a spell-checker won't catch are the ones that can often hurt you most. These are actually *diction* errors—incorrect word choices in which you have confused one word with another that it closely resembles. In such cases, you have spelled the word correctly, but it's the wrong word. Since it means something other than what you've intended, you end up misleading your readers.

The best way to avoid this problem is to memorize the differences between pairs of words that are commonly confused with each other but have distinct meanings. The following examples illustrate a few of the most common and serious of these errors. Most handbooks contain a glossary of usage that *cites* more of these *sites* of confusion.

Spelling/Diction Error: *It's* versus *Its*

Although you can't tell a book by it's cover, its fairly easy to get the general idea from the introduction.

Correction

Although you can't tell a book by *its* cover, *it's* fairly easy to get the general idea from the introduction.

[apostrophe dropped from possessive and added to contraction]

It's is a contraction for *it is. Its* is a possessive pronoun meaning "belonging to it." If you confuse the two, *it's* likely that your sentence will, at least initially, mislead *its* readers. (See BWE 7.)

Spelling/Diction Error: *Their* versus *There* versus *They're*

Their are ways of learning about the cuisine of northern India besides going their to watch the master chefs and learn there secrets—assuming their willing to share them.

Correction

There are ways of learning about the cuisine of northern India besides going *there* to watch the master chefs and learn *their* secrets—assuming *they're* willing to share them.

[expletive *there*, adverb *there*, possessive pronoun *their*, and contraction *they're* inserted appropriately]

There as an adverb normally refers to a place; *there* can also be used as an *expletive* to introduce a clause, as in the first usage of the correction. (See the discussion of expletives in chapter 9, the section "Cutting the Fat.") *Their* is a possessive pronoun meaning "belonging to them." *They're* is a contraction for *they are.*

Spelling/Diction Error: *Then* versus *Than*

If a person would rather break a law then obey it, than he or she must be willing to face the consequences.

Correction

If a person would rather break a law *than* obey it, *then* he or she must be willing to face the consequences.

[comparative *than* distinguished from temporal *then*]

Than is a conjunction used with comparisons: rather x *than* y. *Then* is an adverb used to indicate what comes next in relation to time: first x, *then* y.

Spelling/Diction Error: *Effect* versus *Affect*

It is simply the case that BWEs adversely effect the way that readers judge what a writer has to say. It follows that writers who include lots of BWEs in their prose may not have calculated the disastrous affects of these mistakes.

Correction

It is simply the case that BWEs adversely *affect* the way that readers judge what a writer has to say. It follows that writers who include lots of BWEs in their prose may not have calculated the disastrous *effects* of these mistakes.

[verb *affect* and noun *effects* inserted appropriately]

In their most common usages, *affect* is a verb meaning "to influence" and *effect* is a noun meaning "the result of an action or cause." The confusion of *affect* and *effect* is enlarged by the fact that both of these words have secondary meanings: the verb *to effect* means "to cause or bring about"; the noun *affect* is used in psychology to mean "emotion or feeling." Thus, if you confuse these two words, you will inadvertently make a meaning radically different from the one you intend.

GLOSSARY OF GRAMMATICAL TERMS

adjective An adjective is a part of speech that usually modifies a noun or pronoun: for example, *blue, boring,* and *boisterous.*

adverb An adverb is a part of speech that modifies an adjective, adverb, or verb: for example, *heavily, habitually,* and *very.*

clauses (independent and dependent) A clause is any group of words that contains both a **subject** and a **predicate.** An **independent clause** (also known as a **main clause**) can stand alone as a sentence. For example,

The most famous revolutionaries of this century have all, in one way or another, offered a vision of a classless society.

The subject of this independent clause is *revolutionaries,* the verb is *have offered,* and the direct object is *vision.* By contrast, a **dependent** (or **subordinate**) **clause** is any group of words containing a subject and verb that cannot stand alone as a separate sentence because it depends on an independent clause to complete its meaning. The following sentence adds two dependent clauses to our previous example.

> The most famous revolutionaries of this century have all, in one way or another, offered a vision of a classless society, *although* most historians would agree *that* this ideal has never been achieved.

The origin of the word *depend* is "to hang": a dependent clause literally hangs on the independent clause. In the example above, neither *although most historians would agree* nor *that this ideal has never been achieved* can stand independently. The *that* clause relies on the *although* clause, which in turn relies on the main clause. *That* and *although* function as **subordinating conjunctions;** by eliminating them, we could rewrite the sentence to contain three independent clauses:

> The most famous revolutionaries of this century have all, in one way or another, offered a vision of a classless society. Most historians would agree on one judgment about this ideal: it has never been achieved.

comma splice   A comma splice consists of two independent clauses connected ("spliced") with a comma. See *BWE 2.*

conjunctions (coordinating and subordinating)   A conjunction is a part of speech that connects words, phrases, or clauses: for example, *and, but, although.* The conjunction in some way defines that connection: for example, *and* links; *but* separates. All conjunctions define connections in one of two basic ways. **Coordinating conjunctions** connect words or groups of words that have equal grammatical importance. The coordinating conjunctions are *and, but, or, nor, for, so,* and *yet.* **Subordi-**

nating conjunctions introduce a dependent clause and connect it to a main clause. Here is a partial list of the most common subordinating conjunctions: *after, although, as, as if, as long as, because, before, if, rather than, since, than, that, though, unless, until, when, where, whether,* and *while.*

conjunctive adverb   A conjunctive adverb is a word that links two independent clauses (as a conjunction) but also modifies the clause it introduces (as an adverb). Some of the most common conjunctive adverbs are *consequently, furthermore, however, moreover, nevertheless, similarly, therefore,* and *thus.* Phrases can also serve this function, such as *for example* and *on the other hand.* When conjunctive adverbs are used to link two independent clauses, they always require a semicolon:

> Many pharmaceutical chains now offer their own generic versions of common drugs; however, many consumers continue to spend more for name brands that contain the same active ingredients as the generics.

When conjunctive adverbs occur within an independent clause, however, they are enclosed in a pair of commas, as is the case with the use of *however* earlier in this sentence.

coordination   Coordination refers to grammatically equal words, phrases, or clauses. Coordinate constructions are used to give elements in a sentence equal weight or importance. In the sentence "The tall, thin judge required the witness to answer the lawyer's question, but the witness refused," *The tall, thin judge required the witness to answer the lawyer's question* and *but the witness refused* are coordinate clauses; *tall* and *thin* are coordinate adjectives.

dependent clause (see **clauses)**

direct object   The direct object is a noun or pronoun that receives the action carried by the verb and performed by the subject. In the sentence "Certain mushrooms can kill you," *you* is the direct object.

fused (or **run-on) sentence**   A fused sentence combines two independent clauses with no conjunction or punctuation. See *BWE 2.*

gerund (see **verbals)**

independent clause (see **clauses)**

infinitive (see **verbals)**

main clause (see **clauses)**

noun   A noun is a part of speech that names a person *(woman)*, place *(town)*, thing *(book)*, idea *(justice)*, quality *(irony)*, or action *(betrayal)*.

object of the preposition (see **preposition)**

participle and **participial phrase** (see **verbals)**

phrase   A phrase is a group of words occurring in a meaningful sequence that lacks either a subject or a predicate. This absence distinguishes it from a clause, which contains both a subject and a predicate. Phrases function in sentences as adjectives, adverbs, nouns, or verbs. They are customarily classified according to the part of speech of their key word: *over the mountain* is a **prepositional phrase;** *running for office* is a **participial phrase;** *had been disciplined* is a **verb phrase;** *desktop graphics* is a **noun phrase;** and so forth.

predicate   The predicate contains the verb of a sentence or clause, making some kind of statement about the subject. The predicate of the preceding sentence is *contains the verb, . . . making some kind of statement about the subject.* The simple predicate—the verb to which the other words in the sentence are attached—is *contains.*

preposition, prepositional phrase   A preposition is a part of speech that links a noun or pronoun to some other word in the sentence. Prepositions usually express a relationship of time *(after)* or space *(above)* or direction *(toward)*. The noun to which the preposition is attached is known as the **object of the preposition.** A preposition, its object, and any modifiers comprise a **prepositional phrase.** "*With* love *from* me *to* you" strings together three prepositional phrases. Here is a partial list of some of the most common prepositions: *about, above, across, after, among, at, before, behind, between, by, during, for, from, in, into, like, of, on, out, over, since, through, to, toward, under, until, up, upon, with, within,* and *without.*

pronoun   A pronoun is a part of speech that substitutes for a noun. Examples are: *I, you, he, she, it, we,* and *they.*

run-on (or **fused) sentence**   A run-on sentence combines two independent clauses with no conjunction or punctuation. See *BWE 2.*

sentence   A sentence is a unit of expression that can stand independently. It contains two parts, a **subject** and a **predicate.** The shortest sentence in the Bible, for example, is "Jesus wept." *Jesus* is the subject; *wept* is the predicate.

sentence fragment   A sentence fragment is a group of words punctuated like a complete sentence but lacking the necessary structure; it is only a part of a sentence. "Walking down the road" or "The origin of the problem" are both fragments because neither contains both a **subject** and a **predicate.** See *BWE 1.*

subject   The subject, in most cases a noun or pronoun, names the doer of the action in a sentence or identifies what the predicate is about. The subject of the previous sentence, for example, is *The subject, in most cases a noun or pronoun.* The simple subject of that sentence—the noun to which the other words in the sentence are attached—is *subject.*

subordination, subordinating conjunctions Subordination refers to the placement of certain grammatical units, particularly phrases and clauses, at a lower, less important structural level than other elements. As with coordination, the grammatical ranking carries conceptual significance as well: whatever is grammatically subordinated appears less important than the information carried in the main clause. In the following example, the 486 personal computer is subordinated both grammatically and conceptually to the Pentium-based PC:

Although 486-based personal computers continue to improve in speed, the new Pentium-based PC systems have thoroughly outclassed them.

Here *Although* is a **subordinating conjunction** that introduces a subordinate clause, also known as a **dependent clause.**

verb A verb is a part of speech that describes an action *(goes)*, states how something was affected by an action *(became angered)*, or expresses a state of being *(is)*.

verbals (participles, gerunds, and infinitives) Verbals are words derived from verbs. They are verb forms that look like verbs but instead function as nouns, adjectives, or adverbs.

An **infinitive**—composed of the root form of a verb plus *to (to be, to vote)*—becomes a verbal when it is used as a noun *(To eat is essential)*, an adjective *(These are the books to read)*, or an adverb *(He was too sick to walk)*.

Similarly, a **participle**—usually composed of the root form of a verb plus *-ing* (present participle) or *-ed* (past participle)—becomes a verbal when used as an adjective. It can occur as a single word, modifying a noun, as in *faltering negotiations* or *finished business.* But it also occurs in a **participial phrase,** consisting of the participle, its object, and any modifiers. Here are two examples:

Having been tried and convicted, the criminal was sentenced to life imprisonment.

Following the path of most resistance, the masochist took deep pleasure in his frustration.

Having been tried and convicted is a participial phrase that modifies *criminal; Following the path of most resistance* is a participial phrase that modifies *masochist.*

The third form of verbal, the **gerund,** resembles the participle. Like the participle, it adds *-ing* to the root form of the verb, but unlike the participle, it is used as a noun. In the sentence "Swimming is extraordinarily aerobic," the gerund *swimming* functions as the subject. Again like participles, gerunds can occur in phrases. The gerund phrases are italicized in the following example: *"Watching a film adaptation* takes less effort than *reading the book* from which it was made."

In using a verbal, remember that although it resembles a verb, it cannot function alone as the verb in a sentence: *Being a military genius* is a fragment, not a sentence.

GUIDELINES FOR REVISING FOR CORRECTNESS

1. In correcting grammar, seek to discover the patterns of error in your writing, and unlearn the logic that has led you to make certain kinds of errors recurrently.
2. Check the draft for errors that obscure the boundaries of sentences: fragments, comma splices, and run-ons. Begin by isolating the simple subject and predicate in the main clause(s) of every sentence (to make sure they exist); this check will also

help you to spot faulty predication and errors in subject-verb agreement. Then check to see that each independent clause is separated from others by a period, comma plus coordinating conjunction, or semicolon.

3. Check your sentences for ambiguity (capable of being read in more than one way) by deliberately trying to misread them. If your sentence can be read to mean something other than what you intended, the most common causes are misplaced and dangling modifiers and errors in pronoun reference.

4. Fix errors in pronoun reference and misplaced modifiers by making sure that every pronoun has only one clear antecedent and that every modifying word or phrase is placed as close as possible to the part of the sentence it modifies.

5. Avoid dangling modifiers by making sure that the noun or pronoun being modified is actually present in the sentence. Avoid broad reference by adding the appropriate noun or noun phrase after the pronoun *this*. (You can greatly improve the clarity of your prose just by avoiding use of the vague *this*, especially at the beginnings of sentences.)

6. Check that commas are separating dependent clauses, long prepositional phrases, or other modifying elements from the main clause. A comma is not a pause; its function is to help readers locate your sentence's main (independent) clause(s).

7. Enclose nonrestrictive modifiers placed between the subject and predicate of a sentence in a pair of commas or—for more emphasis—in a pair of dashes. A nonrestrictive modifier is a phrase that can be deleted from the sentence without changing the sentence's meaning.

APPENDIX A

DOCUMENTATION STYLES

THIS APPENDIX TREATS THE technical side of using sources. The first three sections of this appendix deal with specific features of two of the more common styles: the MLA (Modern Language Association), which uses the author-work format, and the APA (American Psychological Association), which uses the author-date format. Section I examines MLA and APA styles for in-text citations—that is, for crediting sources in the body of your paper. Section II discusses MLA and APA styles for end-of-text references—that is, for the reference section that provides full bibliographic information on your sources, usually placed at the end of your paper or report. Section III explores the MLA and APA styles for citation of electronic sources, such as on-line databases. Section IV presents the basics of some other important documentation styles, including principal variants of the number-reference system, as well as the Chicago style, based on the *Chicago Manual of Style.*

Once you begin doing most of your writing in a particular discipline, you may want to purchase the more detailed style guide adhered to by that discipline. Toward this end, we have included at the end of this appendix, as Section V, a brief bibliography of style manuals. Because documentation styles differ not only from discipline to discipline but also even from journal to journal within a discipline, you should consult your professor about which documentation format he or she wishes you to use in a given course.

Larger questions of form, such as the disciplinary format for reports in the sciences and social sciences, are beyond the scope of this appendix. They are addressed at length, however, elsewhere in the book. For advice on formats governing the organization of an entire paper, see Chapter 3, "Questions of Format," and the sections titled Voices from Across the Curriculum, which appear throughout the text. For illustrations of how to integrate quotations into your text, and for discussions of what you need to cite, what you don't, and why, see Chapter 8, "Using Sources." Chapter 8 also addresses the larger matter of using (in the sense of "conversing with") sources, rather than just including them.

From this appendix you will learn how to document most of the kinds of research materials you are likely to use in college writing. The appendix is arranged in a way that should allow you to quickly grasp the chief organizing principles by which each of the major types of documentation styles operates. Although this appendix cannot cover everything, it can provide you with perspective on the *logic* of various documentation styles. Once acquainted with this logic, you will be better able to follow and understand the more compendious style guides of particular disciplines.

SECTION I: IN-TEXT CITATIONS (MLA AND APA)

In-text citations indicate in shorthand form in the body of your paper the source you are using. All in-text citations direct your readers to the complete citation located in a list of references at the end of the paper or report. Although the MLA and APA styles use slightly different forms, both insert brief identifying information within parentheses at the end of a sentence. Within each style the form varies a little depending on the type of source being cited. To keep attention focused on the form, we use variations of one basic sentence for all examples of MLA in-text citations and another sentence for all examples of APA in-text citations.

MLA In-Text Citations

1. Single author

For both books and articles, include the author's name and the page number (without the abbreviation "p."). Note that there is no intervening punctuation between name and page and that the parentheses precede the period or other punctuation. If the sentence ends with a direct quotation, the parentheses come after the quotation marks but before the closing period. Also note that no punctuation occurs between the last word of the quotation and the closing quotation mark:

> The influence of Seamus Heaney on younger poets in Northern Ireland has been widely acknowledged, but Patrick Kavanagh's "plain-speaking, pastoral" influence on him is "less recognized" (Smith 74).

In this case, "(Smith 74)" indicates the author's last name and the page number on which the cited passage appears. The end-of-text reference list is organized alphabetically by authors' last names. A reader could look up Smith in this list to find complete bibliographical information on this source (such as publisher and date).

If the author's name has been mentioned in the sentence, you should include only the page number:

> According to Smith, Kavanagh's "plain-speaking, pastoral style influenced Heaney" (74).

One exception to these rules occurs with quotations of more than four typed lines. These are set off from the text by indenting one inch from the left margin and typing them double-spaced without quotation marks. The citation in such cases should appear in parentheses two spaces *after* the final punctuation. For example:

> Kavanagh's plain-speaking, pastoral style influenced Heaney. In such poems as Heaney's "Digging," we encounter the presence of a rural voice offering mordant commentary on his father's literal and figurative roots. It is less recognized, however, that we encounter the same mordant tone in Kavanagh's "The Great Hunger." (Smith 74)

2. Two or three authors of a single work

List them all:

> (Smith, Jones, and Adams 74).

Note that MLA spells out the word "and"; some other documentation styles, such as APA, specify an ampersand (&) in place of the "and."

3. More than three authors of a single work

Use the first author's name and "et al." This phrase, which means "and others," is neither italicized nor placed in quotes: (Smith et al. 74).

4. Two or more works by the same author

Include a short version of the title to identify which work by the same author you are citing. Generally speaking, shorten the title by taking out the first few words, rather than lifting out the key terms. If the original title were *Belfast Poets and the Anxiety of Influence,* you could use "(Smith, *Belfast Poets* 74)."

5. A multivolume work

Include the volume number, followed by a colon and the page: (Smith 2: 74).

6. Unknown author

In the case of unsigned articles (usually brief newspaper or magazine pieces), use a short version of the title: ("Belfast Poets" 74).

7. Quoting a source's quotation

When you quote a quotation (commonly known as an indirect source), add the abbreviation "qtd. in."

According to Harriet Smith, the "plain-speaking, pastoral style" of Irish poet Patrick Kavanagh heavily influenced Seamus Heaney (qtd. in Marsh 57).

8. More than one work in a single citation

Separate the works with a semicolon, alphabetized by the authors' last names:

The influence of Patrick Kavanagh on Seamus Heaney's poetry usually centers on issues of class consciousness and regional identity (Marsh 82; Smith 74).

APA In-Text Citations

1. Single author

For both books and articles, include the author's name, followed by a comma, and then the date of publication. If you are quoting or referring to a specific passage, include the page number as well, separated from the date by a comma and the abbreviation "p." followed by a space. In short, unlike MLA style, APA includes a comma after the author's name, the date of publication, and, preceded by another comma, the abbreviation "p."

Studies of students' changing attitudes towards the small colleges that they attend suggest that their loyalty to the institution declines steadily over a four-year period, whereas their loyalty to individual professors or departments increases "markedly, by as much as 25 percent over the last two years" (Brown, 1994, p. 41).

As in MLA style, (1) the parentheses precede the period or other end punctuation of the sentence being documented; (2) if the sentence ends with a direct quotation, the parentheses come after the quotation marks but still before the period; and (3) no punctuation occurs between the last word of the quotation and the closing quotation mark.

If the author's name has been mentioned in the sentence, include only the date in the parentheses immediately following the author's name:

Brown (1992) documents the decline in students' institutional loyalty.

Alternatively, you could avoid parenthetical citation altogether:

In his 1992 study, Brown documents the decline in students' institutional loyalty.

One exception to these rules occurs with quotations of forty words or more. These are set off from the text by indenting five spaces from the left margin and typing single-space without quotation marks. The citation in such cases should appear in parentheses one space *after* the final punctuation. For example:

Brown documents the decline in students' institutional loyalty. In a survey of entering and graduating college students, Brown found that graduating seniors, while reporting their highest loyalty to individual faculty members within their majors, indicated significant decreases in enthusiasm for the institution at large from what they had reported as first-year students. (1992)

2. Multiple authors

For a work with two authors, include both names every time, connected with an ampersand (&): (Brown & Greene, 1995).

For a work with three, four, or five authors, include all names in the first reference: (Brown, Greene, Blue, Orange, & Square, 1995). In subsequent references use only the first author followed by "et al." (followed by a comma) and the year: (Brown et al., 1995).

For a work with six or more authors, use only the first author's name followed by "et al." for all citations.

3. Two or more works by the same author

The date within the parenthetical citation will distinguish which of the two works by the same author you are referring to. In the case of two or more works by the same author in the same year, the in-text citation should distinguish them with "a" and "b" (and so on): (Brown, 1994a). In the case of two or more works by the same author published in different years, list the years separately and sequentially: (Brown, 1992, 1993).

4. A corporate author or government agency

If the name is long, write it out the first time; then abbreviate it in subsequent citations: (United States Department of Agriculture, 1992, p. 117). Subsequently, use "(USDA, 1992, p. 231)."

5. Unknown author

As with MLA style, use the first few words of the title for unsigned pieces (usually brief newspaper or magazine articles). If the original title was "What went wrong during their four years in college?" you would simply use "("What went wrong," 1992, p. 69)." Note: capitalize only the first word of the title.

6. Citing a source's quotation

To document material that your source quotes from another source (commonly known as an indirect source), identify the original source in your text by author's name, and in your citation precede your source with the phrase "cited in."

> Orange observes that data about students' institutional loyalty must be adjusted not only for school size but also for "such elusive factors as campus ambience" (cited in Brown, 1994, p. 12).

7. More than one work in a single citation

Alphabetize authors' last names and separate them with semicolons: (Brown, 1994; Greene, 1992, 1993; Orange, 1991). The two dates after Greene indicate two articles by that author. If you are citing two articles by the same author written in the same year, use "a" and "b" after the dates: (Taupe 1996a, 1996b). See item 3.

SECTION II: END-OF-TEXT LISTS OF REFERENCES (MLA AND APA)

All citations made in the body of your paper or report (in-text citations) are keyed to a list of references located at the end. This list, titled *Works Cited* in MLA style and *References* in APA style, begins on a separate page. It presents in alphabetical order (by the author's last name) all sources cited in the body of the text and includes full publishing information for each source.

Manuscript form: Both forms of end-of-text references center the title—the MLA an inch from the top of the page with two spaces before the first entry and the APA two inches from the top with four spaces between the title and the first entry. Both forms double-space within and between entries. The first line of the reference in each format is not indented; subsequent lines for the reference are indented five spaces in MLA style and three spaces in APA style.

MLA Works Cited

In general, MLA style divides entries into three parts: author, title, and publication data. Each part is separated by a period from the others.

1. Book by a single author

> Douglas, Ann. *Terrible Honesty: Mongrel Manhattan in the 1920s.* New York: Farrar, Straus and Giroux, 1995.

Note that the subtitle is included in the reference, separated from the title by a colon (and two spaces).

More than one work by a single author

Organize the works alphabetically by the first major word in the titles. Provide the author's name with the first title, and then, for subsequent entries, insert three hyphens followed by a period (---.) in place of the author's name.

2. Book by multiple authors

For two or three authors, the form is the same as that for books by a single author, except that the names of authors after the first are not inverted: Marsh, Alec, and Linda Miller.

For more than three authors, include only the name of the first author followed by "et al.": Marsh, Alec, et al.

3. Book by corporate author

Use the name of the corporation as the author (for example, American Medical Association).

4. Book by unknown author

Alphabetize by the first significant word of the title.

5. Book with translator and/or editor in addition to author

Translation:

Calvino, Italo. *Italian Folk Tales.* Trans. George Martin. New York: Pantheon, 1981.

Although not required, some or all of the original publication data may be added at the end of the entry. In the case of Calvino's book, after "1981." you could add

Trans. of *Fiabe italiane.* 1956.

Book with author and editor:

Durkheim, Emile. *Suicide: A Study in Sociology.* Trans. John Spaulding. Ed. George Simpson. New York: The Free Press, 1951.

Note: When a book has both a translator and an editor, the translator's name precedes the editor's.

6. Selection in anthology or edited collection

Alphabetize according to the author of the selection, then list its title, and then provide the title, editor(s), publication data of the book in which it appears, plus the page numbers of the entire selection.

Levi-Strauss, Claude. "The Structural Study of Myth." *Critical Theory Since 1965.* Eds. Hazard Adams and Leroy Searle. Tallahassee: Florida State UP, 1986. 809-22.

When you know where the selection originally appeared, you can give that publication information first and then supply the information on the source you actually consulted, preceded by "Rpt. in" (meaning "Reprinted in"). In this case, include the page numbers of both the source you are citing and the original source. For example:

Levi-Strauss, Claude. "The Structural Study of Myth." *Journal of American Folklore* 68, no. 270 (October-December 1955): 428-44. Rpt. in *Critical Theory Since 1965.* Eds. Hazard Adams and Leroy Searle. Tallahassee: Florida State UP, 1986. 809-22.

Do not include only the original source when you have actually consulted only the reprinted version. Notice that "UP" is the standard abbreviation for "University Press."

7. Multivolume work

List the total number of volumes after the title; at the end of the entry, identify the volume used.

> Cawley, A. C. "The Staging of Medieval Drama." *The Revels History of Drama in English*. 3 vols. Ed. Lois Potter. London and New York: Methuen, 1983. Vol 1. 1–66.

8. Book in a series

The title page of your source may indicate that the book is part of a series. In such cases, give the name of the series and the number marking the book's place in that series.

> Fast, Robin Riley, and Christine Mack Gordon, eds. *Approaches to Teaching Dickinson's Poetry*. Approaches to Teaching World Literature 26. New York: MLA, 1989.

9. Editions of books after the first edition and republished books

Editions:

If the book is not a first edition, specify the edition by number (2nd ed.), year (1989 ed.), or other distinguishing characteristic ("Rev. ed." for "Revised edition," "Abr. ed." for "Abridged edition"). You will find such information on the title page.

> Hodges, John C., et al. *Harbrace College Handbook*. 12th ed. Fort Worth: Harcourt Brace College Publishers, 1994.

Republished book

If a book is republished—for example, a paperback reissue of a hardcover—include the original publication date after the title and before the publication information of the book you have actually used.

> Kavanagh, Patrick. *Collected Poems*. 1964. New York: W.W. Norton & Co., 1973.

10. Government publication

If no author is listed, start with the name of the government and the name of the agency. In the case of U.S. documents, the publisher is the Government Printing Office (GPO) in Washington, D.C.

> United States. Dept. of Transportation. *National Transportation Statistics*. Washington: GPO, 1990.

If you know the author's name, include it either at the beginning of the entry or after the title, preceded by the word "by."

11. Articles in periodicals

References for articles differ from those for books in a few small ways:

- Article titles go inside quotation marks.
- No punctuation follows the name of the periodical.
- A colon precedes the page numbers.

Article in a journal:

Most journals are issued monthly or quarterly and are either separately or continuously paginated. In the latter, the page numbers of each issue within a given year begin where the previous issue ended:

> Cressy, David. "Foucault, Stone, Shakespeare and Social History." *English Literary Renaissance* 21 (1991): 121–33.

The number "21" is the volume number. Although the title page also includes an issue number and a season, it is not necessary to include this information about continuously paginated journals.

When the journal is separately paginated, include the issue number immediately after the volume number (separated by a period):

> Lazere, Donald. "Back to Basics: A Force for Oppression or Liberation?" *College English* 54.1 (1992): 7–21.

Note: because magazines and journals are documented somewhat differently, you need to know how to categorize periodicals as either one or the other. The distinction between magazine and journal is usually made on the basis of their intended audiences. Periodicals aimed at a specialized, usually scholarly audience are designated as journals, while periodicals written for a general readership are usually classified as magazines. *English Literary Renaissance* (cited above) is a journal. *Newsweek* is a magazine.

Article in an encyclopedia:

Begin with the author's name if the article is signed; otherwise, begin with the title of the article. For well-known reference works like the *Encyclopaedia Britannica,* you do not need to include full publication information, just the date of the edition you consulted. If the articles are arranged alphabetically, do not include volume numbers or page numbers.

> "Bats." *The New Book of Knowledge.* 1981 ed.

Article in a monthly or weekly magazine:

Articles in magazines are cited like articles in journals, except that you do not include volume and issue numbers for magazines. You do, however, include more information on the date of publication. Magazines, as opposed to journals, are usually intended for a general audience. (See note above on distinguishing magazines from journals.)

> McPhee, John. "The Gravel Page." *The New Yorker* 29 Jan. 1996: 44–52.

The only difference between monthly and weekly magazines is that monthly magazines do not include a day of the month, just month and year.

If you are citing a magazine (or newspaper) article printed on nonconsecutive pages—for example, pages 11-16 and then pages 52-58—give only the first page number followed by a plus sign (11+).

Article in a newspaper:

The format for newspapers is the same as for magazines, except that the page reference indicates the number or letter of the section containing the article. Anonymous articles are alphabetized by the first significant word in the title.

> Foreman, Bill. "Sculpture Evokes Memories of Young Bombing Victims." *Morning Call* [Allentown, PA] 11 Feb. 1996: A17.

If the city is not identified in the paper's name, indicate it in square brackets after the title. If there is no section letter (as with the weekend editions of the *New York Times,* which are continuously paginated), simply indicate the page number as it appears at the top of the page. If the paper has more than one daily edition, include this information (for example, "late ed.") after the date but before the colon preceding the page number.

Newspaper editorial or letter to the editor:

Cite editorials and letters to the editor as you would an article, except that you should also include the word "Editorial" or "Letter" just before the name of the periodical. Do not underline either of these words, and separate them from other information with a period. Signed editorials or letters begin with author's name.

> "Unforgotten Crimes in Nigeria." Editorial. *New York Times* 10 Feb. 1996: 22.

12. Reviews

To cite a review, include the reviewer's name (if available), the title of the review (if given), followed by the words "Rev. of," the title of the work reviewed, and the name of the author. Then the source of the review (and *not* the work reviewed) is given as in any citation of a book or periodical.

> Rorty, Richard. "Color-Blind in the Marketplace." Rev. of *The End of Racism: Principles for a Multiracial Society,* by Dinesh D'Souza. *New York Times Book Review* 24 Sept. 1995: 9.

There are a number of variations on this model, depending on what is being reviewed. If it is an edited text, for example, you would substitute "ed." for "by"; if a film, "dir." for "by" before the title of the work(s) under review. As with other sources, if the review is unsigned, begin with and alphabetize by the title of the review. If the review is untitled, begin with "Rev. of" and alphabetize by the title of the work being reviewed.

13. Interviews

For published interviews, start with the name of the person being interviewed, followed by the title (or, if untitled, the word "Interview"). Then add the name of the interviewer, followed by the source, which is cited as with any periodical.

If it is a broadcast interview, include the name of the program, the station, and the date. For unpublished interviews, follow the name of the person interviewed with the phrase "Personal Interview" (or "Telephone Interview") followed by the date.

Adams, Anna. Interview. *Community Outreach.* WVIA, Allentown, PA 12 Jan. 1996.

Adams, Anna. Personal Interview. 26 Feb. 1996.

14. Electronic sources
See Section III.

APA References

The APA style divides entries into the following parts: author (using initials only for first and middle names), year of publication (in parentheses), title, and publication data. Each part is separated from the others by a period. In alphabetizing the *References* list, place entries for a single author before entries that he or she has coauthored, and arrange multiple entries by a single author by beginning with the earliest work. If there are two or more works by the same author in the same year, designate them with an "a" and a "b" (and so on) directly after the year. For all sequential entries by an author after the first, substitute three hyphens followed by a period (---.) for his or her name. See the discussion of manuscript form in the introduction to Section II for information on spacing and indenting.

1. Book by a single author

Tannen, D. (1991). *You just don't understand: Women and men in conversation.* New York: Ballantine Books.

Note that the subtitle is included in the reference, separated from the title by a colon (and two spaces), and that only the first letter of the title and subtitle are capitalized (although proper nouns would be capitalized as necessary). See the discussion of APA *References* above for the details of citing multiple entries by the same author.

2. Book by multiple authors

Ginsburg, H., & Opper, S. (1969). *Piaget's theory of intellectual development: An introduction.* Englewood Cliffs, NJ: Prentice-Hall.

Include all authors' names (although "et al." is used for in-text citations with three or more authors), separate them with commas, and use an ampersand (&) before the last author cited. Note that unlike in MLA form, all authors' names are cited with the last name first, and initials are used in place of first and middle names.

3. Book by corporate author
Use the name of the corporation as the author (for example, World Health Organization).

4. Book by unknown author
Alphabetize by the first significant word of the title.

5. Book with translator or editor

Gimpel, J. (1984). *The cathedral builders.* (T. Waugh, Trans.). New York: Harper Colophon Books.

Note that the name of the translator is located within parentheses and appears in normal rather than inverted order after the title and before the publication data.

For a book with an author and an editor, the editor is treated exactly the same as the translator in the previous example. In place of "Trans.," use "Ed."

6. Edited book

Arac, J. (Ed.). (1988). *After Foucault: Humanistic knowledge, postmodern challenges.* New Brunswick, NJ: Rutgers University Press.

7. Article or chapter in an edited book

Sawicki, J. (1988). Feminism and the Power of Foucauldian Discourse. In J. Arac (Ed.), *After Foucault: Humanistic knowledge, postmodern challenges* (pp. 161–178). New Brunswick, NJ: Rutgers University Press.

Notice that you list and alphabetize according to the author of the article, that there are no quotation marks around the title of the article, and that there is no punctuation between the article title and the inclusive page numbers listed inside parentheses, prefaced by "pp."

8. Multivolume work

Johnson, B. D. (1978.) *National party platforms* (Vol. 1). Urbana: University of Illinois Press.

Note that the volume number follows the title and is placed in parentheses and that no punctuation intervenes between the title and the parentheses. A period follows the closing parenthesis.

9. Editions of books after the first edition

Binkley, W. E. (1962). *American political parties: Their natural history* (4th ed.). New York: Knopf.

Note that the edition number follows the title and is placed in parentheses and that no punctuation intervenes between the title and the parentheses. A period follows the closing parenthesis.

10. Government document

U.S. Congress, Joint Committee on Printing. (1950). *Biographical directory of the American Congress, 1774-1949* (81st Cong., House Document no. 607). Washington, D.C.: U. S. Government Printing Office.

As exemplified above, if there is a report number, include it parenthetically immediately after the title, with no intervening punctuation.

11. Articles in periodicals

References for articles differ from those for books in a few small ways:

- Article titles are neither underlined (italicized) nor enclosed in quotation marks.
- Capitalize the first word and all significant words in the names of periodicals.

- Underline or italicize the volume number (which is separated by a comma from the title of the journal) to distinguish it from the page reference.
- For periodicals with volume numbers, include the page numbers of the entire article, separated by a comma from the preceding volume number. Do not use "pp."
- For periodicals without volume numbers, use "p." or "pp." before the page number(s).

Article in a journal:

Baumeister, R. (1987). How the self became a problem: A psychological review of historical research. *Journal of Personality and Psychology, 52,* 163-176.

For articles by two or more authors, use commas to connect the authors, and precede the last one with a comma and an ampersand.

If the journal is paginated by issue (rather than annually), place the issue number in parentheses following the volume number.

Wallston, B. S. (1981). What are the questions in psychology of women? A feminist approach to research. *Psychology of Women Quarterly, 5*(4), 597-617.

Article in a monthly or weekly magazine:

Include the month and the year and, if a weekly magazine, the day as well. Do not abbreviate the month.

Rupley, S. (1995, September 26). Net worth: On-line investing. *PC Magazine, 14*(16), 29.

Article in a newspaper:

Include the complete date, and list the section number with the page numbers, using the abbreviation "p." or "pp."

Foreman, B. (1996, 11 February). Sculpture evokes memories of young bombing victims. *The Morning Call* [Allentown, PA], p. A17.

Newspaper editorial or letter to the editor:

Faltysek. R. B. (1995, December 19). The price of company loyalty. [Letter to the editor.] *Tulsa World,* p. 13.

If the letter has no title, simply include the bracketed identification. If the paper does not have section numbers, just list the page number.

Article in an encyclopedia:

If the entry has no author, begin with the entry title.

Irrigation. (1981). *The new book of knowledge.* (Vol. 9, pp. 408-410). Danbury, CT: Grolier.

Remember that although all significant words in journal and magazine titles are capitalized, only the first word of a book title (and of its subtitle) is capitalized.

12. Reviews

If the review itself has a title, locate it in front of the bracketed title of the subject being reviewed. Also indicate within the brackets the kind of work being reviewed.

> Gorra, M. (1995, November 5). Taking the Freud out of Mother Goose. [Review of the book *From the beast to the blonde: On fairy tales and their tellers.*] *The New York Times Book Review,* pp. 7, 9.

If the subject being reviewed were a film, you would use the phrase "Review of the film." If the review is untitled, use the title of the subject being reviewed, but place it within brackets (to indicate that it is not the title of the review).

Note: Capitalize only the first word of a review title unless, as in the example above, the title contains proper nouns.

13. Interviews

> Cleph, G. (1996). Drumming in my sleep. [Interview with Douglas Ovens]. *Po-Mo Percussion, 10,* 26-33.

If the interview is unpublished, do not include it in *References.* Instead, mention the nature and date of the interview within the text of the paper.

14. Abstracts

Rather than use only an abstract culled from a collection of abstracts, it is preferable to use the entire original article as a source. If you have used only an abstract from a collection, cite it in parentheses at the end of the entry. You would cite the article just as you would any article and then add, for example,

> (From *PsychSCAN: Neuropsychology,* 1996, 5, Abstract No. 422.)

This citation lets your readers know that you are using only the abstract.

15. Electronic sources

See Section III.

SECTION III: DOCUMENTING ELECTRONIC SOURCES

As of 1994, there were at least 10,000 databases and more than 500 electronic publications, including journals, magazines, and newsletters. Increasingly, research is being conducted electronically. One fairly comprehensive reference for electronic publications is the *Gale Directory of Databases,* which describes each type of service with addresses. Also see the most recent edition of Lisabeth A. King, Diane Kovacs et al., *Directory of Electronic Journals, Newsletters, and Academic Discussion Lists,* edited by Ann Okerson (Washington: Assn. of Research Libs.). This kind of information can also be found in one of the popular Internet (Net) directories, such as Eric Braun's *The Internet Directory* (New York: Fawcett).

The rapid growth of electronic media has outpaced the ability of various codifying bodies (APA, MLA, and other professional organizations) to keep up with them. Consequently, there is not yet any standard for referencing on-line information, and the guidelines now available will continue to evolve. This process may be rendered less chaotic when/if a standard citation form is arrived at by the International Standards Organization (ISO).

Although we will outline for you current methods of citing materials on databases, computer programs, and CD-ROM, your best bet for obtaining the most recent citation information is to locate the World Wide Web (www) site of the particular codifying organization whose style guide you are using. More detailed hard-copy information on citing electronic sources is provided by Xia Li and Nancy B. Crane, *Electronic Style: A Guide to Citing Electronic Information* (Westport: Meckler, 1993), but the most current information is available on the Net itself; consult your Internet service provider or university Internet guru on how to use "search engines" to track down this information. The best information we could find at press time was at

> http://neal.cstateu.edu/history/cite.html

for Chicago and APA style and

> http://www.cas.usf.edu/english/walker.mla.html

for MLA.

The citation formats for electronic sources differ from those used for print sources in a few primary ways:

- The method of accessing the information is included in what is called an *availability statement*. This statement replaces the publication information typically provided for text references. You provide the information sufficient to retrieve the source.
- In APA style the phrase "[On-line]" (in square brackets) comes directly after the title and before the availability statement. MLA also includes this information but prints the word without a hyphen and without square brackets: Online.
- When an electronic source is available in both print and nonprint formats, generally list both.
- Citing the exact date for an electronic source is more complicated than for printed texts. Generally, list the most recent update of the information, since electronic data are frequently revised. When a date cannot be determined, supply the date of your search (also known as the access date).

MLA Documentation of Electronic Sources

Standard format:

1. Name of the author, if given.
2. For a nonprint source, the title of the material accessed, inside quotation marks, followed by the date of the material, if given.

    If there is also a printed version of the source, provide the publication information in this slot, including the title and date. The nonprint information follows. The date of the nonprint information generally comes after the title of the database or other service from which the information was obtained but before the availability statement (discussed in item 7).

3. The title of the database, underlined. If the source is an electronic journal or newsletter or conference, include the title, underlined, followed by volume and issue numbers, year or date of publication (in parentheses), and number of pages or paragraphs (if given) or "n. pag." (which stands for "no pagination").
4. Publication medium (CD-ROM or Diskette or Online) in parentheses.
5. Name of the vendor or publisher (with city of publication) or computer service.
6. Electronic publication date or, in the case of publications on diskette, year of publication. If you are using a computer service, list the date of access in this slot.
7. Availability statement. The current *MLA Handbook for Writers of Research Papers,* 4th ed., indicates that you may supplement the citation with the electronic address used to access the document, introduced by the word "Available." Some professors require this information. Although MLA entries normally end with a period, omit it here because adding a period to a path statement will hinder retrieval (the computer will read the period as part of the code).

Notice that, prior to the availability statement, you will already have told your readers the title of the database, if you were using one, and the name of the vendor or publisher or computer service. The availability statement basically repeats this information along with other information, such as file numbers and E-mail addresses, that would allow your reader to gain access to your source.

> Kupisch, Susan J. "Stepping In." Paper presented as part of the symposium <u>Disrupted and Reorganized Families</u> at the annual meeting of the Southeast Psychological Association, Atlanta, Ga. (23-26 Mar. 1983): n. pag. Online. Dialog. ERIC. ED 233276.

In this case, the citation informs readers that the article can be accessed from a database called ERIC. The word "Dialog" is the name of the vendor of the electronic document service. ERIC is the service itself. The letters and numbers following identify the particular document.

Here are a couple more examples:

> Shearson Lehman Brothers, Inc. "Reebok: Company Report." 29 July 1993. <u>General Business File.</u> CD-ROM. Information Access. Nov. 1993.
> "Middle Ages." <u>Academic American Encyclopedia.</u> Online. Prodigy. 30 Mar. 1992.

If the Shearson Lehman Brothers report had been on diskette, the word "Diskette" would appear in place of "CD-ROM" in the first example above. In that same example, the first date is the date of publication; the date at the end of the entry is a user access date. In the second example, an article from an on-line encyclopedia, "Prodigy" is the computer service through which the user accessed the encyclopedia.

APA Documentation of Electronic Sources

Standard format:

1. Name of author.

2. Date, in parentheses, of the year of publication or, in cases of revision, the most recent update. If you cannot determine the date, use the date of your search.

3. Title of article. This slot may also be filled with the title of a chapter.

4. Name of periodical, underlined, followed by the phrase "[On-line]" (in brackets and hyphenated), a comma, and the volume number, also underlined. If the source is a chapter from a book, the title of the full work, underlined, fills this slot. If the article is on CD-ROM, use "[CD-ROM]" in this slot in place of "[On-line]."

5. Availability statement, prefaced by the word "Available" and a colon before specifying the path. This statement replaces the place and name of the publisher used in text references. Supply the information necessary for someone else to retrieve the source, such as the protocol (for example, FTP), the directory, and the file name.

Here are two examples:

Shearson Lehman Brothers, Inc. (1993). "Reebok: Company Report." *General Business File.* [CD-ROM]. Available: Information Access.

Tupisch, Susan J. (1983). "Stepping in." Paper presented as part of the symposium *Disrupted and Reorganized Families* at the annual meeting of the Psychological Association, Atlanta, Ga. [On-line]. Available: Dialog. ERIC. ED 233276.

Availability statements are sometimes rather complex. Here is a fairly straightforward example: Steve Summit maintains the FAQ (Frequently Asked Questions) list for the Usenet group comp.lang.c. This FAQ is available at several sites, but the canonical version is the one at the Massachusetts Institute of Technology. It resides at an address dedicated to FAQs known as rtfm (an acronym for Read The Flipping Manual) and might be cited as

Summit, S. (1996). C.L.C-FAQ [On-line]. Available: by anonymous FTP from rtfm.mit.edu/pub/usenet-by-group/comp.lang.c/C-FAQ-list

Other forms of electronic correspondence—from bulletin boards, E-mail messages, and discussion groups—are not included in the *References* list. Instead, cite them as personal communication within the text.

SECTION IV: OTHER DOCUMENTATION STYLES

The Number-Reference System

The documentation style used most frequently in the natural sciences is known as the number system or the number-reference system. There are several versions of this system, but they all share a single principle: sources are numbered within the text, and these numbers correspond to a reference list given at the end of the paper. Depending on the particular version of the system you are using, these numbers are inserted within the text at the pertinent place in the sentence, using parentheses, brackets, or a superscript. In the text, you number your references in the order that you mention them, so the first source you cite is "(1)," the third "(3)," and so forth. If you use the same source more than once, repeat its original number (don't give it a new number).

At the end of the paper, in a section named *References,* list your sources in the order of their appearance in the text. (If the reference list includes comments, title it *References and Notes.*) Don't list references more than once, even if you refer to them more than once in the paper. Numbers in the reference list are followed by a period (that is, drop the parentheses or brackets used for your in-text citations).

The largest difference among numbers systems is that some of them arrange the *References* list in alphabetical order, numbered consecutively. In-text numbers then correspond to the numbers in the *References* list, rather than running consecutively in order of appearance.

The basic rules for citation are as follows:

1. The author's name is given as initials and entire last name; the order is not inverted. Join two authors with "and"; omit the "and" for three to five authors. For six or more authors, use only the first author named and follow that name with "et al."
2. A comma separates the author's name from the title of the book or periodical. The title is underlined; the first word and all other significant words are capitalized (not prepositions or the articles *a, an,* and *the*). Accepted abbreviations of journal titles may be used. (You will find such abbreviations in bibliographies and will rapidly learn to recognize the abbreviated forms of the titles of the most commonly used journals in a given discipline.) Note that the actual title of the article in a periodical is not included.
3. In citing a book, the publication information follows the title with no intervening punctuation and is enclosed in parentheses. It includes the publisher, place of publication, and date separated by commas. A comma follows the parentheses and then the page or pages, using the abbreviations "p." for page or "pp." for pages. Place a period at the end.
4. In citing a journal or magazine, give the volume number in bold type, followed by a comma, then the first page number (with no "p."), and then, enclosed within parentheses, the date (the year, the month and year, or the day, month, and year, as applicable). Place a period at the end.

Here are a few examples:

1. A. Rothenberg and B. Greenberg, <u>The Index of Scientific Writings on Creativity: General, 1566-1974</u> (Archon Books, Hamden, CT, 1976), pp. 34-39.
2. F. Pine, <u>Journal of Nervous and Mental Disease</u>, **134**, 506 (1962).

The different sciences vary to some extent in their particular use of the number-reference system. In CBE (Council of Biology Editors) format, for example, the titles of books are not underlined and only the first word is capitalized. Similarly, journal titles are not underlined but are capitalized, and article titles are included in the citation. See the bibliography in Section V.

The Chicago Style

Similar in many respects to MLA style, the Chicago format, as found in *The Chicago Manual of Style,* is the one most often used by scholars publishing in history, art, music, philosophy, and some social sciences. The style uses notes that appear at the bottom of the page as footnotes or at the end of the paper as endnotes (on a separate page titled *Notes)*. Each footnote or endnote is marked in the text with a superscript numeral at the end of the sentence in which the citation occurs; the superscript numerals refer to the correspondingly numbered footnotes or endnotes. The Chicago style provides full bibliographic citations at the end of the paper in a section titled *Bibliography.*

The author's name appears in its normal word order in footnotes and endnotes but in inverted order in bibliographic entries. The author and the title are separated by a comma in the notes and by a period in the bibliography. Publication information—including place, publisher, and date (in that order) —is enclosed in parentheses in the note, but not in the bibliography, where it is set off by a period. Page numbers appear only in the notes without "p." or "pp." and are set off from the publication information (within the parentheses) by a comma. If you refer to a source in your notes more than once, use only the author's last name and an abbreviated version of the title; exclude the publication information.

Sample notes (footnote or endnote):

[1] Harris Gaylord Warren, *Herbert Hoover and the Great Depression* (New York: Oxford University Press, 1959), 67-68.

[2] Marver H. Bernstein, "Political Ideas of Selected American Business Journals," *Public Opinion Quarterly* 17 (summer 1953): 258-61.

[3] Bernstein, "Political Ideas," 259.

Sample bibliographical entries:

Bernstein, Marver H. "Political Ideas of Selected American Business Journals." *Public Opinion Quarterly* 17 (summer 1953): 258-67.

Warren, Harris Gaylord. *Herbert Hoover and the Great Depression.* New York: Oxford University Press, 1959.

SECTION V: BIBLIOGRAPHY OF STYLE MANUALS

The following bibliography contains a sampling of the major disciplinary style guides. These are usually available in the reference room of the library. Following each entry, in brackets, are the disciplines most likely to use the particular guide. Some disciplines accept more than one documentation style, and disciplines often prescribe their own variations on a standard style, as is the case, for example, with music's use of Chicago style.

American Chemical Society. *American Chemical Society Style Guide and Handbook.* Washington, D.C.: American Chemical Society, 1985. **[chemistry]**

American Institute of Physics. *Style Manual for Guidance in the Preparation of Papers.* 4th ed. New York: American Institute of Physics, 1990. **[physics]**

American Mathematical Society. *A Manual for Authors of Mathematical Papers.* 8th ed. Providence: American Mathematical Society, 1984. **[mathematics]**

American Psychological Association. *Publication Manual of the American Psychological Association*. 4th ed. Washington, D.C.: American Psychological Assn., 1994. **[psychology, many other social sciences]**

Associated Press Staff. *Associated Press Photojournalism Stylebook*. Reading, MA: Addison-Wesley, 1990. **[journalism]**

The Chicago Manual of Style. 14th ed. Chicago: University of Chicago Press, 1993. **[history, art, music, philosophy]**

Columbia Law Review. *A Uniform System of Citation*. 15th ed. Cambridge: Harvard Law Review, 1991. **[law]**

Council of Biology Editors. Style Manual Committee. *CBE Style Manual: A Guide for Authors, Editors, and Publishers in the Biological Sciences*. 5th ed. Bethesda: Council of Biology Editors, 1983. **[biology]**

Dodd, Janet S., ed. *ACS Style Guide: A Manual for Authors and Editors*. Washington, D.C.: American Chemical Society, 1985. **[chemistry]**

Gibaldi, Joseph. *MLA Handbook for Writers of Research Papers*. 4th ed. New York: The Modern Language Assn. of America, 1995. **[English, classics, foreign languages]**

Goldstein, Norm, ed. *Associated Press Stylebook & Libel Manual*. 4th ed. Reading, MA: Addison-Wesley, 1994. **[journalism]**

Holoman, D. Kern. *Writing About Music: A Style Sheet from the Editors of 19th-Century Music.* Berkeley: University of California Press, 1988. **[music]**

International Steering Committee of Medical Editors. "Uniform Requirements for Manuscripts Submitted to Biomedical Journals." *Annals of Internal Medicine* 90 (1978): 95-99. **[medicine]**

Lane, Michael K., et al. *Style Manual for Political Science*. Washington, D.C.: American Political Science Association, 1993. **[political science]**

Turabian, Kate L. *A Manual for Writers of Term Papers, Theses, and Dissertations*. 5th ed. Chicago: University of Chicago Press, 1987.**[interdisciplinary]**

The University of Chicago Manual of Legal Citation. Chicago: University of Chicago Law Review, 1989. **[law]**

GLOSSARY of LOGICAL TERMS and FALLACIES

THE PROBLEM WITH TRYING to think about thinking is that we are often put off by the perception that we must first be equipped with a large arsenal of terms and specialized techniques. If your aim is to undertake a study of what philosophers, psychologists, linguists, and others have had to say about human reasoning, you would indeed need a substantial technical vocabulary. If, however, your aim is to become more aware of yourself and others in the act of thinking, you can accomplish this goal with a more modest set of conceptual tools.

This appendix offers you two sets of vocabulary for talking and thinking about thinking. The first of these is a Glossary of Logical Terms describing kinds of arguments (ways of relating reasons and evidence to conclusions) and the primary parts of arguments. This list is prefaced by a short summary of this book's guidelines for producing good (by which we mean fair and accurate) thinking.

The other vocabulary set is a Glossary of Logical Fallacies. This glossary focuses on explanations of the best-known fallacy labels—the names used to charge another's argument (or your own) with various kinds of faulty reasoning and (deliberate or accidental) deception. (The term *fallacia* is Latin for deceit.)

Learning to spot and name logical fallacies will not, unto itself, make you a better writer and thinker. Before you can concern yourself with catching errors—grammatical, logical, or whatever—you have to give yourself the chance to generate some observations and tentative conclusions to work with. Some of these may well turn out to be fallacious, but if you follow the strategies outlined in this book for arriving at, testing, and evolving ideas, the false moves that may occur in the early phases of your writing process will be replaced by more carefully reasoned analysis. If you become obsessively concerned with errors too early in the writing process, you will have difficulty recognizing and recording any of your thinking. Your best bet is to create a space in which you can record your initial responses without worrying whether they are right or wrong, relevant or irrelevant. Later on in the writing process—after you've discovered some of the responses you might wish to make—you can start evaluating your arguments.

It is clearly to your advantage, however, to know the terms that others commonly use to talk about arguments. Although an understanding of common errors in thinking won't generate ideas for you, such an understanding will definitely make you better at revising your work and more sensitive to your own assumptions and word choice. At the very least, if someone charges you with equivocating or with having a non sequitur, you will have some idea how to respond.

Taken together, the two glossaries will make you more aware of how arguments work, and where, typically, they go wrong. Preceding these glossaries we offer the following set of guidelines, principles that this book presents throughout as your best means of producing clear and logical thinking.

PRODUCING GOOD THINKING: SOME NECESSARY HABITS OF MIND

There is no formula—no single set of procedures—that will automatically improve your thinking. There are, however, some habits of mind, some basic ways of approaching ideas and information that are necessary to the production of good thinking. The most important of these is the willingness to ask questions—especially about one's own assumptions—and to repeatedly reconsider conclusions. All of the following recommendations are in the service of this essential disposition.

1. *Suspend judgment.* Seek to understand before you judge. Make understanding a higher priority than judging.
2. *Avoid oversimplification.* Qualify (limit and refine) your generalizations. Seek out evidence that conflicts with your claims, and use it to evolve more accurate claims.
3. *Examine assumptions.* Reason back to and question the (often unstated) assumptions that underlie your claims.
4. *Don't treat opinions as facts.* Distinguish between evidence (data) and claims (ideas and judgments about the data). You have no doubt heard people say, when challenged about an opinion stated as though it were an obvious fact, that they are entitled to their opinions. It is true that not all of our convictions can be supported with reasons and evidence. In academic and other forms of analytical writing, however, you must substantiate your opinions or acknowledge them as unsubstantiatable.
5. *Support claims with evidence.* Don't assume that the meaning and the truth of your claims are self-evident. Share your thought process with your readers. Let them see how you arrived at your claims and why you think the evidence means what you say it does.
6. *Question either/or statements.* Dividing possible views on a subject into two opposing sides often forces a choice between black and white when some shade of gray is fairer and more accurate. Before deciding which side of an issue you think is right, consider whether the issue has been adequately and appropriately defined.
7. *Choose and define your terms carefully.* Much of what goes wrong in reasoning is the product of sloppy (vague, inaccurate) and/or deliberately misleading terminology. Try thinking of your words as doorways and your arguments as the corridors these doorways lead to. See, for instance, our example in Chapter 9 of what happens when a writer chooses the word "ambivalent" rather than "ambiguous" to describe a presidential policy. The time you invest in locating and defining your doorways is time you won't waste getting stuck in unproductive corridors or having to retrace your steps.

GLOSSARY OF LOGICAL TERMS

In this and the following glossary, **boldface** type indicates the primary term discussed, and *italic* type identifies terms treated elsewhere in the glossaries.

assumption. An assumption is a statement accepted or supposed as true. A writer's willingness to articulate and test assumptions determines, in large part, the quality of the writing he or she can produce. Much poor thinking, and thus poor writing, results from leaping to conclusions from inadequately examined—often unstated and unrecognized—assumptions. The conclusions of an argument are valid only insofar as they are based on supportable assumptions. For further discussion and examples of dealing with assumptions, see Chapter 5, especially "Two Ways to Improve the Logic of Your Theses Statements"; also see "Developing a Thesis by Reasoning Back to Premises" in Chapter 4 and "Linking Evidence and Claims" in Chapter 7.

deduction. Deductive reasoning begins with a generalization that is applied to a specific instance in order to draw a conclusion about that instance. Deduction is a process aimed at predicting one phenomenon from another and at inferring consequences. The revision process is largely deductive. Revision tests the adequacy of a general principle (thesis) by determining how well this principle accounts for particulars that the writer observes in a subject. For further discussion and examples of deduction, see Chapters 3 and 4; also see *dilemma, disjunctive syllogism, induction, inference, modus ponens, modus tollens, premise,* and *syllogism.* In the Glossary of Logical Fallacies, see two kinds of invalid deductive arguments—*affirming the consequent* and *denying the antecedent.*

dilemma. Dilemma, a form of deductive argument, formulates a required choice between two or more unattractive alternatives. In symbolic terms, a dilemma is set up as:

p or *q.*
If *p* then *r.*
If *q* then *s.*
Therefore, *r* or *s.*

In concrete terms,

p or *q:* The U.S. government should either send troops to Bosnia or not.
If *p* then *r:* If troops are sent, American soldiers will die, and the situation still may not be resolved.
If *q* then *s:* If troops are not sent, America's international prestige may suffer, and the killing may go on interminably.
Therefore, *r* or *s:* Therefore, American soldiers will die, and the situation still may not be resolved; or America's international prestige may suffer, and the killing may go on interminably.

In the conclusion to this dilemma, the government will fail no matter what it does. One way out of the dilemma is a maneuver called going "between the horns," in which some alternative course of action (something between the two extremes of sending troops or doing nothing) would be proposed. The government might, for example, lessen the damage to its prestige without having American soldiers take on too great a share of the responsibility by organizing an international force, as was done in the Gulf War.

As an argumentative strategy, the dilemma is often used to argue for the maintenance of the status quo. An argument against funding space weapons on the grounds that it would simply escalate an arms race in which various powers already possess the ability to destroy the earth many times over might formulate its position using a dilemma.

disjunctive syllogism. The disjunctive syllogism form of deduction begins by asserting two or more alternatives, known as disjuncts, as the major premise. The minor premise then negates one of these disjuncts, leaving the remaining one for the conclusion. Here the formula is:

> *p* or *q*.
> Not *p*.
> Therefore, *q*.

(There may be more than two disjuncts: the major premise might assert, for example, five alternatives, and the minor might reject three, leaving two for the conclusion.) If we replace the symbols with actual premises, we get:

> We must find more sources of fossil fuel, or we must locate new sources of energy, or we must radically reduce energy demands.
> We can't find more sources of fossil fuel, and we can't reduce energy demands beyond a certain point.
> Therefore, we must locate new sources of energy.

As with all either/or thinking, the problem in arguing disjunctively is that you may have misrepresented the issue and/or left out a key alternative (such as nuclear or solar energy in our example). See the discussion of reductive binaries and false dichotomies in Chapter 2 ("Binaries: Either/Or Questions") and Chapter 4 ("Strategies for Developing a Thesis by Reasoning Back to Premises").

enthymeme. An enthymeme is a *syllogism* with an unstated premise or an unstated conclusion. The statement "The animal is equally at home in both air and water, so it must be an amphibian" is an enthymeme. The missing part of the syllogism is the major premise: "All animals that are equally at home in both air and water are amphibians." The statement "Because Jane is a woman she cannot participate in military action" is also an enthymeme. This example reveals the potential problem with enthymemes—that they can conceal debatable premises, in this case, that women are too delicate (or emotional or weak) to participate in battle. Such premises need examining.

evidence. Evidence is the data on which a conclusion may be based. As Chapter 7 illustrates, evidence and claims must achieve a certain balance—too many claims with insufficient data or a mass of data without explicit claims produces weak analyses.

The relation between facts and opinions (evidence and conclusions) is not as straightforward as it might seem, because "facts" can't be easily separated from interpretation and speculation. What we already believe to be true often determines what we are prepared to see as fact. See in Chapter 7, "Voices from Across the Curriculum: What Counts as Evidence?"

hypothesis. A hypothesis is a tentative conclusion, a proposed explanation that its author will test against evidence. The advice of this book is to treat your ideas as hypotheses to be tested rather than as obvious truths.

implication. An implication is an indication, a meaning that is suggested rather than openly and directly stated. Articulating and reasoning from (inferring the meaning and consequences of) implications is one of the primary activities of analysis. Analysis aims at making the implicit explicit. See *inference*. For extended examples of the process of pursuing implications, see Chapters 1 and 4.

induction. Inductive reasoning begins with particulars (facts, observations) and draws a general conclusion about them. Induction is a process aimed at forming theories about the meaning of things. The scientific method, for example, uses induction to evolve explanations for observed phenomenon such as the higher incidence of heart attacks among men than women. The proposed explanation (general principle) is then tested <u>deductively</u> according to the pattern: if theory X is true, then such-and-such should follow. If the particular results predicted by the theory do not occur when the theory is put to the test, the scientist knows that something is probably wrong with his or her induction. A deductive premise is only as good as the inductive reasoning that produced it. (See, in Chapter 4, our discussion of a student essay on the meaning of Velázquez's painting, *Las Meninas,* for an example of how inductive reasoning works in the writing process.)

inductive leap. An inductive leap is the mental move one makes from particulars to a theory about the larger class to which the particulars seem to belong. Induction always involves a leap; that's why it is important to demonstrate the representativeness of your particular example(s). The learning process is to a significant extent inductive, which is to say experimental. A child, for example, after touching a hot iron, will learn to be careful of things with electrical cords. See *hasty generalization, overgeneralization,* and *composition* in the Glossary of Logical Fallacies.

inference. An inference is a conclusion derived by reasoning from something known or assumed (data and premises) to something else that follows from it. Inferences are related to but not the same as implications. An implication suggests but does not directly state a meaning that a reader or viewer or listener infers. I imply what you infer: the implication occurs at the sending end of the message and the inference at the receiving end. A raised eyebrow might <u>imply</u> a curious or skeptical attitude. From the raised eyebrow an observer might <u>infer</u> a curious or skeptical attitude.

modus ponens (the mode of affirming). The simplest form of deductive argument, modus ponens can be stated in the following formula, in which the first line is known as the major *premise,* the second line is the minor premise, and the third line is the conclusion:

If p then q.

p.

Therefore, q.

Replacing the symbols with actual terms, we get:

If airbags become standard equipment on automobiles, traffic fatalities should decrease.

Airbags are becoming standard equipment on automobiles.
Therefore, traffic fatalities should decrease.

This argument may or may not be true, depending on how adequately (reasonably) its premises are explained, but its form is valid.

modus tollens (the mode of denying). A kind of deductive argument, the formula for which is:

If p then q.
Not p.
Therefore, not q.

Here is an example:

If the defendant were innocent, then he would have consented to a lie-detector test.
The defendant did not consent to a lie-detector test.
Therefore, the defendant is not innocent.

The form is valid, but the example illustrates that there is more to developing and evaluating an argument than valid form. In this case, the major premise assumes a cause-effect relationship that does not necessarily follow. A person may well have reasons other than guilt for not submitting to a lie-detector test—fear that the tests are not always accurate, for example. The closer you come to demonstrably factual premises, the more effective modus tollens will be. For example,

If the illness was caused by bacteria, it would respond to antibiotics.
The illness did not respond to antibiotics.
Therefore, the illness was not caused by bacteria.

Even in this case, though, the illness might have been caused by bacteria that were resistant to available antibiotics.

premise. A premise is a proposition upon which an argument is based and from which the argument's conclusion is drawn. In other words, a premise is an assumption the truth of which an argument depends on for its success. The technical definition of a deductive argument asserts that if the premises are true, the conclusion must be true. It follows that to disprove a deductive argument, you need to present reasons for believing one or more of its premises are false. In order to agree with a deductive argument, writers generally show how possible objections to one or more of its premises fail. See *syllogism*.

reductio ad absurdum (reduction to absurdity). A reductio (a version of *modus tollens*) promotes its conclusion by demonstrating that denying the conclusion would lead to absurdity. In symbolic terms, the argument proceeds as follows:

To prove p:
Assume that p is false (not p).
Derive implication q from the assumption that p is false.
Show q is false (absurd).
Conclude p.

Here is an example of reductio in concrete terms:

> What you want to prove: There should be some limitations on the sale of sexually explicit materials.
>
> What you (pretend to) assume: There should be no limitations on the sale of sexually explicit materials.
>
> Implication (typically overstated) derived: Eight-year-old children could not be restricted from bringing pictures of explicit sexual activity to school for show-and-tell.
>
> Show the implication is false (absurd): Children obviously should not be permitted to buy and carry whatever kind of sexually explicit materials they can get their hands on.
>
> Conclude: There should be some limitations on the sale of sexually explicit materials.

syllogism. A syllogism is an argument expressed in the form of two propositions (its *premises)* that contain a common or middle term with a third proposition called the conclusion, which results necessarily from the other two. For example:

> major premise: All accountants must pass the CPA exam.
> minor premise: Paula is an accountant.
>   ["accountant" is the common or middle term]
> conclusion: Paula has passed the CPA exam.

Although the three parts of the syllogism may not be explicitly stated, they can be deduced from the conclusion. Consider, for example, the following piece of academic conventional wisdom:

> Students should be required to take foreign language courses.

It is a useful component of logical thinking to deduce the syllogism that is underneath this statement. Here is one version of such a syllogism:

> major premise: Courses that broaden students' experience of other cultures should be required.
> minor premise: Foreign language courses broaden students' experience of other cultures.
> conclusion: Therefore, foreign language courses should be required.

The operative term in thinking syllogistically is validity. It is crucial to realize that validity is not the same thing as truth. In a valid argument, if the premises are true, then the conclusion must also be true. Validity, in other words, has to do with the relations among statements in an argument. An argument can be valid but not true or true but not valid. The most common type of false argument that is nevertheless valid is one in which one or more of the premises are untrue, or at least open to question. The syllogism about foreign language courses, for example, is valid but not necessarily true. It is not self-evident that all courses that broaden students' experience of other cultures, such as a course on the kinship patterns of Trobriand Islanders, should be required. An argument that is true but not valid arrives at an incontestable conclusion, but the relation between premises and conclusions does not require us to believe that the conclusion is true. For example:

> major premise: Some men are left-handed.
> minor premise: Some women are left-handed.
> conclusion: Some left-handers are better at math than right-handers.

Although all three statements are true, the conclusion doesn't follow from the premises. How do you test for validity? If the conclusion can be shown to be false while the premises are true, then the argument is invalid (since in a valid argument the conclusion must be true if the premises are true). Consider the following example:

> major premise: All Christians celebrate Easter.
> minor premise: Smith is Christian.
> conclusion: Smith celebrates Easter.

The first step in testing for validity is to try to negate the conclusion. If Smith does not celebrate Easter, but the major and minor premise can be shown to be true, then the argument is invalid. In this case, the obvious problem is that the major premise is not necessarily true: to make such an argument, you would need, at the least, to determine what the key word "celebrate" means. See *Toulmin model*.

Toulmin model. The Toulmin model of argument, established by Stephen Toulmin, is thought by some to be better suited to writers than the syllogistic model because it places more emphasis on the relationship between writer and readers, anticipating their assumptions and objections. The Toulmin model replaces the three terms of the *syllogism* with the following three terms:

> claim: Whatever it is you are trying to prove.
> grounds: The data to be used in proving the claim.
> warrant: The logic by which you connect grounds and claim.

Here is an example with the slots filled in:

> claim: The government should support recycling programs.
> grounds: We live in a world of dwindling resources.
> warrant: Recycling is an efficient means of conserving resources.

Generally speaking, the grounds of an argument should be something that readers would be willing to grant the status of fact or virtual fact. Similarly, the *warrant* is an idea that most readers would either accept or be persuaded by logical reasoning to accept as true. As with syllogistic reasoning, if both the warrant and the grounds are accepted as true, the claim should follow.

It is worth noting that the more complicated any of the three terms become, the more complex the chains of reasoning that will be necessary to support them. So, for example, although readers might accept that the need to conserve resources and the value of recycling in this respect point to the conclusion that we should have recycling, readers might not accept the part of the claim not explicitly backed by the grounds and warrant—that government-funded recycling programs are the way to go. A simpler claim (recycling programs should be supported) would be easier to establish; a more complicated claim (recycling should be supported at all levels of government) would require additional supporting arguments with more grounds and warrants.

warrant. A warrant is a statement that provides a reason for believing that a claim (conclusion) made about *evidence* is true. A warrant, in other words, connects the grounds of an argument—the data—with the claim. Similar to the major *premise* of a *syllogism,* the warrant is an assumption that the writer believes readers will accept as true.

GLOSSARY OF LOGICAL FALLACIES

The following glossary of logical fallacies is organized into two broad categories.

1. **Derailers** are assertions or appeals that "derail" a logical argument by sidetracking it. Included in this category are various kinds of deceptive appeals and ways of clouding or digressing from an issue with irrelevant claims or misleading terms.
2. **Chain problems** are faulty links in the "chain" of argumentation. Included in this category are various kinds of missteps in the way an argument uses and organizes its premises and conclusions.

Under derailers, we include such things as appeals to pity or fear or popularity (the "bandwagon" tactic we all learn as children—"everyone's doing it"). Under chain problems we include the fallacy called begging the question (circular reasoning), in which the conclusion of an argument is used as one of its premises.

As will be evident, these two large categories often overlap. Nevertheless, we think these categories provide a useful way of organizing your thinking about logical fallacies in terms of where and how (by means of what kind of maneuver) they occur.

Derailers

ad hominem. From the Latin for "against the man," ad hominem attacks an argument by casting aspersions on the person who presents it, rather than dealing with the issues it raises. For example: "James Joyce's novels should be banned. After all, he lived out of wedlock with Nora Barnacle for over twenty years."

appeal to authority. Although appealing to authority can be a legitimate form of persuasion, such appeals can sometimes derail the reader. It is, for example, reasonable to cite President Clinton's view on foreign policy, since that is an area of his expertise, but it is a fallacy to authorize his view on the likelihood that the Baltimore Orioles will win the pennant. Even in cases in which the authority cited is appropriate to the matter at hand, that citation is no substitute for an argument. You would want to cite Clinton's reasoning on foreign policy, not just his conclusion.

appeal to fear. An appeal to fear uses a threat of harm, usually irrelevant to the issue at hand, to persuade an audience to a position. When a college president says that faculty members criticizing the new evening educational program should consider that their disloyalty may jeopardize the college's financial status and thus the faculty's salary base, he is using an appeal to fear. The ability of the college to pay a faculty member's salary is not relevant to the evaluation of the relative merits of the new program.

appeal to ignorance. An appeal to ignorance invites readers to draw a conclusion on the basis of something that they don't actually know. You couldn't argue against the death penalty on the grounds that a number of innocent people had been wrongly executed because this would be to assert as evidence something that we don't know. Alternatively, this fallacy can hold that if there is no proof against something being the case, it must be the case. For example, "Since you can't prove there aren't extraterrestrials among us, I'm sure that there are."

appeal to pity. An appeal to pity plays on our sympathy rather than inviting us to view a position rationally. Take, for example, the case of the student who tells a professor, "I really need an A in this course; otherwise, my parents will force me to quit school and get a job."

appeal to popularity (bandwagon). Popularity is not a reliable indicator of value, nor is consensus an adequate measure of truth. When a hamburger megacorporation announces the sale of its trillionth burger, it has not established that the burger is either good or good for you.

appeal to tradition. One can appeal fallaciously not only to the authority of a person but also to the authority of a tradition. A practice may have been established in the past and surrounded with ritual, but that does not make the practice a reasonable one. Because the first-year students on a college campus have always been required to live segregated into first-year dormitories, it does not follow that this tradition should be continued.

equivocation. Equivocation confuses an argument by slipping between two meanings for a single word or phrase. For example: "Only man is capable of religious faith. No woman is a man. Therefore, no woman is capable of religious faith." Here the first use of "man" is generic, intended to be gender neutral, while the second use is decidedly masculine. One specialized form of equivocation results in what are sometimes called **weasel words.** A weasel word is one that has been used so loosely that it ceases to have much of any meaning (the term derives from the weasel's reputed practice of sucking the contents from an egg without destroying the shell). The word "natural," for example, can mean good, pure, and unsullied, but it can also refer to the ways of nature (flora and fauna). Such terms—"love," "reality," and "experience" are others—invite equivocation because they mean so many different things to different people.

false analogy. An analogy becomes false when it is overextended: there is a point of resemblance at one juncture, but the writer then goes on to assume that the two items compared will necessarily resemble each other in most other respects. The greater the differences between the two items, the weaker the argument will be. If you argue that a professional baseball player is like a slave because he is owned by a team, which can force him to wear his hair and dress for road trips in specified ways, you ignore other crucial facts: that unlike a slave, he is paid large amounts of money for his labor, that he chose this occupation in the first place, and so on.

poisoning the well. The fallacy of poisoning the well occurs when a writer attacks a position by shifting the focus from its merits to its source or origin (the "well"). You are poisoning the well if you argue that a system of national health care is harmful to individual freedom <u>because</u> such systems have been used in socialist countries.

Such an argument does not evaluate the strengths and weaknesses of a particular program; it dismisses the position through association with an origin the audience might distrust. A related fallacy, the **genetic fallacy,** argues against a claim by noting that its origin is tarnished or its inventor unworthy of respect. The fact that Nixon's administration was proven guilty of corruption in the Watergate hearings does not invalidate his China policy. See *ad hominem.*

red herring. The term "red herring" derives from an old hunting practice of dragging a herring across a path to distract the hounds from their quarry. A red herring is an issue that diverts an argument by introducing irrelevant concerns (whether the writer has raised them intentionally or accidentally). The prosecutor in an assault case introduces a red herring when he or she mentions that the accused was once charged with tax evasion. Similarly, in evaluating the relative merits of single-malt scotch whiskies, it would be a red herring to raise the issue of whether the scotches were produced by small distilleries or international conglomerates.

straw man. When you oversimplify or otherwise misrepresent an opposing viewpoint with the deliberate aim of making it easier to attack, you have constructed a straw man. Suppose a reference librarian cautions you against overrelying on electronic databases when you do research, on the grounds that databases tend to treat complex matters too superficially. You would be converting this argument to a straw man if you attacked the librarian's position as antiquated and antitechnological. See "Gambit 1: Challenge a Commonly Held View" in Chapter 6 and "Strategy 3: Converse with Your Sources" in Chapter 8.

Chain Problems

affirming the consequent. This deductive fallacy takes the following form:

If *p* then *q:* If a film appeals to the lowest common denominator, it will be a success at the box office.
q: Howards End was a success at the box office.
Therefore *p:* Therefore, *Howards End* appealed to the lowest common denominator.

In fact, *Howards End* appealed to a markedly literate audience. As this example illustrates, both premises can be true and the conclusion false because the argument overlooks other explanations. See *denying the antecedent.*

begging the question. To beg the question is to argue in a circle by asking readers to accept without argument a point that is actually at stake. This kind of fallacious argument hides its conclusion among its assumptions. For example, "*Huckleberry Finn* should be banned from school libraries as obscene because it uses obscene language" begs the question by presenting as obviously true issues that are actually in question: the definition of obscenity and the assumption that the obscene should be banned because it is obscene.

composition. The composition fallacy assumes that what is true of the parts is also true of the whole. A commonly cited example of the composition fallacy is that an all-star team composed of the best player at each position would be the best team. This reasoning ignores the critical role that teamwork plays in winning games. For another example, consider the argument that if government price supports for dairy products and grains are good, then all price supports are good. Because some products may merit price support, it does not mean that all price supports are worthwhile. See *division.*

denying the antecedent. The deductive fallacy of denying the antecedent takes the following form:

> If *p* then *q:* If a film appeals to the lowest common denominator, it will be a success at the box office.
>
> Not *p:* A given film does not appeal to the lowest common denominator.
>
> Therefore, not *q:* Therefore, the film will not be a success at the box office.

As this example illustrates, both premises can be true and the conclusion false because the argument overlooks other explanations. See *affirming the consequent;* in the Glossary of Logical Terms, also see *modus tollens,* which resembles denying the antecedent but is a valid form of deduction.

division. You commit the fallacy of division when you assume that what is true of a class of things is necessarily true of its members. In syllogistic form: "Cambridge has a reputation for fine scholarship. Reginald attended Cambridge. Therefore, Reginald is a fine scholar." See *composition.*

false cause. The error of false cause is produced by assuming that two events are causally connected when such causal connection does not necessarily exist. One of the most common forms of this fallacy—known as **post hoc, ergo propter hoc** (Latin for "after this, therefore because of this")—assumes that because *A* precedes *B* in time, A causes B. For example, it was once thought that the sun shining on a pile of garbage caused the garbage to conceive flies. This is what Shakespeare's Hamlet refers to when he tells Polonius, "If the sun breed maggots in a dead dog, being a good kissing carrion, . . . let [your daughter] not walk i' the sun . . . as your daughter may conceive" (2.2.182–84). As this example also illustrates, typically in false cause some significant alternative has not been considered, such as the presence of flies' eggs in the garbage. Similarly, it does not follow that if a person watches television and then commits a crime, television watching necessarily causes crime; there are numerous other causes to be considered.

false dilemma. A false dilemma reduces the alternative explanations to two, when in fact there are more than two. This move is often unfair, as when protesters raising questions about American foreign policy are told to love their country or leave it. See the discussion of binaries and false dichotomies in Chapters 2 and 4. Also see *dilemma* in the Glossary of Logical Terms.

genetic fallacy. See *poisoning the well* and *ad hominem.*

hasty generalization. When you move prematurely from too little evidence to a broad conclusion, you have fallen into hasty generalization. Much of this book addresses ways of avoiding this fallacy, also known as an unwarranted inductive leap. In particular see "Demonstrate the Representativeness of Your Example" in Chapter 7; also see *induction* in the Glossary of Logical Terms.

non sequitur. "Non sequitur" is Latin for "it does not follow." A non sequitur usually refers to a misstep in a chain of logical reasoning—in particular, to a faulty deduction of an erroneous conclusion from the premises. For example: "Sarah is a brilliant and beautiful young woman. Therefore, she will have a happy life." In fact, there is a chance that these traits will make her the target of envy and aggression and thus not lead to happiness.

overgeneralization. An overgeneralization is an inadequately qualified claim. It may be true that some heavy drinkers are alcoholics, but it would not be fair to claim that all heavy drinking is or leads to alcoholism. As a rule, be wary of "totalizing" or global pronouncements; the bigger the generalization, the more likely it will admit of exceptions. See, for example, the process of qualifying a claim illustrated in the discussion of *Educating Rita* in Chapter 4.

One particular form of overgeneralization, the **sweeping generalization,** occurs when a writer overextends the reach of the claim. The claim itself may be adequately qualified, but the problem comes in an overly broad application of that generalization, suggesting that it applies in every case when it applies only in some. See Chapter 5, "Weak Thesis Type 4: The Thesis Makes an Overly Broad Claim."

post hoc, ergo propter hoc. See *false cause.*

simple cause/complex effect. One of the most common problems of thinking, the fallacy of simple cause/complex effect involves assigning a single cause to a complex phenomenon that cannot be so easily explained. A widespread version of this fallacy is seen in arguments that blame individual figures for broad historical events, for example, "Eisenhower caused America to be involved in the Vietnam War." Such a claim ignores the cold war ethos, the long history of colonialism in Southeast Asia, and a multitude of other factors. See *false cause.*

slippery slope. In the slippery slope fallacy, the writer asserts that allowing one thing to happen will necessarily lead to a disastrous sequence of events. This fallacy turns up often in arguments about government regulations and policies. During the Vietnam War, for example, the domino theory was a classic example of slippery slope: if one country were allowed to fall under communist rule, the entire region would inevitably follow suit. Similarly, the argument that the decriminalization of drug use will lead to skyrocketing addiction is an example of slippery slope. Such has not proved to be the case in countries where heroin addicts can have access to the drug by prescription.

sweeping generalization. See *overgeneralization.*

weasel words. See *equivocation.*

INDEX

A

Abstract (versus concrete) diction, 165–166
Abstracts
    in science writing, 98–99
Active and passive voice, 171–175
Adverbs, conjunctive, 194–195
Agree/disagree questions
    problems with, 32
    refocusing of, 32
    See also Binaries
American Psychological Association (APA)
    documentation style, 212–214, 219–222
    report format, 47–49, 99, 109–110
Analysis
    common charges against, 7–9
    compared with argument, 4, 9–12, 92–93
    compared with expressive writing, 9–10, 14, 27–31
    compared with summary, 5, 12–14, 25–27
    definitions of, 1–3, 24
    and the writing process, 5–7
Analytical process
    accepting uncertainty, 6
    making the implicit explicit, 4–5
    prewriting, 7
    sample prewriting questions, 5–6
Analyzing versus judging, 3, 87–89
Argument
    circular (begging the question), 117
    debate model, problems with, 92–93
    deductive, 231, 50–52
    forms of, 231–237
    inductive, 233, 50–52
    versus opinion, 4
    thesis in argument versus analysis, 9–12

Toulmin model, 236–237
    See also Critical thinking, Fallacies, Logic
Assignments. *See* Topics
Audience
    and introductions and conclusions, 95, 106–107
    and kinds of writing, 9–10

B

Basic Writing Errors (BWEs)
    comma errors, 202–204
    comma splices, 193–195
    errors in pronoun reference, 198–200
    errors in subject/verb agreement, 195–197
    errors in using possessive apostrophes, 201–202
    misplaced modifiers and dangling participles, 200–201
    sentence fragments, 190–192
    shifts in sentence structure (faulty predication), 197
    spelling/diction errors, 204–205
Begging the question (circular argument), 239
Bibliography
    end-of-text listing of references
        APA, 219–222
        MLA 214–219
    manuscript form for, 214
    of style manuals in various disciplines, 227–228
Binaries
    function of in thinking, 31
    implied in topics, 32–33
    reductive thinking, 32

Binaries *(continued)*
strategies for using, 32–34
Biology, writing in
discussion section of reports, 109–110
formats, 47–48
introductory paragraphs, 98–99

C

Circular argument (begging the question), 117
Citation
end-of-text, 214–222
in-text, 211–214
See also Documentation styles
Claims
distinguished from evidence, 118
unsubstantiated, 117–119
Clichés (conventional wisdom), 83–84
Close reading (explication), 92
Comma splice, 193–195
Comparison and contrast
advantage of 34
asking "so what?", 35
compared with definition, 34
difference within similarity, 22,
134–135
problems with, 34–35
strategies for using, 35–37
Complex sentence, 180–181
Compound sentence, 180–181
Computer (electronic) sources
documentation of, 222–225
Conclusions
across the curriculum, 110–112
concessions in, 113
function of, 106–109
raising new points in, 112
in science writing, 109–110
typical problems with, 112–113
Conclusions, strategies
broader implications and significance,
108–109
coming full circle, 106, 111–112
culminating "so what?", 106–109, 113
guidelines, 113–114
identifying limitations, 108–109
thesis in, 108–109
three things to do, 110–111
Conjunctive adverbs, 194–195, 206
Critical thinking

false dichotomies, 78
guidelines (some templates), 77–79, 67,
52–53
two ways to improve the logic of thesis
statements, 89–91
unstated assumptions, 91
See also Fallacies, Logic, Thinking

D

Deductive arguments, 231, 50–52
Definition
advantages of, 34
problems with, 34–35
strategies for using, 37
Developing a thesis
by reasoning back to premises, 73–79
in an exploratory draft, 63–67
through successive complication, 68–71
Dichotomies, false, 78
See also Binaries
Diction
concrete and abstract, 165–166
errors, 164
jargon, 167–168
latinate, 166
sexism, 164–165, 198–199
shades of meaning, 164–165
tone, 185–186
Disciplinary difference. *See* Voices from Across
the Curriculum
Discourse communities and formats, 46
Documentation styles
APA (American Psychological
Association), 212–214, 219–222
bibliography of style manuals, 227–228
Chicago, 226–227
for electronic sources, 222–225
manuscript form for APA and MLA, 214
MLA (Modern Language Association),
211–212, 214–219
number-reference, 225–226

E

Economics, writing in
formats in, 48
hypothesis and conclusions, 58–59
limiting introductory claims, 103
putting the thesis in context, 92

Either/or questions (binaries)
  advantages of, 31
  agree/disagree, 32
  problems with, 31
Endnotes, 226–227
Equivocation, 238
Essay exams
  agree/disagree and either/or, 32–34
  argument versus analysis, 9–12
  comparing and contrasting, 35–37, 22
  definitions, 37–38
  finding unstated questions, 20–21
  focusing, 20, 26–27
  interpreting the questions, 10–12
Etymology, 116, 164–166
Evidence
  analyzing in depth (10 on 1), 124–128
  demonstrating representativeness, 128–130
  film analogy (pan, track, and zoom), 130
  function of, 117–119
  guidelines for analyzing, 136
  ideology and methodology, 122–123
  making details speak, 119–121
  suggestive versus conclusive, 136
Evolving thesis, 56–58

F

Facts
  versus judgments and interpretation,
    118–119
Fallacies, glossary of
  ad hominem, 237
  appeal to authority, 237
  appeal to fear, 237
  appeal to ignorance, 238
  appeal to pity, 238
  appeal to popularity, 238
  appeal to tradition, 238
  equivocation, 238
  false analogy, 238
  false dilemma, 240
  hasty generalization, 240
  non sequitur, 240–241
  overgeneralization, 241
  post hoc, ergo propter hoc (false cause),
    241
  simple cause/complex effect, 241
  slippery slope, 241
  weasel words, 238, 241

False analogy, 238
Film, 68–73, 130, 148
First-person *I* pro and con, 169–170
Five-paragraph form
  problems with, 44–46
Footnotes, 226–227
Form
  for documenting sources, 210–228
  five-paragraph, 44–46
  reports in the sciences, 47–49, 99,
    109–110
  See also Formats
Formats
  advantages of, 42–43
  for analytical writing, 52–53
  APA (American Psychological
    Association), 47–48
  discourse communities, 46–49
  induction and deduction, 50–52
  in the natural sciences, 47
  problems with, 43
  in the social sciences, 47–48
Fragments, 190–192
Freewriting, 23–24

G

Grammar
  glossary of terms, 205–208
  See also Basic Writing Errors, Sentence
    structure
Guidelines for Writing Analytically
  analyzing evidence, 136
  constructing effective topics, 38–39
  finding and developing a thesis, 79–80
  introductions and conclusions, 113–114
  revising for correctness, 208–209
  stylistic revision, 187
  using formats, 52–53
  using sources, 158

H

Heuristics
  definition of, 42–43
  formats as, 42
  See also Strategies
Hypothesis, 233
  evolving thesis as hypothesis and
    conclusion, 58–59
  treating thesis as, 88–89

I

Ideas
    versus opinion, 4, 28, 87–89
    and uncertainty, 19
    what ideas do, 19
    where to find them, 19
Ideology
    effect of on information-gathering, 123
Implication, 233
    in analysis, 4–5
    and asking "so what?", 65–66
    in concluding paragraphs, 53, 110–111,
      108–109
    and inference, 233
    "reading between the lines," 8–9
Induction and deduction
    as common thought patterns, 50–52, 231,
      233
    diagrams, 51
Inductive leap, 128–129, 233
Inference, 233
    and implication, 233
Introductions
    across the curriculum, 98–101
    avoiding strong claims, 102–103
    function of, 96–97
    typical problems with, 101–103
    using research in, 98
    and the writing process, 96
Introductions, strategies
    challenging a commonly held view, 104
    establishing significance of topic 97–98,
      113
    funnel, 96–97
    guidelines, 113
    leading with second best example,
      104–105
    procedural openings, 99–101
    raising an issue, not settling it, 96,
      102–103
    in science writing, 98–99
    starting with definition, 104
    thesis in, 96–101
    See also Straw man

J

Jargon, 167–168
Journals, 24

L

Logic (critical thinking)
    deduction, 231, 50–52
    dilemma, 231–232
    disjunctive syllogism, 232
    enthymeme, 232
    fallacies, glossary of, 237–241
    induction, 233, 50–52
    modus ponens, 233–234
    modus tollens, 234
    premise, 234
    syllogism, 235–236
    terms, glossary of, 231–237
    Toulmin model, 236–237
    warrant, 237
Logical fallacies. *See* Fallacies

M

Modern Language Association (MLA)
    documentation style, 211–212, 214–219

N

Non sequitur, 240–241
Nonstandard English, 196

O

Organization
    in an analytical essay, 52–53
    of early drafts, 63
    placement and evolution of thesis, 77–80,
      55–57
    See also Formats
Oversimplification, how to avoid, 19–22

P

Parallelism
    antithesis, 182
    faulty parallelism, 182
Personal response (topics)
    advantages of, 27–28
    compared with analysis, 9–10, 14
    problems with, 28
    ways of achieving critical detachment, 30
Persuasion
    argument versus analysis, 9–10
    using evidence to test as well as prove,
      115–119

Plagiarism, avoiding, 142
Political science, writing in
building on anomalies in introductions,
97–98
conclusions, 108–109
ideas versus opinions, 4
procedural openings, 4
what counts as evidence, 121–124
Post hoc, ergo propter hoc (false cause), 241
Premises, 234
developing a thesis by reasoning back to
premises, 73–77, 79
Prewriting, 7
advantages of, 22–24
to find and interpret topics, 22–24
freewriting, 23–24
journals, 24
starting points, 24
Pronouns
ambiguous reference, 198–199
antecedent problem, 198
broad reference, 199–200
chart of, 168
and sexism, 198
using first-person, 169–170
Psychology, writing in
abstracts, 98–99
discussion section of reports, 109–110
formats, 47–48
introductory paragraphs, 98
Punctuation
colon, 192, 194
comma errors, 202–204
comma splice, 193–195
dash, 192
semicolon, 192–194

Q

Qualifying generalizations, 121
Quotation
in concluding paragraphs, 113
integrating into a paper, 143–145
versus paraphrase, 156–158
problems in using, 137–139, 146–148

R

Reasoning back to premises
developing thesis by, 73–77, 79

Red herring, 239
Reductio ad absurdum, 234–235
Research
analysis of, 146–158
documentation of, 142, 210–228
paper, 152–156
value of, 139
See also Sources
Revising for correctness
guidelines, 208–209
technical revision as a form of conceptual
revision, 159–161
See also Basic Writing Errors
Revision
conceptual versus technical, 159–161
making a thesis evolve, 56–58, 63–67
modes of, 60
step-by-step sample revision, 67–68
for style, 161–163, 187
Rhetoric
appeals, 237–238
of introductions and conclusions, 95,
106–107
and kinds of writing, 9–10
and style, 162–165, 185–186
Rogers, Carl (on argument and evaluation), 3
Run-on (fused) sentence, 193–195

S

Science, writing in
discussion sections of reports, 109–110
formats in, 47–49
types of lab reports, 99
Sentence fragments, 190–192
Sentence structure (syntax)
active and passive voice, 171–175
coordination, subordination and order of
clauses, 175–177
cumulative sentence, 184–185
cutting the fat, 177–178
expletive constructions, 177–178
four basic sentence types
simple, 179
complex, 180–181
compound, 180
compound-complex, 181
parallel structure, 181–182
antithesis, 182
faulty parallelism, 182

Sentence structure *(continued)*
    passive voice, pro and con, 172
    passive voice in science writing, 172
    periodic sentence, 182–184
    static and active verbs, 174–175
    thesis statements, 86
Sexism
    diction, 164–165
    pronouns, 198–199
Sources, using
    analysis of sources, 146
    brief list of how-tos, 138–139
    citing, 210–228
    conversation analogy, 138–139
    finding, 140–141
    guidelines for, 158
    reference tools, 140
    research paper (an example), 152–156
    six strategies for critical analysis of
        sources, 146–152, 156–158
    six techniques for integrating quotation,
        143–145
    typical problems in using, 137
Standard English, 196–197
Strategies for
    analyzing evidence, 124–130
    critical analysis of sources, 146
    defining, 37–38
    developing a thesis by reasoning back to
        premises, 73–79
    developing a thesis through successive
        complication, 68–71
    finding a thesis in an exploratory draft,
        63–68
    fixing weak thesis statements, 81–93
    handling complexity, 19–22
    integrating quotation, 143–145
    making personal response analytical, 28–30
    making summaries analytical, 26–27
    organizing an analytical essay, 52–53
    using binaries, 32–34
    using comparison and contrast, 36–37
    using formats in exploratory drafts, 49–50
    writing conclusions, 106–111
    writing introductions, 104–106
Straw man
    as opening gambit, 149
    problems with, 239
    and use of sources, 149

Style
    bibliography of style manuals, 227–228
    definition of, 161–163
    levels of, 162–163
    revising for, 160–161
    See also Diction, Sentence structure
Stylistic revision
    guidelines, 187
Subject/verb agreement, 195–197
Summary, 5, 12–14, 25–27
    depth versus breadth, 26–27
    functions of, 25
    strategies for using, 26–27
    typical problems with, 25–26
Syllogism, 235–236
    disjunctive, 233
    enthymeme, 233
Syntax. *See* Sentence structure

T

Thesis
    in argument versus analysis, 9–12
    as camera lens, 57
    in conclusions, 78, 52–53, 108–109
    definitions of, 55–58, 79–80
    and false dichotomies, 78
    as hypothesis and conclusion, 56, 58–59
    in introductions, 52–53, 77, 96–101
    a standard format for developing, 52–53
    and the writing process, 60–63, 68–69
Thesis, weak
    definitions, 81
    categorical thinking, 89
    conventional wisdom, 83–84
    guidelines in recognizing and fixing, 93
    improving logic of, 89–71
    overly broad, 85
    statements of intention, 82
    statements of fact, 82–83
    types of, 82–89
    word choice in, 86
Thinking
    and feeling, 7
    categorical, 89
    deductively, 231, 50–52
    fallacies, 237–240
    guidelines for good thinking, 230
    inductively, 233, 50–52

kinds of arguments, 231–237
    oppositional, 92–93
    and value judgments, 89
Tone, 185–186
    formal and informal, 162–163
    and word choice, 164
Topics (writing assignments)
    argument, 4, 9–12
    assigned versus open, 17–18
    avoiding oversimplification, 19–22
    binaries (either/or questions), 31–34
    comparison and contrast, 34–37, 22
    definition, 34–37
    finding unstated questions in, 20–21
    guidelines for constructing and
      interpreting, 38–39
    interpreting directions, 9–12, 17–18, 25
    key words in, 9–12, 25
    personal response, 9–10, 14, 27–31
    summary, 5, 12–14, 25–27

rules governing sexual conduct, 74–79
tax laws, 73–74
television programming and censorship,
    89–91
media: coverage of Tienanmen Square,
    127–128
paintings, as statement, 13–14, 60–68
Warrant (in Toulmin model of argument), 237
Word Choice. *See* Diction

V

Verbals
    gerund, 191, 208
    participial phrase, 191, 208
Voice, active and passive, 171–175
Voices from Across the Curriculum
    citing sources, 142
    the evolving thesis as hypothesis and
      conclusion, 58–59
    finding sources, 140–141
    formats in the natural and social sciences,
      47–49
    ideas versus opinions, 4
    integrating sources, 152
    reasoning back to premises, 79
    what counts as evidence, 121–124

W

Writing About
    advertising,, 4–5
    cultural history and religion: flood stories,
      130–133
    film, as narrative, 68–73, 148
    history and historians, 146–148, 150–151
    issues
      big money in baseball, 119–121
      research and teaching in higher
        education, 152–157